"The hard ... work of non-attachment ... leads to ... total freedom."
— Judaism

"No other virtue [is] better than a pure detachment from all things."
— Christianity

"Detachment is not that you should own nothing, but that nothing should own you." — Islam

"What is happiness? Detachment." — Hinduism

"The one who is non-possessive and unattached is the one that I call priestly." — The Buddha

"The Integral Way depends on decreasing, not increasing. To correct your mind, rely on not-doing." — Taoism

UNDOING: FREEING YOURSELF FROM YOURSELF

James E. Royster, PhD

Edited by: Constance England and Ray Moore

Metateric Books

DEDICATION:

To all who are eager to face the truth of who they've become, willing to admit their faults and limitations, and courageous enough to change by releasing the old in order to rediscover their never-changing, original essence.

Gratitude and Acknowledgements

My gratitude begins with our shared human life, with which – given its utter magnificence – there is nothing comparable or even imaginable. Since *Undoing* is an attempt to uncover this magnificence, everyone who has played a part in the book has contributed to it from the magnificence of their own uniqueness – particularly my parents and siblings, extended family and friends, teachers and mentors, colleagues, saints and sages of the world, all of whom have left their mark as only each could.

Those who have given their personal testimonies rank high for contributing to the living significance of the principles set forth. The actual demonstration of the effectiveness of detachment and forgiveness in personal life is more convincing than any mere assertion or promise. My thankfulness is unbound to those who have revealed themselves openly and deeply, at times even at personal risk. *Undoing* would be less interesting without their courage and contribution.

This book has benefited immensely from the volunteered and competent editing of two very special friends, Connie England, accomplished poet and selfless giver well along in life's transformational possibilities, and Ray Moore, a former teacher of exceptional skill, insight and a prolific writer. That they have taken great amounts of time from their respective lives to review my text and offer truly helpful comments remains, and will always remain, exceedingly high in my appreciation and gratitude.

Friends who have shared perspectives incorporated into the text include: Bernd and Silke Pohlmann-Eden, John Miller, Jacob De-Hoog…

Editors' note: And to the many others that Dr. Royster would have included if he had completed this final page. "Gratitude and Acknowledgements" is presented here as found after his death.

Copyright 2018. All rights reserved

Contents

Foreword 1
Prologue: Reader Beware 2
Preface: What's Coming 3
Chapter One: Who Am I? 9
    Part I: The Cosmic Big Picture 9
    Part II: Human Consciousness, the Even Bigger Picture 12
Chapter Two: Attachment: Why We Need It; Why We Don't 41
    Part I: Agent of Identity and the Ego 42
    Part II: The Liberating Power of Detachment 65
    Part III: Nonattachment and its Benefits 73
Chapter Three: Testimonials: Attachment and Detachment 79
Chapter Four: Forgiveness: Neutralizing Grudges and Grievances ... 107
    Part I. Unforgiveness – Its Power Undermined 107
    Part II. Three Dimensions of Forgiveness 108
    Part III: Forgiveness in the World Religions 113
    Part IV. Forgiveness Outside Formal Religion 126
    Part V. Science Investigates Forgiveness 128
    Part VI: How to Develop Forgiveness 130
Chapter Five: Forgiveness Testimonials 135
Chapter Six: Death, The Final Detachment? 163
    Part I: Setting the Framework for Our Investigation 163
    Part II: Evidence for Life After Death 167
    Part III: Peaceful Transitions to the Afterlife 183
Epilogue: How Far Do We Take Detachment? 195
    On Detaching from God 195
Postscript 198
Bibliography 199

Foreword

As he wrote this book, Dr. Royster became acutely aware of his own experience of attachment. After completing the last chapter on the final letting go, that which we all face at the end of life, he learned that he had an inoperable tumor and had only days to live. Immediate family drew near, and the Hospice doctor inquired in a most direct way, "What do you have yet unfinished?" Dr. Royster answered, "My book, *Undoing*."

Through a Skype conference, two dedicated friends who had previously made editorial suggestions and were familiar with publishing stepped forward, and committed to carry the manuscript to publication. One of Dr. Royster's final sentences was spoken at the conclusion of that meeting: "Amazing what open-hearted people can accomplish," he said.

Dr. Royster's final days were peaceful. He requested no interference in the process and reported no pain to the surprise of doctors. At times he was heard exclaiming, "Fascinating!" as he observed the process of the body letting go into what is beyond this life.

* * * *

Earlier in his life, after completing his Masters in Theology, Professor James E. Royster (Emeritus) served as an educational Christian missionary with his young family in India, Egypt, and Kenya where he was significantly impressed by the spiritual lives of the people he met.

Dr. Royster later received his PhD in world religions, teaching at various colleges for thirty-one years, while specializing in the spirituality and wisdom traditions of the East. He retired from Cleveland State University in 2002 to complete his first book, *Have This Mind: Supreme Happiness, Ultimate Realization, and the Four Great Religions – An Integral Adventure* (Balboa Press, 2014) which represents his professorial efforts and later formed the basis of study classes with a significant following of university students and retirees.

During his professorial career, Dr. Royster pioneered a study series entitled "Spirituality and Human Transformation" leading small groups of dedicated students on six week wilderness monastic retreats.

Dr. Royster lived as a scholar/pioneer/spiritual practitioner, fulfilling his passion for teaching and writing, while exploring and mastering the mind.

Prologue: Reader Beware

In recognition of the myriad of beliefs and practices held by we humans, *Undoing* acknowledges as proper and legitimate whatever specific views are being voiced at any given moment, and it does so without approving or condemning. Given the genetic makeup, the situations, the conditioning, and the choices that make up our past, whatever is currently believed could not be different. This means that the content of *Undoing* will be addressing a seemingly endless range of beliefs and practices. Consequently, *there is probably something here for everyone* and probably nothing here that will appeal to everyone. Every human being is a unique individual with a one-of-a-kind set of beliefs. Unfortunately, this is seldom realized to the point of allowing others to be as they are until they are inclined ... within themselves ... to make changes. *Undoing* honors this principle and offers suggestions on how we can facilitate change *within ourselves*.

* * * *

The words that follow will affect your well-being. They will enhance it, or disturb it, or destroy it. They will enhance it if you take the teachings seriously and apply them. You will find yourself freer as you shed once necessary and beneficial aspects of your personality that have ceased to be either necessary or beneficial. Life will become bigger and richer. Your happiness will grow; your relationships will improve; your energy and enthusiasm will heighten. Without condoning, you will become more accepting of what is, and not so upset at things you once disliked, did not believe, or that caused suffering.

The notions that follow will disturb your well-being if you read them too hurriedly, unthinkingly, without pause, reflection, or consideration. They will disturb if you second-guess them or try them half-heartedly, if skepticism overrides your initial openness, or if distraction leads you to dismiss them.

The content will destroy the modicum of well-being that you now think you have if you scoff at these concepts and practices, if you reject them outright, or if you refuse even to consider them. They will destroy your well-being if you are so content with the life you are now living that you find no room for improvement, no need for more easeful relationships with others, and no desire for more zest and joy.

Preface: What's Coming

Although the title does not indicate this, *Undoing* is selectively autobiographical, a partial narrative of my life journey from birth and childhood in a struggling but ambitious post-Depression Era family in a Detroit suburb to comfortable retirement in a large Florida 55+ community of successful, middle class, and for the most part, content (if not happy) adults. That's just about as much objective history as you'll receive. The rest of the occasional self-revelation centers in my intellectual and spiritual growth, which is offered as an example of what is available to anyone interested. For me personally, the heart of the book is the universal spiritual depth found in the world's religions; the personal narrative is just the carrier of the intention and reason for writing.

* * * *

At the outset, I want to state the purpose and scope of *Undoing: Freeing Yourself from Yourself* so readers can decide up front whether to read on or not. Some of my academic friends may expect more from this book than I intend. It is not an academic treatise. My former book, *Have This Mind: Supreme Happiness, Ultimate Realization, and the Four Great Religions—An Integral Adventure,* represents my professorial efforts. *Undoing* draws from that period in my life and goes on to share my current "integral adventure" incorporating additional insight and experiences from my post-academic years. This book does use some modified scholarly features but does so in an un-obstructing way. Anyone who wants to trace a reference to its source is able to do so, but there are no extensive notes, no traditional bibliography, and no index. My primary intention is to offer reflections that inform, inspire, and challenge readers to take up and practice a transforming, integral adventure that opens into the fullness of life – but only if they're inclined. What follows is not for everyone.

Socrates is credited with the bold claim: "The unexamined life is not worth living." I whole-heartedly agree. And yet in contemporary society, particularly in the West, it seems that most people live their lives in 'quiet mediocrity,' by which I mean almost completely in reference to the external world. Routine, formal, outer, exoteric beliefs and rituals dominate even religion, which ought to promote self-reflection. As a result, the mind becomes so riveted on extraneous issues that little awareness is directed to one's own inherent nature. The media, movies, magazines, athletics, shopping, entertainment, politics, international conflict, civil discord, the rich and glamorous – all of these draw our attention away from our inner world. The distracting effect of outward-directed attention inevitably leads to discouragement, depression, and fear, and is far removed from the genuine happiness that is one's birthright. How can one be happy in the midst of all of this? Thomas Jefferson's reference in the Declaration of Independence to "the pursuit of happiness" only complicates the problem if one assumes that true happiness can be found in the outer world. *Undoing* offers a path to unconditional happiness, a fullness and richness of life that is independent of external conditions.

Undoing sets forth some of what I've learned over the past eight decades. Herein is my personal 'philosophy of life,' which includes an integral, thoughtful sampling of religion, psychology, philosophy, world literature, world travel, and especially, spirituality. My effort is to present a consistent, comprehensive worldview that does not so much critique other worldviews as offer instead an alternative to such cultural features as materialism, commercialism, parochialism, party politics, competition, etc., ways of life devoid of deep meaning and genuine happiness. What follows is hopefully a dialogue between you and me, a sharing of my experience and reflections with a thoughtful reader. It is a formulation of what I've discovered that promotes a personally meaningful and affirming life. It all fits together harmoniously in my heart and mind, motivating me to write, to teach, and to share my conclusions with any who may be interested.

Undoing focuses on a single, transformative principle that is emphasized in all of the major religions, a principle of wide applicability as life unfolds through ascending levels of maturation, all the way from magical (Easter Bunny), mythical (God created the world in six days), rational (reality accords with reason), pluralistic (other religions also have truth), to integral (everything fits together harmoniously), and beyond. In other words, this principle works at the early stages of minimal maturity all the way through to ultimate realization. In fact, this principle and process is *the* crucial factor in all forms of movement toward more comprehensive, compassionate, and caring modes of being.

I trust that nothing written here (or in any of my writing) is construed to mean that I think or claim that I have personally achieved and realized everything about which I've written; that is far from the case. I am, however, confident that everything I've written is possible, available, and true to human nature for each and all of us. To much of this, I can attest personally, and I know all of it to be authentic, reliable, and fully capable of self-realization.

So, enough already! What is this all-important principle? It is detachment – the letting go of that which served beneficially, maybe even protectively, for a time but which now tends to limit and hold one back from the fullness and joy of life. Here's an example of how simple and basic the principle is: We must detach from learning the alphabet in order to move on to learn to read. What's the point of reciting the ABC's repeatedly after one knows them? Why keep believing something you used to believe after discovering that it stands in the way of accepting a more inclusive view, one more rational and compassionate? Why keep doing something you've discovered isn't satisfying?

Nasr ad-Din is a mythical sage-fool in Middle East culture. A friend once found him in the market with his clothes wet from sweating, his skin beet red, tears flowing down his face, all the while eating red hot pepper after red hot pepper from a basket. The friend exclaimed: "Nasr ad-Din, what are you doing?" Nasr ad-Din answered: "I keep hoping I'll find a sweet one." This story illustrates how Nasr ad-Din became stuck in repeating an unproductive behavior. To demonstrate the real-life relevance of detachment, many contemporary examples – in the form of personal testimonials – will be used to describe its application and ensuing benefit.

I was brought up to believe that my family and church taught and lived Truth, while the vast majority of other people around the world, and even most in our own country, believed and lived by myths, fanciful ideas and practices far from the truth. Two scholar-writers corrected this gross distortion and misunderstanding for me. They were (in the academic arena) Mircea Eliade of the University of Chicago and (in the broader culture) Joseph Campbell, each longstanding specialists in world mythology.

Campbell summarized the purpose of valid, living mythologies as fourfold: (1) to provide a meaningful worldview; (2) to show how we fit into the natural world; (3) to give guidance on how to get along with others; and (4) to outline a way of becoming fully human. Just in case it's not apparent, to live a meaningful life, one must have a mythology. Mythologies differ radically throughout the world, but all are meaningful for those who believe and live by them, even though they may not appear sensible or be beneficial for others. I offer *Undoing* as a workable mythology, or, in more familiar terms, an approach to life leading to ever-increasing happiness and unconditional love.

For those with the time and inclination, I heartily recommend that the book be read in its entirety and in the order presented; there is an inherent logic in its development. As you will see, the book moves from the broad to the specific, from principle to application, and from ideal to manifestation. However, it does not need to be read straight through. Your personal objectives will indicate how much you read and in what order. The focus of each chapter is well defined, thereby allowing you to be selective.

All in all, *Undoing* is intended to be specific and practical.

* * * *

As the title indicates, Chapter One raises the most important question of everyone's life, even though it often goes unaddressed: Who am I? Far too many of us tread through life assuming our identity unquestioningly, allowing family, education, religion, culture, politics, etc., to define us. I know this has certainly been true for me. This first chapter sets our individual identity in the context of the identity we share with all humans. We will then look at our position and role as humans in the massive, complex, and mysterious universe. The most important point in the chapter and in the book identifies our birthright identity, that which is our foundation, our core, our essential nature. The rest of book addresses the way to discover this true Self and the way to manifest it in our daily life.

The chapter contains views that may seem elusive and abstract and therefore require thoughtful reflection. Einstein is credited with saying: "Everything must be made as simple as possible, but not simpler." By all means, yes. The most crucial ideas introduced here pertain to our deepest, truest nature as human beings, our most essential qualities and values, and how we can recognize and affirm them. These concepts will be new for some. If there is initial questioning and hesitancy, ongoing consideration and self-exploration (including experimentation as appropriate) may lead to understanding and profound changes in self-conception. Truth may begin as a proposition, but it only becomes fully acknowledged when discovered to "bear fruit" in the living. The chapter closes with further clarification by means of questions and observations that may have been provoked by some of the notions in the chapter.

Chapter Two summarizes the typical human lifetime by identifying the most significant factor operating in the earlier phases, namely the ego, the self-sense that causes so many personal and interpersonal difficulties. We also discover the naturally emerging stages of life as our experience broadens and deepens, as we engage life in its adventurous unfolding. Briefly stated, the chapter shows the need for attachment, and then the need to give it up – to detach. This ongoing, reciprocating dynamic of taking on and releasing constitutes the means by which identity is made, unmade, and remade, on and on as long as we're continuing to grow and mature.

Real life examples of attachment and detachment make up Chapter Three. These testimonials demonstrate how specific individuals have discovered their limiting attachments and how they have detached from them, thereby discovering more joy, peace, and freedom. The extent and significance of these contrasting life practices, attachment and detachment, becomes evident through these personal accounts.

Chapter Four focuses on a specific form of attachment that is especially widespread and destructive. Because of the preferences everyone develops, we naturally sharpen our critical tools according to them and constantly judge what doesn't meet our personal standards and expectations. "I don't like this; I don't like that." "Why isn't there more of this and less of that?" "What's wrong with him, with her, with them?" "Why don't they corral their dog; make their kids obey?" "Why do they hang out with such people; always look so sloppy?" On occasions, our dislikes become so toxic that they lead to insult, abuse, and suffering.

Likes and dislikes, from the seemingly innocent to the harshly extreme, block accurate understanding of oneself, others, and life itself. Projection and criticism create such a distorted picture that a kind of blindness sets in. Life is engaged with so much negativity that some acquaintances may pull away to preserve their own contentment. We address this common issue from the standpoint of its remedy – forgiveness for ourselves and for those we have judged.

Chapter Five presents real life examples of forgiveness, testimonials of and about forgiveness that exemplify the extraordinary benefits that ensue from this ameliorating practice. Apologizing and offering forgiveness to someone wronged, seeking and/or opening to forgiveness when offered, and forgiving oneself may be difficult at first, but the gains are invaluable, as these testimonials demonstrate. I once spoke with a counselor of the abused who claimed that certain acts of violence are so horrendous that forgiveness would be wrong, even that it would be impossible. These examples prove otherwise.

Chapter Six deals with the last event of *this* lifetime. Many Westerners, including some Christians, believe that death is the end of life. Increasing numbers, however, are coming to a different conclusion, one for which there is growing evidence. We will investigate some of the evidence suggesting that death is a transition, not an end. Whether death is seen as an absolute end or as a transition, detachment is an invaluable tool. Whether ending now or continuing, these final days and hours will give rise to increased fear and suffering if one 'hangs on' or resists the unfolding sensations, if one dreads and bemoans the inevitable. Having practiced detachment in the past, one is better prepared to face with equanimity and acceptance the mystery that arises during the dying process. The chapter concludes with descriptions of dying experiences, and gives two examples from people who appear to have died peacefully.

The Epilogue draws the principles and practice of *Undoing* to a conclusion, adds a striking and challenging perspective, and offers a few final words to consider – to think about or not.

Chapter One: Who Am I?

> To be nobody but yourself in a world which is doing its best ... to make you everybody else means to fight the hardest battle which any human being can fight.
> (e. e. cummings)

This chapter concerns the most crucial of all questions, one that is often not considered or is poorly considered.

> Without the Cosmos, the planet would not be.
> Without the planet, life would not be.
> Without life, humans would not be.
> Without consciousness, I would not be.

* * * *

These opening statements need unpacking. In terms of size, we humans are minuscule and inconsequential in the expansive and expanding universe. In terms of the role we occupy, we are monumental. This chapter addresses our identity from two standpoints: first, how we normally understand ourselves; second, in terms of the deeper, essential, rarely recognized quality that makes us unique and distinctive in the cosmos. When asked, "Who are you?" we usually give our name and then say something about our body and/or mind, something like, "I'm a man and an American." But this doesn't get at what is most important, our identity as a conscious being. The chapter investigates this most crucial quality – crucial because it is seldom acknowledged and is of ultimate import.

Part I: The Cosmic Big Picture

A. The Physical Universe

We live in the natural world, the physical universe, and therefore begin with creation stories. Every religion, from tribal to the world religions, has its creation story explaining how it all began. These stories have been regarded as largely mythic (i.e., untrue) by those who don't understand the significance of a living mythology. As we saw in the Preface, Joseph Campbell established the value of living mythologies by showing how they provide meaning for those who hold them, meaning that is necessary for life to be significant and to have purpose. By focusing on the two biggest pictures, cosmos and consciousness, this chapter offers a contemporary mythology: a meaningful understanding of reality that meets the four values that Campbell identifies.

Those who have matured to at least the rational stage of human development depend today on science for their understanding of creation and the natural world. Many others remain locked in conventional religion and read scripture in fundamentalist and literalistic fashion (e.g., according the myths existing at the time of the scripture's origin). They see irreconcilable conflict between science and religion and tend either to ignore or to reject science outright. These folks have not 'undone' or re-interpreted the stories of religion taught during their childhood, fables that are still preached dogmatically in fundamentalist churches today.

Those open to contemporary science, including the philosophy of science, face multiple views of how the cosmos operates. One radical view is that we live in a multiverse made up of many parallel universes, the actual number of which is unknown. Some hold that universes come and go over vast eons, never actually beginning or ending, just transitioning. Some contend that black holes lead to other universes. Still others believe that the cosmos never began because it *always was/is*, with no beginning and no ending – infinite and eternal.

Another notion is that this so-called physical universe doesn't really exist: it's actually an illusion, a phantasmagoria projected by the mind with no more reality than a dream. In more 'scientific' terms, we humans and everything in the universe are a hologram, empty and suspended in space. All of this, some theorize, is recorded and projected from the exterior of black holes.

Happily, we don't need to resolve these different views. Our objective is more manageable: to discover and negotiate a way of life that works regardless of which theory is actually true. To illustrate this, we will assume the consensus view of most scientists that our cosmos began with the Big Bang. This so-called Bang initiated a cosmos that began 13.7 billion years ago, a cosmos where darkness prevailed for millions of years. When the first stars formed, they organized into ever-expanding galaxies. Our home, the Milky Way, 160,000 light years across, is one of the smaller galaxies among the 200 billion in the currently observable universe. Light travels at 186,000 miles per second. The size of 160 thousand light years is beyond my ability to imagine. At the same time that our earth, one of 50 billion planets in our galaxy, is orbiting around the sun, the sun is itself orbiting around the center of the galaxy, once every 225-250 million years. Such is the inconceivable magnitude of our home.

This home, even though it operates according to the laws of mathematics, physics, chemistry, etc., remains to a great extent undecipherable and mysterious. In spite of all that has been learned about the universe since the beginning of modern science in the early sixteenth century, when Copernicus announced that the sun not the earth is the center of the universe, our universe has continued to perplex and mystify. For example, the space between galaxies and planets, what we ordinarily regard as 'empty' space, is declared to be 'dark energy' and 'dark matter.' Cosmologists believe that the universe is made up of 78% dark energy and 27% dark matter, leaving only 5% as 'normal' matter. J. B. S. Haldane, a British evolutionary biologist, spoke for many when he declared that "the universe is not only queerer than we suppose, but queerer than we *can* suppose."

Our universe is equally inconceivable when we turn our attention in the other direction, to its miniscule dimensions. We now enter the subatomic realm by means of quantum science, which uses nanotechnology to search the hidden dimensions of that which cannot be seen by the naked eye. Here subatomic particles such as photons exhibit behavior so counter-intuitive that Nobel Prize winning physicist Richard Feynman once said: "I think I can safely say that nobody understands quantum mechanics." For example, subatomic particles exhibit both/and behavior; each is simultaneously a wave and a particle, seen as one or the other depending on how our awareness registers it.

To conclude this short foray into our physical world, the world of science, do note that whether moving up and out or down and in, we find more and more of what we usually call space than what we regard as matter. We've seen that the universe is perhaps 95% space, with only 5% actual matter. When this apparent matter, comprised as it is of atoms, is subjected to further investigation it turns out to be, again, largely empty. What does it mean to regard something as empty? Atoms, making up everything that exists, are themselves almost entirely empty. And when the nucleus, and the particles (electrons, neutrons and protons) that constantly orbit in the atoms, are studied, these too are mostly space. They do contain quarks, which can be mathematically established but not observed. The universe seems to be increasing spaciousness with nothing really solid or stationery.

B. Life Emerges, Then Consciousness

We have looked so far only at the physical universe. What about life, which is qualitatively different from matter? Around 3.8 billion years ago, life emerged through a chemical processes in the sea. This extraordinary event, when "inert stuff jumped to live stuff," marked the unfathomable magnificence of life, so often taken for granted. It is beyond man's rational mind to understand all that has evolve from that moment. And thus far, life (as we know it) exists only here on our earth.

The primal life that emerged eons ago is vastly different from human life. Much, much later than this earliest evidence of life, we humans appeared as Homo sapiens, nearly 200,000 years ago. Into this unimaginatively huge, intricate, complex, and mysterious universe – estimated to provide life to eleven million different species – we humans made our entrance.

What is the justification for this opening excursion into the physical universe, especially in a book treating an individual psychospiritual principle and practice? It is to address the question: *Are we humans any more important than any other species or feature, organic or inorganic, occupying this planet in this galaxy in this universe?* How could we be more important, given the inarguable interconnectedness of all that is? By what rationale could we be more important than the sun, or gravity, or insects? What would happen to us in their absence? If the least of these arbitrarily selected features of the cosmos disappeared (insects, for example), we humans would soon follow. The entire plant and animal life on which humans depend would vanish without pollination. On the other hand, if humans disappeared, the insect world would hardly notice, and perhaps might even thrive (with no pesticides and more organic decay). So where do we stand in the value scheme of this complex, interactive earth? Are even insects more important than humans?

Be not alarmed; the answer is a resounding, "No!" Why? Because we are conscious! We are aware! We know that we exist! Our consciousness, so far as we know, is unlike that of any other creature; it is more extensive, more complex. We are the universe, conscious of itself. What could be more special and extraordinary than this?

A few contemporary scientists stress our presence and role in the universe in an even more startling fashion. Not only are we conscious humans the culmination of the universe's lengthy unfolding, we are Universe. All that has transpired from helium and nitrogen, to stars and planets, to plants and animals has occurred *in order to produce you and me, all of this is in us as us – the cosmos is us*. The evolutionary and interconnected principles of the universe have 'conspired' to create you and me to *be aware,* and to *be aware that we are aware*. Other beings are aware, but so far as we know they are not aware of being in a state of awareness.

Part II: Human Consciousness, the Even Bigger Picture

The earliest evidence of self-awareness cannot be convincingly established; it is too elusive and can only be surmised from skeletal remains and human artifacts, sources too concrete and restricted to reveal a non-material, spiritual quality. Nonetheless, some authorities venture to suggest that self-awareness can be seen in the earliest art and artifacts (perhaps 100,000 years ago), or the earliest writing (5500 years ago), or coherent writing (Homer's epic stories *The Iliad* and *The Odyssey* around the twelfth-century BCE). A few centuries later, certain evidence of self-consciousness is established by the advice of the Delphic Oracle, "Know Thyself."

The question of identity has continued to be posed throughout history, and has produced an endless supply of answers. Ramana Maharshi, Hindu sage and saint of the last century, declared it to be the question leading to life's ultimate truth. Why is it such a crucial question? Because it determines, more than any other possible question, how we're going to live this human life. Everything begins and ends with identity: who I think I am.

As we work and play to become somebody, we oscillate between being like others (we want/need to be liked) and being unique, different and (hopefully) special. Dr. Seuss got the unique part right when he said: "There is no one alive who is youer than you." Oscar Wilde rightly observed: "Be yourself; everyone else is already taken." Anthropologist Margaret Mead observed: "Always remember that you are absolutely unique. Just like everyone else." The comedian, Lily Tomlin jokes: "I always wanted to be somebody. Now I see that I should have been more specific." The ready availability of pointed quotations such as these on identity itself suggests the value of self-knowledge.

Identity is not only a crucial question but an extremely difficult one to answer. The professions and disciplines tend to offer limited answers: philosophers get lost in tangential issues; psychologists debate within a theoretical framework; sociologists lose the individual in the group; economists focus on bottom line and buying power; politicians reduce us to votes and reelection; theologians work within scriptural confinement. So who can thoroughly and accurately answer a question that may not be answerable? After all, any answer is hardly free from some degree of vested interest on the part of the responder. So I'll be clear up front. My interest is to formulate an understanding founded in our essential identity, an identity that fosters a meaningful life and excludes nothing, that provides a sense of personal contentment and ease in living.

The process of identity formation begins very early in life, well before we become rational enough to reflect deliberately on such matters. One evening after supper, while my dad was studying to become a journeyman electrician, and I was a two- or three-year-old playing noisily on the floor, he asked me, then told me, and then demanded that I be quiet. When I still wasn't as quiet as he needed, he forcefully commanded that I go sit in the corner and not move a muscle. I obeyed as far as he was able to see me, but wiggled my toes in my shoes. I already, unknowingly, held a view of my identity as a separate person with some degree of self-dignity; my dad (whom I loved, admired, and wanted to be like) could not rule me. This action on my part shows an ego already formed and growing. In subsequent stages of development, the ego continues to shape our self-sense, more or less without much thought given to the process.

However, when we begin to think for ourselves, the rational stage has been entered and identity formation becomes more deliberate, even if it is not always clearly recognized as such. For me, and probably for most of us, this started in high school and expanded in college. Rare and fortunate is the person who continues throughout life to reformulate his or her identity.

We could begin an objective investigation of our personal identity with the question, "When did I begin?" But we soon find that every possible answer ends up being arbitrary and leading to endless debate: at conception; at birth; when parents decided to have children, fell in love, cohabited; how about their parents, the parents of their parents, ad infinitum? This question pertains to consciousness itself and not one's personal consciousness, one's self-sense. If we're going to start with a reasonably answerable question, it has to be: "When did *I* begin to be *me*?"

Every one of us became self-consciousness when we realized for the first time (now a long-lost memory) that we could respond to someone and then they would respond to us – to me specifically. It all starts and continues with the dynamic process of interacting from inside to what is outside: "I can affect what's out there"; "I'm not a nothing because I do something and something responds"; "Mom will come when I cry"; "When I smile at others, they smile at me." All of this, of course, is without words; language comes later. Identity begins when we begin to interact with our surroundings. From this time on, we are developing our me-ness, our assumed and subtle sense of "I am."

Identity formation is a natural, inevitable, and necessary process, so much so that it takes place without our even realizing that it is occurring. To be human is to create/make/concoct/fabricate personhood and a personality, and to build character (of one sort or another). To be a healthy, normal human, we must create a self and an ego. They are most often identical, but not always. And neither of them is *the* Self, our original, essential/divine identity. The rest of this book clarifies the personality and offers a process for recognizing *the* Self – but only after we discover and admit that the self we've become carries too much confusion, difficulty, conflict, and suffering. We want a change, a way out of being stuck as just this 'me.' Life's got to hold more than this! It does!

The *most* fundamental feature of our humanness is consciousness, more properly indicated as pure consciousness, original and unsullied, perfect and complete. Pure consciousness is consciousness without content. It is awareness devoid of anything appearing in it, or anything that can be named. We're talking now about consciousness as an essential state of being, as a generic way of identifying what it means most fundamentally to be a living human being. Pure consciousness is prior to every other thing that might be said about human nature. It is prior to gender, reason, emotion, intention, imagination; prior to family, nationality, religion, education, profession; prior to anything and everything that characterizes our humanity; prior to everything we have learned and can learn; prior to experience.

We need to investigate consciousness further since it definitely tends to be overlooked. It comes as a surprise to the vast majority of us when we discover and acknowledge for the first time that we are, indeed, foremost and inarguably *consciousness*. When I've introduced this over the years in my classes, I've gotten no feedback that anyone had already singled out this crucial fact. Very, very few are aware that it is what we *are*, prior to our bodies, our minds, all that we otherwise are, and all that makes up our world. Consciousness is what registers everything of which we become aware. Consciousness is the vast, empty 'field' in which everything appears. Several analogies suggest how foundational pure or contentless consciousness actually is: it is like the silence in which sounds appear, like the empty sky in which clouds appear, like a calm ocean in which waves appear, or a lake distinguished from its fish, turtles, weeds, etc. Another analogy exists with a mirror. In itself, a mirror is empty, reflecting nothing. However, anything and everything that arises in front of a mirror is reflected in its exact form, undistorted unless the mirror itself is distorted. But, of course, there are no distortions in pure consciousness. However, as consciousness reflects human enterprising, distortions seem to appear due to judgments based on prevailing human standards and expectations. From this, endless problems occur.

The main point emphasized here is that consciousness registers whatever appears before it, and that we can only be aware of that which appears in it. If anything does not arise there, it does not exist for us. This can be demonstrated by investigating your own consciousness ... not its content, but consciousness itself. If you exercise sufficient sensitivity and acuity, you will discover that your consciousness as consciousness does not have boundaries, internally or externally; it is without demarcation. You will also discover that it is not touched by time. All demarcations and time distinctions, to the extent that they occur, do so as content within consciousness. And note that the absence of boundary and the absence of time are how we define infinity and eternity, the essential qualities usually attributed to God, or what might better be termed Ultimacy. Ultimacy identifies the central referent in the religious, spiritual, and wisdom traditions of the world. The merit of the word lies in the fact that it is non-specific and not limited by human idea (*HTM* 23-34).

I am contending here that the essential qualities of God/Ultimacy are identical to our own essential nature as pure consciousness. Herein lies our spirituality. We are first and foremost spiritual beings because our foundational identity derives from and is shared with the Source of all that is, itself Pure Spirit. We are part and parcel of this Pure Spirit, integral with It, integral *as* It. I am not suggesting that we are identical to God; both God and we have features that are distinguishable from each other (God can create a cosmos: we can't. We have preferences: God doesn't). What I am pointing out is that our *essential* nature – prior to all that we otherwise are and become – is what we also ascribe to Ultimacy, to what most know as God. "Self" is one of the most widely used words in the spiritual and wisdom traditions for this inborn nature that is and reflects Ultimacy. Self is the pure consciousness and potentiality of Ultimacy, inherent in each of us. This is the unchanging Self that is clouded over by the identities constructed by every human in every culture, the self that becomes 'me.'

* * * *

Let us now outline, and then investigate more deeply, the 'Big Picture' in terms of our uniquely human qualities: (1) with our conscious entry into time and space, we *seem* to be a body; (2) this rudimentary consciousness or awareness, prior to language, enables response to the inner and outer world; (3) there is a spiritual quality to this consciousness since it is devoid of any feature indicative of the material or concrete; (4) implicit also in pure consciousness are knowing and being; and (5) equally inherent in pure consciousness is happiness, contentment, tranquility, and love. These are inborn qualities, as yet unexperienced, unrecognized, and unacknowledged. They can only be experienced, recognized, and acknowledged as they arise as *content* in the vastness of pure consciousness, as they emerge from the formless into the world of form, from pure subjectivity to objectivity. These exceptional human qualities (spiritual, knowing, being, happiness, contentment, tranquility, and love) warrant further comment.

* * * *

In the meantime, however, a prior question: Did the cosmos and the potential for consciousness begin with the Big Bang? Scientists tend to assume that it did, even though science as science cannot answer the question. In the philosophy of science, the question of origin becomes more relevant: What caused the Big Bang? When religion enters the discussion, God becomes the initiating cause. Virtually every religion offers its particular creation story. Traditional Jews, Christians, and Muslims offer the Eden story. Hindus have several creation accounts: one view is that universes come and go, endlessly, always have and always will; another postulates four progressively deteriorating eons of unimaginable length until the cosmos finally disappears into vacuity, and after an immeasurable period of nothingness, another round of existence begins. The Buddha taught that such questions as the origin of the world are speculative and unanswerable, a waste of effort and misdirected. Better to find out why we are so often discontented and suffer from this and that; better to get free of our problems, dissatisfaction, and misery than get lost in conjecture. For example, in the immediacy of the event, if hit by a poisoned arrow, he noted, we don't need to know the kind of poison and who shot it, we need to get the arrow removed and the poison out. The Buddha had already provided a meaningful worldview and a corresponding diagnosis of the human predicament and its resolution. Additionally, he had emphasized the great opportunity of being human. With all this in place, he then zeroed in on the central issue: how to live in conformity to reality; how to undo our mistaken views and behaviors.

* * * *

Why have we investigated the cosmos when we really want to know how best to live our lives? Why are we investigating consciousness when it's how to live a happy and meaningful life that we want to know? What has all this got to do with "undoing and freeing us from ourselves?" The Buddha's story provides a clue. So does the contribution of Joseph Campbell. We'll draw from each, and introduce another helpful source.

If we have a sense of the immensity, magnificence, and mysterious quality of the universe, coupled with an accurate understanding of who we are and how we fit into this unimaginably huge cosmos, we then have a worldview that allows us to envision how we can, individually and together, remove whatever seems to block our full, appreciative awareness of life, and take advantage the opportunities here and now to realize unalloyed happiness. The poisoned arrow is keeping us from discovering and being what/who we are by nature. By fully recognizing and understanding that, we discover the insights and motivation to pursue a fuller, freer, happier life. One of the most influential and widely studied spiritual texts today is *A Course in Miracles*. The miracle it discloses "does nothing. All it does is ... undo." The *Course* (reputedly revealed by Jesus to a Jewish psychologist at Columbia University in the 1970s) is based on each person's willingness to admit: "I have done this thing, and it is this I would undo" (*W*. Ch. 27, VIII. 11, 6).

As we have seen, consciousness is our 'rock-bottom' identity, that which constitutes our essential nature. Without it, we would not be. Consciousness and existence go hand in hand. This consciousness that we are is at least as spacious as the universe itself: our awareness contains the entire, expanding universe. We can even sense infinity, that which is beyond the universe. When we think it, however, it is simply a thought, not infinity itself. On the other hand, as we have seen, our consciousness as consciousness is 'marked' by infinity and eternity, without boundary and without time.

Thought and Language: Crucial but Misleading

Admittedly, we cannot know for certain how the cosmos began, nor can we unify the many contrasting views – religious, philosophical, and scientific. A prior question might be broached: Why do we want to know? A quick answer is that we are curious by nature. We want to know how we fit into the natural world. There is, however, a still more vital question that stands prior to our drive to know and to learn. If we're going to think about anything, and think we must, we need to understand a bit about thinking itself. How does it proceed? How does it function? What are its strengths and weakness? These questions lead to two more questions: (1) Is there a limiting, unnoticed feature of thinking that conditions its operation? and (2) Is there anything intrinsic to thinking itself that distorts its observations and conclusions? The answer to the last two questions is decidedly "Yes."

In spite of the intrinsic mutuality of all that makes up the universe, its undeniable interconnectedness, and the inalterable and relentless application of the law of cause and effect, *all thinking* is based on isolating one thing from another. The uni-verse is a single, harmonious, interacting whole, and yet thinking divides it up into seemingly discrete and separate parts. This inevitable feature of thinking is so foundational and crucial to its very nature that we are unaware of its operation – and its distorting effects.

This contrast between the nature of the universe and our thinking is so crucial that it deserves, perhaps requires, further repetition in order to integrate it into our emerging re-definition of our identity. Life is a single, interactive, unfolding process, everything changing, everything effecting and being affected. Nothing is separate; nothing is static. But we don't engage life on its actual terms because our thinking assumes that it is made up of this and that, that and this, each thing standing separate and apart from everything else. At the risk of redundancy, I emphasize this because it is so fundamental to our entire interaction with life, however and wherever we meet it.

The very nature of thought and language – *all thought, all language* – is to divide into parts, to set one thing over against other things, and, to that extent, to record and project a world of difference, contrast, contradiction, opposition, competition, combat, and even war. Thinking, the background of all speaking and writing, draws on the number of words in each person's mind that represent the vast number of things with which the individual is familiar. The total number of words signifying the number of identifiable 'things' in the world – inner and outer – is beyond counting. In itself, however, our world is un-fragmented, interconnected, interactive, unfolding multiplicity—yet thinking keeps us from directly seeing this.

In order to engage life happily and meaningfully, we must reduce the massive, ever-changing and fragmented world within which we live to one that is orderly and makes sense. Fragmented multiplicity must be broken down into sensible, manageable categories. Duality is the most fundamental form of multiplicity that is still multiple but not single, not one. The most common term indicating oneness in contrast to multiplicity is nonduality. Nonduality and duality name the two different states of consciousness that mark every human being, and about which there is much more to clarify.

Specifying and dualizing are the conjoined means by which the thinking mind enables us to make sense of our lives in the world. They are the primary operative principles of the thinking mind. I have to write about them as if they are two different functions because thinking itself requires it. Actually, they operate as a single principle because anything of which we're going to be aware and about which we are thinking/talking must be both separated in the world and in our mind from everything else. Naming one thing – any and all things – seems to be a single process to us but is actually twofold when we talk about it because thinking and talking require this. Thinking and talking cannot and do not happen apart from this unconscious, natural process of dualizing.

We depend on thinking and talking as the primary means by which we interact with each other and the world. They are essential but limited because, as we've discovered, they distort reality even as they report it. What are some of the implications of this discovery? Strictly speaking, there should be no nouns in language because there is nothing specific in life, nothing fixed and unchanging. By definition, a noun is meant to specify, to name something specific. But nothing *is* specific in the strict sense of the term. Nothing is actually separated from its surroundings, not just in terms of the space it inhabits but also temporally, its coming to be and its ceasing to be. From this standpoint, there should be no 'the' in any language since the word is intended to designate something definite. Perhaps English more than others languages supports this distortion since it is purported to have more nouns than any other language.

Dictionaries demonstrate the inherent, pervasive connectivity and mobility in the natural world and in life. Every word in a dictionary is 'defined' in relation to other words in the dictionary. No word serves as the foundation for all the others. Where is the solid, changeless foundation, or absolute starting point, providing support for this now evident but non-apparent mutuality? There is none. Thus, we are forced to conclude that reality/life is primarily relational and changing. Everything that seems specific is actually in a changing relationship with other so-called 'specific things.' It is relational 'all the way up and all the way down and all the way out.'

We typically think of ourselves as single individuals in a massive universe. Actually, we are made up of inter-active, ever-changing parts in an inter-active, ever-changing universe. We are beings of constant change in a universe of constant change, only seemingly a single person living as a seemingly isolated part in the wholeness of the universe. Why don't we recognize this? Because the compartmentalizing operation of the thinking mind has commandeered the fullness of our nature, a fullness that mirrors the fullness of the universe itself. This fullness is our pure consciousness, our awareness as awareness, distinguished from the multitudinous content that ordinarily occupies our mind.

As we've seen, we live in a fragmented world of endless multiplicity. We take this world for granted; it seems to be the way things are. Where there is multiplicity there is going to be contrast and contradiction; it is inevitable. We take this to be the nature of reality as well. But it's not. The 'stuff' of reality is actually complementary. Apart from our projection of human preferences and values onto the universe, reality operates harmoniously. Even so-called disruptions in the natural world are necessary, regular events that become absorbed into the larger harmony. Cut into the cosmos at any point and everything is seen to complement everything else, all the way out and up and down. Technically, this is called 'holarchy,' parts making up wholes, which are parts of still larger wholes, all the way up, down, and out.

Decades ago when I first began to study the world's religions, particularly Hinduism and Buddhism, I was surprised and a bit alarmed when I discovered their seeming endless numbers of gods and goddess, especially those that were so horrendous and frightening when I met them in sculpture, paintings, and literature. In India, for example, this imagery decorates buses, inside and out, and graphically adorns temples. As I moved more deeply into these and other traditions, particularly Taoism, it became clear that these divine figures simply represented actual – that is, real – aspects of the world and life as we encounter it. These religions and wisdom traditions were acknowledging life as we meet it in its fullness ... without projecting and imposing our human preference for the good and rejection of the bad. They were dealing with life as it is, recognizing the human projection of pros and cons and providing a realistic way of understand, overcoming, and transcending the apparent duality. There may be no more important element in our common Western worldview to *undo* than this one of expecting life to match our preferences. Reality is as it is, not as we want it to be.

As we've seen, our immediate, apparent world is a world of duality, duality being the minimal reduction of the nearly infinite multiplicity that we assume extends to infinity. If the thinking mind tries to reduce the dual to one, the first digit in the counting series, this one becomes simply the one in contrast to the many and remains in the world of multiplicity, and, therefore, is not *the* One of nonduality.

Actually, however, each of us is One. In and as the One we are the One of the Universe and Beyond, a single One that can only be known beyond the dualizing mind, while resting in and as pure consciousness. The requirement of sequential thinking creates the inability to convey accurately the absolute impossibility of not distinguishing one thing from another in/as an awareness of One, of being One. This can occur 'experientially' only by releasing the world of multiplicity and resting in and as pure consciousness.

In and as pure consciousness, there is only One. This is where our essential identity lies as well as several other absolutely fundamental qualities of our humanness. An intrinsic mutuality, even identity, prevails among these qualities within the realm of Oneness. They are, minimally: consciousness, spirituality, knowing, being, love, happiness, contentment, and tranquility. Thinking/writing/talking require that they be treated serially.

The very fact that we're able to reflect on the qualities of consciousness, given the intrinsic limitation in thinking, indicates that we are not trapped in this limitation. We can rest in an awareness that is not caught in the limitation, thereby transcending it and uncovering the magnificent reality that is our essential identity – who/what we are by birthright.

Consciousness as Spiritual

Why begin by emphasizing the *spiritual* nature of our humanness? There are several reasons. One practical reason is that many, perhaps even most, who claim to be spiritual, do so without any experiential sense of what that spirituality actually is. If questioned, many will be unable to name a specific feature of their spiritual sense, but may hesitantly refer to some 'hidden' something or other, maybe something as nebulous as: "It's a gift of the Holy Spirit"; "It's somewhere in the unconscious"; or "It's beyond our awareness." At least the latter comment uses the right terminology even as it fails to see that *it is our awareness that is our spirituality*. What possibly could be more spiritual than consciousness itself? When we see that consciousness (that which we are most fundamentally and essentially) is also our spirituality, we recognize how absolutely crucial this is to human life as we know and live it. Spirituality cannot be separated from consciousness. To be one is to be the other. Consciousness/spirituality is single, in contrast to how the thinking mind and communication are forced to render it.

Spirituality as spirituality – unmanifested, unarticulated – is without content, just as pure consciousness is without content. Our subjectivity as subjectivity is also identical to pure consciousness itself and our spiritual root. When consciousness/spirituality/subjectivity takes on content, that content becomes what we are able to say about ourselves as religiously self-conscious beings. The content constitutes part of our unique personhood, who we are as a specific somebody, our distinctive features and traits. The manifested spiritual components in most cases will take on the form of a traditional religious faith: perhaps Methodist or Roman Catholic in the West, Muslim in Egypt, Hindu in India. Regardless of the outer form it takes, at root level in all that is human, consciousness itself is spiritual and subjective.

While consciousness as spirituality is the *sine qua non* of all human experience, as we've contended here, some may still fail to recognize the implications following from this. Perhaps the most important is that our body and thinking mind are *not* the most basic features of our humanness. Instead, they are 'tools' or 'mechanisms' that provide the opportunity for the expression, activation, and manifestation of our consciousness/spirituality/ subjectivity. Even as an automobile enables the activities of our life to expand but requires attentive care, so do our body and mind.

If unmodified consciousness is our base nature, why do we spend so much time, money, concern, and worry over the manifested modifications, the 'machinery,' that allows us to live a life that is centrally spiritual and, at best, secondarily physical? Is it not because we identify with our bodies as if that is who we are? We attach to the body because it seems so obvious. Human experience focuses naturally on objects, the outside world, rather than attend to our subjective, inner self – without which we could not even be aware of the outer world. We only come to know ourselves accurately when we open to our inner self. This process is enriched as we investigate what others have discovered about the inner self.

* * * *

Part of the evidence that I personally find so convincing regarding the centrality and foundational quality of our spirituality resides in the values that are recognized universally as the highest and most commendable: happiness, love, sincerity, honesty, integrity, justice, generosity, and patience, to mention a few. Every world religion champions these qualities to one extent or another. There is nothing material about any of them: they are entirely the 'stuff' of consciousness/spirituality. To be sure, they can be manifested in objective, even material form, and it is wondrous and commendable when that happens. These manifestations, however, begin in our spiritual nature, more commonly regarded as our mental-psychological-emotional nature, which is also spiritual and non-material.

To put the matter in its most comprehensive form: everything that occurs in the mind, in consciousness, is non-material, non-physical, non-concrete, and therefore spiritual. The content of the mind is without dimension and cannot be weighed or measured. How then can it be anything but spiritual? This is where we live our lives. This is actuality … who/what we are. The time/space expression in our inwardness is an appearance, a secondary level of reality. Our outer lives are real in the objective dimension, but are not primary as is our conscious/spiritual identity. Totally without any inherent materiality, our inner life, our subjectivity, is essentially spiritual. As such, it is our core nature. As spiritual beings, we are currently having a human experience, open to all the surprises and wonders that accompany this extraordinary adventure.

* * * *

The foundation for the worldview depicted here resides in the realization of our essential nature as spiritual beings. This is a prerequisite also for the discovery of our inherent happiness. We are increasingly acknowledging the priority of our spirituality over our humanness; that is, we are spiritual beings first and human beings secondarily. We *have* a body, we *have* a mind; but we *are* spirit. Evidence that we are fundamentally spirit is both implicit and explicit throughout this book. Our prevailing culture certainly doesn't support this view and there are ready arguments against it. A survey of the world's spiritual and wisdom traditions, however, provides plenty of evidence, certainly enough to begin at least to give the view thoughtful consideration.

Given the focus of the news media on the unusual, the exceptional, the fearful, and the negative, it's not easy in today's world to remain positive and hopeful. Without a doubt, there's a lot in the world that is horrendous, a lot that stimulates fear, a lot that is discouraging. At the same time, however, I'm amazed and deeply impressed with the extensive interest in and commitment to spirituality that has arisen worldwide in the last few decades.

The number of publications (books, journals, magazines), organizations (professional and lay), periodic meetings (in large assemblies and in private homes), and individuals who have given themselves almost full-time to personal discovery and enhancement of their spirituality is truly amazing. An Amazon search for spiritual books results in more than 512,000 titles. Some of the better-known teachers attract so many eager followers that attendance at their public meeting has to be managed by lottery. Adyashanti, an American who focuses on Zen Buddhism while drawing widely from other traditions, is a case in point. When the Dalai Lama speaks, thousand attend. In 1970, when I began teaching personal transformation from a worldwide perspective at Western College in Ohio, this interest and growth was just beginning. When I moved five years later to Cleveland State University, academic interest had expanded so significantly that multiple courses attracting hundreds of students were offered. Since that time, interest has blossomed culture-wide and worldwide.

Another example of this extraordinary growth is seen in the popularity of *A Course in Miracles* and its radical reinterpretation of Christianity. Purportedly revealed, as we've seen, by Jesus to Dr. Helen Schucman, an atheist psychologist in New York City, the content of this book exceeds 2,000 pages and is far from simple in its formulations. More than 2,000 study groups have formed since the mid-1970s and meet regularly, often weekly, in over 75 countries to explore the spiritual message of the *Course*. Large numbers of books have been written to interpret and expand the frequently enigmatic meaning and significance of the basic principles of this text. The teachings tend to be a reinterpretation and universalizing of standard Christian belief, but with an inclusive emphasis on spirit rather than doctrine or ritual.

Our spiritual nature and our happiness are so interconnected that either one is also the other. If we truly recognize our intrinsic spirituality and give full reign to its development, we are simultaneously happy. If our happiness is unrelated to any circumstance, if it is unconditioned, it is simultaneously an integral quality of our spirituality. In other words: to be spiritual is to be happy; to be happy is to be spiritual.

Humans typically postulate a natural happiness on the part of newborn babies, even while knowing that babies cannot articulate such subtle inner states, states that they can come to speak about only as language develops. By then, of course, the inborn state may have all but disappeared.

Damaging and occluding experiences inevitably occur to suppress awareness of our original happiness. There is compelling evidence, however, that this inborn state always exists as our essential nature, though perhaps beyond immediate awareness, and that it can be rediscovered. *Undoing* is devoted to this end – a guide to remembering who/what we are.

As adults, we know what happy experiences and spiritual experiences are. We easily and frequently talk about them. This is partly true because these are experiences that come and go, sometimes present and sometimes absent. Each one also has an opposite, at least what we regard as an opposite. We know what it's like to be unhappy and we certainly recognize feelings, intention, events, and situations that seem far from spiritual. In the past, we've all had our happy state shattered, for example, by a critical comment, and seen cases where someone who claims to be spiritual becomes guilty of behavior that indicates otherwise. The underdeveloped spirituality and happiness found in a broadly secular society seems obvious to those who know themselves to be spiritual beings. Some social psychologists and religious leaders conclude that rampant commercialism, alcoholism, drug abuse, sexual preoccupation, criminal activity, etc., are fundamentally symptoms of a spiritual void in the lives of those burdened by such obsessions.

* * * *

Every authentic religion offers a path from the fragmented world of discord and discontent to a world that is harmonious and One – that is, to Ultimacy, to God. In the Christian world, this journey back to Origin has been described in multiple ways, most often centering on salvation as a way of neutralizing sin. Today, only the most traditional of Christians believe in this centuries-old approach. This is certainly not to imply that what has been regarded as sinful throughout the ages is no longer found in society or within/among people. Rather, the stigma associated with the word 'sin' can be so harsh that it may induce an extreme negativity and alienation, an attitude inhibiting the free-flowing expressions of love.

Today, particularly where a sense of community and belonging prevail, we are more likely to consider this kind of disharmonious behavior as wrong-doing, as mistaken, as hurtful, as giving rise to suffering, rather than as sinful. What invariably happens whether it is called sin or mistake, is a disruption of oneness, harmony, accord, and always injects estrangement, alienation, and disaffection into the situation. For this reason, I prefer 'reconciliation' as a better term today for what historically has been called 'salvation' (*HTM* 285-351). A change in designation in no way lessens the impact and seriousness of this unfortunate feature in human relationships, and in no way lessens the need for forgiveness, a vital and necessary practice to be treated in an upcoming chapter.

Shifting so-called sin from the strictly religious arena (where it tends to be regarded as evil) to the educational realm (where it is considered a mistake) provides a significantly different solution than salvation. When a mistake occurs, an opportunity for understanding arises. Remorse and guilt are out of the picture. Consequently, there's no need to invoke a longstanding, irrational myth of salvation based on an ecclesial interpretation of an event (the crucifixion of Jesus) that took place some 2000 years ago. It now becomes a matter of re-education in present time, a broadening and deepening of understanding. This, in turn, brings love more readily into play. The Vietnamese saint, Thich Nhat Hanh, points out: "Understanding makes love and compassion possible, and when love and compassion are present understanding deepens" (*LBLC* 180). Understanding keeps open the on-going, never-ending path to full realization of our essential nature, without the burden of guilt.

Thus, salvation, redemption, and reconciliation are three ways of speaking about a process that is crucial in Christianity because it is the way one is restored to a right relationship to God if disruption has occurred. Doctrinally, this restoration is seen to reside in the work of Jesus the Christ as the one and only Son of God who is simultaneously fully divine and fully human. Theologically, this view is known as the incarnation, and held to be the unique nature of Jesus the Christ and of him only, a claim that cannot be substantiated because it has been made of others, both before, during, and after the time of Christianity's origin. For example, Heracles and Perseus were human sons of the Greek God Zeus and believed to be divine and human. In Hinduism, Krishna is known as an incarnation of Vishnu. Many other Hindu deities are human incarnations of the gods and goddesses that stand higher in the pantheon lineage.

My own view extending into young adulthood was that of traditional Christian doctrine. As a newly ordained clergyman, I preached sermons calling on sinners to come to the altar and be saved by Jesus. Needless to say, for me preaching of that type ended many decades ago. Today, not only do I reject the exclusivity of Jesus as divine, I also deny the exclusive identification of incarnation with Jesus. I now contend that every person is simultaneously human and divine. Even broader is my claim that everything in the universe is an incarnation (i.e., a manifestation or embodiment) of the universe's initiating force; everything reflects the stamp of its origin.

Each of us, whether Christian or not, can envision ourselves at birth as integrally divine and human, divine in the form of a newborn human. Our initial nature is divine/human, an identity that is integrally one. We are divine because we are the 'product' of the divine (everything created carries the impress of its creator); we are a manifestation of the *essence* of that which created all that is. The *Genesis* creation story asserts that God created us in his own image and likeness: "God said, 'Let us make humankind in our image, according to our likeness'" (1:26). This reference has had profound influence in the Christian mystical traditions, especially in the Eastern Orthodox Church with its focus on *theosis,* or deification (*HTM* 298). However, the *Genesis* passage can also be interpreted to support the contention maintained here: We are all created in the image of God, and, by detaching from the human accretions that hide this image, we manifest our likeness to God.

Being and Knowing

"I am" is the most authentic and comprehensive reply to the question, "Who are you?" In this response, we find two additional qualities of our innate consciousness: being and knowing. These are experientially evident and undeniable. No one could possibly talk us out of knowing that we exist, that we are. And these two nameable qualities are a single self-knowing/being. It is impossible to be and not know that one *is*; it is impossible to know and not be the one who *knows* that he or she is. The duality required by the thinking mind separates what is experientially a single awareness.

With this simple Self/self investigation, we have proven experientially to and for ourselves what the most astute philosophers have discovered and developed in subtle, abstract reasoning. Some of the world's foremost metaphysicians, when reasoning about the nature of being (ontology) and knowing (epistemology), discover and proclaim that they are single being/knowing, just as we have done experientially. Both Ibn al-'Arabī (a Muslim) and Meister Eckhart (a Christian) established this point centuries ago, independently of each other (*HTM* 263f, 401f).

Love

Love is as crucial to living the fullness of life as any quality so far considered. Like our spirituality, it is 'part and parcel' of our intrinsic consciousness. As mature men and women, we know what love is in some of its human expressions but are probably unfamiliar with its centrality in and throughout the universe itself.

If we accept the basic principles of evolution, we can reason backwards from what is known today and conclude that the current emergent and observable features must have been *potentially* existent and *potentially* operative in the earliest phases, though then unapparent. In a parallel manner, the genetic features distinguishing each of us today were present but indistinguishable in the zygote, the tiny cell resulting from the union of egg and sperm, from which each of us developed many years ago. The DNA that marked us then held within itself the information that has come to constitute each one of us in our distinct and unique personhood today.

Similarly, on a planetary scale, philosopher-scientist Richard Dawkins, beginning with what we know of life in the present, journeys backward through evolutionary history to the earliest known organic forms that eventually gave rise to the life we know today, our human life and that of other forms all around us (*AT*). I personally find this history of evolution far more remarkable, more wondrous, more miraculous than any creation story by an imagined superpower and his *nihil fiat* (command out of nothing).

The question arises: What could possibly be analogous to love in the earlier periods of cosmic and biological creation, before humans appeared? And the answer is: coherence, convergence, unification, linking. In every genuine instance of love, some form of separation is overcome and unification achieved. Throughout the universe and on earth, this connecting force is known as gravity; in physics, it's called fusion; in electricity, it's magnetism. It is also the centripetal force. Without this pervasive, joining force, the universe would have spread out too rapidly long ago and not be the universe we know. To be sure, this force does have its opposite: antigravity, fission, diamagnetism, centrifugal. Similarly, based on common understanding, love too has its opposites: fear, anger, frustration, impatience, rejection, etc.

From the standpoint of these parallels, keeping in mind the widespread attracting and uniting effect of these physical processes, we may think of the universe as a setting in which humans are loved by the universe itself, certainly in the sense of providing the conditions and means by which we are able to sustain and fulfill ourselves, and to live happy and meaningful lives. Everything we need to sustain life, even to thrive, is available. We live in a gracious world. That which we require in order to live healthfully, happily, creatively, meaningfully is freely available. If one retorts, "But we have to work for these things," that is true of course; but note also, everything that enables us to work is also given: desire, energy, strength, and opportunity.

The Western world's philosophical tradition also highlights the pervasive role of love in human evolutionary development. Plotinus (Third Century, CE), chief interpreter of Plato's spiritual reflections, identified five stages in the descent of the One into the cosmos: Spirit, Soul, Mind, Body, and Matter. Ascent to the One is a reverse movement through stages of development. Contemporary philosopher Ken Wilber and his colleagues map the individual ascent as one moving from archaic, to magic, to mythic, to rational, to integral. Wilber develops this lineage in two movements, expressed as descending into multiplicity and ascending to oneness. The One descends into the many, thereby setting up the means by which the many might ascend back to the One (*CW* 6). When anything emanates from a source, the return to that source is simply the reverse direction. No matter where we go from home, we get back by either retracing the same route or by any number of alternate routes.

While still rare, the insight that the natural world, even the physical realm, supports love as a universal permeating force is becoming increasingly recognized. Marc Gafni, a contemporary Jewish mystic, champions the same understanding. He writes: "The same love that initiated the big bang is the evolutionary eros that animates all of reality. It is the same love that causes quarks to come together to form atoms. It moves atoms to become molecules, and then later, complex molecules. It moves cells to become multicellular beings. Love, the movement towards higher and higher levels of mutuality, recognition, union, and embrace, is the eros driving all of evolution" (*SIEM* 68). A. H. Almaas (A. Hameed Ali) is another contemporary writer who teaches that the universe provides a loving and supportive context for human life and its unfolding, expanding development (*DHB*, *PE*).

From the standpoint of the social world, it would seem nonsensical to claim that love is inherent and ubiquitous in the world at large. We know only too well that love often seems entirely absent among humans. Perhaps even here, however, it is not. The seeming opposite of love manifests the ingrained presence of love in the universe, manifests it in opposite and contrary forms. When humans fail to live lovingly, trouble and suffering inevitably follow. A very good friend – after two divorces, addiction to alcohol, arrests, and imprisonment – discovered the effects of not living from love. He came face-to-face with the chaos and suffering that inevitably follow from love's absence. Realizing he was on a dead-end path, he turned his life around, took up a religio-spiritual practice, and sought help. He did die, as we all must, but he did so peacefully and with no regrets. Grossly negative ideas, intentions, and actions stem from an ignorance of love as a universal and individual quality. The undesirable result of this kind of negativity gives telling evidence of the supreme value of intra-human, intra-natural world, intra-cosmic love.

A Course in Miracles sets forth the view that every human lives out of either love or fear, two states from which opposite perspectives and emotions are manifest. It also claims that fear is actually a reaction to the mistaken sense that love is absent. The book teaches that *love is the only reality* – all seemingly contrary thought or behavior is the absence of and a call for love. However, in both directions, whether a direct expression of love or a reverse and hidden form, the love may appear in warped form, even grossly distorted. Positively intended love may be offered with conditions that actually harm the recipient. Parental guidance, rather than being supportive and nurturing, sometimes becomes demanding, even deteriorating into abuse.

An example of love made conditional by fear can be seen in my own childhood. Out of fear that I would not learn "proper" behavior and thereby bring embarrassment to them, my parents made what proved to be too many demands too soon. I, in turn, tried to meet their demands but could not and unintentionally developed behaviors unacceptable to them. A so-called 'vicious circle' ensued. Not finding the security and support that a one-, two-, three-year old needs, I unconsciously reacted with thumb sucking. This proved socially embarrassing to my parents, so even more pressure was applied in the form of a bad-tasting coating on my thumb, and then a full thumb wire cover. Frequent scolding only added to my frustration and confusion, increasing my sense of isolation and hurt. Feeling more than ever the need for security and some personal control over my life – all of this unconscious at the time – I unintentionally began to wet the bed at night. This, of course, was no solution, and resulted in just the opposite. With this example, we see how love that was made conditional by fear gave rise to unfortunate results. Love and fear cannot coexist. (I am happy to report that now at eighty-four years the 'terrible' habits acquired long ago have disappeared.)

Far less easily recognized are some other cases of the opposition between love and fear, cases where the need and search for love are so repressed that the seeming absence gets twisted into horrendous acts of hatred, torture, murder, and war. This kind of reversal is apparent when fear becomes aggressive and erupts as confrontation and attack (whether verbal or physical) rather than as withdrawal and protection. An obvious example of this arises when two people compete for the attention and 'love' of another. The common range of reactions, all in the name of love, may run from avoidance to criticism, to open disapproval, to angry words, to spreading lies, to physical fighting. Some citizens who profess love for their nation actually support positions that are contrary to the avowed values of their homeland. We see this today when Americans who affirm the abstract principle of equality act in ways designed to restrict voting rights, to deny equal justice before the law to people marginalized by class or ethnicity, and to reject immigrants and refugees.

The syndrome of intention reversing into its opposite, strange as it may appear at first, is found elsewhere as well. The psychology of projection offers another example. Projection occurs when any part of our actual nature that is not affirmed and healthfully manifested becomes repressed, and eventually shows itself in some distorted form, even as its very opposite. In most societies, perhaps all, the innocent and natural expression of urges that arise in childhood are rebuffed and thwarted by uninformed adults. When the innocent expressions of a child's nature are met with rebuff, children begin to regard this behavior as improper and unacceptable, perhaps thinking they are wrong, deficient, deviant, and, in religious households, bad and sinful. When only suppressed, as in my case, these negative directives can be reviewed from an informed stance and outgrown. When repressed, buried in the unconscious, they constitute issues that may impact the rest of life.

This tragedy occurs when unwise reactions to children's views or behaviors are so extreme that full repression takes place, and the children lose contact with the emotions and urges that were denigrated and rejected. These views or behaviors become so buried that they may emerge someday in a distorted and destructive form. A large percentage of this kind of repression centers in human sexuality. Horrendous as the act is, rape may be an appallingly warped attempt to find love. Fortunately, most adults mirror love so that children witness its manifestation in healthful and socially acceptable behavior.

Let's turn our attention now back to genuine love, the love we feel and manifest when in tune with primal love, the unconditional love that is embedded in our divine/human origin. This quality of love extends freely into all of life, human and non-human, into the entire universe in all its forms and processes. At the same time, when directed to family members and close acquaintances, this universal love takes on personal and individual features. Here too it will not be demanding, demeaning, or harsh, but offer gentle guidance to children and young people who may still need instruction – always with their utmost welfare in mind.

Happiness/Contentment/Tranquility

This trilogy is integral and fully embedded in each of us when we are created – and potentially, fully available to us experientially as we grow and mature. Thought and language (due to their dualizing function) require that each be named separately. Our original condition, however, includes them integral to each other (and simultaneously integral in the potentiality of pure consciousness). Thus, for accurate understanding, the three must not only be individually identified but also seen as a single feature, an integral trilogy in which if any one is present, so will be the other two. They cannot be separated from each other any more than the trilogy itself can be separated from the other qualities making up the essential nature of our origin. [Note: 'integral' is preferred to 'integrated' since the latter implies something that has been done that was not the case previously; the former avoids any such sequential notion.]

There are many ways of being human that do not give rise to a sense of genuine happiness, contentment, and tranquility. Is this also evidence of our spiritual nature? Yes, because the impulse, motivation, and thinking that manifests in negative, harmful action is certainly non-material in itself. However, the difference is that the effects of such behavior are contrary to the love and harmony inherent in the universe as well as contrary to the values principles by the religions and people who hold to basic moral values.

The Gospel of Matthew claims that even when some things are not apparent, they can be discovered: "You will know them by their fruits" (7:16). Not only scripture, but common knowledge also affirms that the inner can be surmised by the outer. In light of the discussion above on love in the universe, it is clear that behavior resulting in harm and suffering is contrary to the overall evolutionary thrust and conditions of the universe. Because this inevitably forfeits genuine happiness, it may be thought of as giving *negative* or *reverse* evidence to the inherent principles of the universe and we humans as discussed above.

To state the matter succinctly: living in conformity and harmony with reality leads to happiness and contentment, but living contrary to the basic principles of reality gives rise to suffering, consternation, and absence of wellbeing. Where there is sufficient wealth and prestige, this may not *seem* to be true. It definitely will be the case, however, for those harmed by the actions of the violators of this fundamental, cosmic principle. Even more concisely: If I'm selfish and want all advantage for myself, I'll not be inwardly content nor will others connected to me; if I'm without any self-preference, we'll all be happy. These contrasting states are evidence of the authenticity of the one and the inauthenticity of the other.

Look into the smiling face of an infant and you can't help but smile back and be lost in that common connection at the base level of our shared and pervasive happiness. For a timeless moment, all personal issues disappear and we know only bliss and tranquility. For the newborn, provided its needs are met, the contentment will continue for a time. However, the child will eventually lose this intimate and original happiness and, like adults, need to rediscover it.

Our immediate feelings of happiness take many different forms, with all of them tinged by this pristine, original happiness that is ours by birthright. Some of us have been conditioned to experience happiness through excellence in sports, achievement in business, top grades in academics, musical preeminence, a prestigious profession, a well paying job, a loving family, a carefree vacation, a notable house, lots of friends. The list could go on and on. The feeling that one stands out from others with some special achievement or quality is crucial to the self-esteem of many, perhaps of most. We do need to feel special and this often takes the form of a special accomplishment. The common feature in each of these 'experiences' of happiness is their dependence on conditions. While each of them reflects our native happiness, in the absence of the conditions (the precipitating circumstances) the experience of happiness might not exist.

Our pristine, birthright happiness is independent of circumstances; it is a steady, permanent quality. Posing a few questions will expose the fundamental difference between original happiness and the temporal happiness derived from conditions. What happens to the so-called happiness that depends on good looks when those looks fade with age or are impacted by illness or accident? What happens to the so-called happiness that comes with the purchase of a flashy new car when it gets old or becomes damaged or needs major repair? What happens to the so-called happiness that depends on athletic prowess, trophies won, business promotion, vacation time, when these all end, as they surely will? Yes, we experience what we *call* happiness in all of these desirable circumstances, but they all come to an end. In contrast, our embedded happiness is ours just because we're human. It is intrinsic to our humanness, timeless and independent of circumstances. If seemingly absent, this happiness/contentment/tranquility may be rediscovered by detaching from who we've learned to *think* we are and thereby *know* who we are as pure consciousness.

The view of the cosmos offered here probably seems reasonable enough, but the human position in it, and pristine human nature in particular, may seem "over-the-top, off-the-wall, pie-in-the-sky" fantasy. To be sure, given all that seems wrong in the world today, it would be easy to dismiss all of this as idle dreaming, too optimistic to have any basis in reality. I can readily imagine some readers, even if they've read this far, fully agreeing with this indictment. My own reflections in support of this view have been presented above.

One last observation: among people I know well, either personally or through reading, whenever they create or produce anything, it's to the best of their ability. It represents their ideal envisionment, highest aspirations, and reflects their noblest values and qualities. Why would the creating source of the universe, including we humans, do anything less than embed in us the best of itself?

In Summation

Being, Knowing, Consciousness, Spirit, Love, Happiness, is a single reality that is distinguishable only by the thinking mind. Apart from the separating feature of the thinking mind, each is integral to all and embedded in the whole. As the essence of our human birthright, this singularity lies dormant until the natural and cultural factors in life's circumstances begin to activate the potential and draw it into manifestation.

Evidence that these qualities constitute our essence lies in the fact that we don't learn them. No one has to teach us what each means. They are latent in us and become present to awareness when something happens that elicits them. Corresponding life events resonate with them and enable them to be re-cognized, known in the customary sense of the term. They are aptly regarded as gnostic in nature (i.e., a knowing that is not learned and therefore carries an authenticity and certitude unchallengeable and fundamentally unlike anything learned).

Why do we seem to forget our original, inborn nature and require this resonance for re-discovery? We discovered the reason earlier when we saw how we build our identity with our identifications, each of them overlaying and hiding our original embedded nature. We discovered that this happens whether it's something we like or dislike, admire or scorn, approve or disapprove. Either way, positive or negative, we build an identity. And this becomes the activity of the ego, the internal demon, to keep this complex of *me-ness* activated.

Interestingly, a few people don't seem to forget their divinity, at least not so quickly and thoroughly. Some children evince exceptional skills and knowledge, for example, prodigies, precocious children exhibiting wisdom beyond their years, children telling strange stories that adults label fantasy. Still others, like the Hindu sage-saint, Ramana Maharshi, rediscovered this knowledge as a teenager, obviously far earlier than many people (and most who don't discover it at all). Some adults claim to have known as a child, to have forgotten, and then rediscovered. For example, the American spiritual adept Franklin Jones (later known as Adi Da) named this childhood experience the "Bright" and later rediscovered it. A friend of mine describes this 'explanation' with one of his favorite quotations: "In the beginning, you knew; then you pretended to forget; then you pretended to forget you forgot; then you forgot you pretend. Remember?"

Undoing is for the sake of remembering ... remembering our original and essential nature. We undo that which has obstructed this original knowledge of our birthright nature, that is, what we have been taught that has served us for a time but is not lasting. Socrates, Plato, and Plotinus, who provided the philosophical foundation for Western culture, introduced *anamnesis* as the means by which we come to know that which is most important, our intrinsic nature. It is not through instruction and learning but by *remembering*. Socrates believed that when we learn we actually rediscover our deepest knowledge from past incarnations. He demonstrated anamnesis by asking a series of geometry questions to a young slave boy who was eventually able to provide answers without any form of instruction, thereby discovering within himself knowledge of which he had not previously been aware, which is exactly the objective of undoing.

Clarifying Notes

The following are Questions and Responses, for those who might want further information about ideas presented in Chapter One.

Q. There is a lot of evidence that we're born with defined propensities, in addition to accumulated inherited tendencies that manifest in the course of our life. What about these in light of the view that we're born as spiritual beings and inherently happy?

R. The evidence for this is quite convincing. This view helps account for the remarkable differences that appear in people and their life situations. But it doesn't distract from the view set forth; it means, however, that these persons – and this includes virtually all of us – will undoubtedly encounter personal qualities and characteristics that will present special attachment challenges and thereby become part of their distinctive path. Attachment is attachment whether it is inborn or learned. Each is susceptible to clarification and release.

Q. Is the order of the specific qualities of our inborn nature significant?

R. There is a degree of arbitrariness in the order. This follows naturally from the integral nature of the qualities as simultaneous and potential in pure consciousness on the one hand, and our requirement and need to investigate them one after the other on the other hand. Spirituality is first because it is so basic, pervasive, and rarely observed. Being and knowing are next because they unite as a logical prerequisite for the subsequent qualities, and everything that we ever experience in life.

Q. Is attachment ever good? What makes it bad?

R. We need attachment to construct a self (distinguished from the Self) and an ego (i.e., an identity), but when we face any real problem, it's because of being too attached. This is when we can detach, not by necessarily doing anything differently, but just by releasing to the universe, to Ultimacy, to God the effects/results of our action. Everything always works out one way or another; ideally, we are learning anew all the time. It's just a matter of continually detaching from what becomes dysfunctional, on and on as we discover the need to do so.

Q. Can we just detach from the ego all at once and thereby simplify the lengthy process?

R. A total and complete detachment is conceivable, but for most of us, given the holding strength of years of learning, conditioning, and habits, it is nearly impossible. A more workable approach is to detach from specifics when they are seen to be unproductive (i.e., give rise to suffering in one or more of its many forms, for oneself and/or others).

Q. Who originally said that we are spiritual beings now having a human experience?

R. The original source seems unknown. It has been attributed to both Pierre Teilhard de Chardin, the French Roman Catholic paleontologist, and to G. I. Gurdjieff, the Russian author and innovative spiritual teacher. The notion appears frequently in spiritual literature. The idea has clearly struck a positive note for many people. Its popularity can be regarded as indicating a growing change in our self-understanding.

Q. If the neonate is born in a state of native happiness and only begins to lose that sense of total well-being when its physical needs are not meet, how as adults can we can rediscover this original happiness in such a way that *regardless of the conditions* of our lives, we can be happy?

R. The child's inherent happiness is disrupted only when it begins to identify with its body and discomfort thereby is experienced. This begins what we might regard as separation from the essential spirituality of the soul and the early formation of the ego, the separate-self sense. As adults, we can transcend the ego and rediscover our essential self to such an extent that we are not distracted – much less, devastated – by what happens in and as the body. Though this is not easy, it is possible, but only when we *know* we are basically divine, and that we *have* a body but we *are not* the body. Separation from the body is exactly the goal sought by the extreme ascetics ... monks who deprive themselves of sleep and food, and the faqirs of India who lay on beds of spikes or hold an arm in the air until it atrophies. Practices of this type are a materialization of the sacred, and neither necessary nor recommended.

Q. What evidence is there supporting the idea of a path "from Ultimacy (God) and back to Ultimacy (God)"?

R. That there is such a return is most evident from the fact that every religious tradition has promoted a path and most have also outlined it in one or more ways. If there were no path, religion and spirituality would be entirely defunct, having offered for millennia something non-existent. The countless thousands of saints and sages who have travelled these paths over the centuries attest to their reality and effectiveness.

If you take up a spiritual practice and discipline, over time you will realize that changes are taking place in your attitudes and actions, changes that allow you to be more content with whatever happens. You will prove to yourself that the embedded qualities of your original nature are manifesting a "return" to the source of your being. There is no better evidence than this.

Q. Why is the word LOVE magnified from the common understanding of an emotion to the foundational force of oneness?

R. When we become thoughtful about what occurs whenever we feel love, we discover that love always involves a reduction of the distance we feel most of the time as we move through life and encounter other people. Initially there seems an absence of any sense of connection with them. This absence of feeling aligned and interconnected is the result of the ego, the separate self-sense that walls us off from the cosmos, including of course, other humans. Undoing the ego is so that we recognize our interconnection and oneness with all that is. Love is the primary and essential 'energy' of unification.

Q. The shift from regarding actions as sinful to seeing them as mistaken is interesting. It removes a lot of the odious associations from sin and opens the door to a more easeful change in attitude and behavior. But does this mean that punishment is now no longer advisable?

R. Yes and no. Punishment alone would be counter-productive and set up a superior-inferior relationship, a situation far from loving. It would be responding to hurt with hurt, never a remedy. This does not mean, however, that the mistake carries no implications for the one who erred. Some loss of privilege might be in order. Apology, recompense, and intention to change would all seem to be appropriate. Finally, the one who erred will certainly benefit from self-forgiveness, and hopefully from the forgiveness of the person wronged.

Q. Are consciousness and mind the same?

R. It is necessary to determine how a particular author uses them. With most authors, consciousness is an all-inclusive term: everything of which one is aware appears in conscious. These authors equate mind to intellectual and other activities of our immediate inner awareness. The mind is conscious as it senses feelings, thinks, remembers, plans, executes, imagines, daydreams, etc. All of these are conscious acts, but they are not pure consciousness because they constitute the content that occupies the 'space' of original, unadulterated consciousness. All mental activity appears within and as consciousness, but only 'base' consciousness, devoid of specifics, is what can be called 'pure consciousness.' In contrast, there are a few writers wanting to highlight the 'nonattached,' or 'pure consciousness' re-discovered by such sages/saints as the Buddha, Jesus the Christ, Lao Tzu, Ibn al-'Arabī, Ramana Maharshi, Dudjom Rinpoche,, and countless others. These writers may also use 'mind' to designate the pure consciousness re-recognized. The Mind/mind of Christ discussed in *Have This Mind* was most definitely the original Mind of pure consciousness, which, when manifested in Jesus of Nazareth, demonstrated the fullness of who He was. 'Mind/mind' aptly symbolizes the purity of our original consciousness integrated with the human mind.

Q. How does our human nature fit into our divine nature? How are we also incarnations along with Jesus the Christ?

R. Everything created has a divine origin and, therefore, mirrors something of the divine. It does not seem that it can it be otherwise. Everything a carpenter builds is a reflection of him and his skill. Accomplished artists leave their identity in their works, even without their signatures if they are distinctive enough in style, content, and media. Every actor portraying Hamlet depicts him uniquely. In a word, a creator is in the creation.

Thus, our origin is divine – the foundation on which/in which our humanness is established and integrated. As human awareness develops within and out of our pure consciousness – itself timeless and boundless – it does so within the framework of our humanness, including time and space. As we become more and more aware, we assume the features of our particular family, religion, school until we have become somebody, a specific identity with a distinct personality. For most, the process continues for a lifetime by means of attachment, aligning with that which is familiar, preferred, traditional, beneficial, enjoyable, supportive, and on and on.

If, however, along the way, we sense our inherent bound-free nature (divine origin), and wish to become free of the attachments that leave us bound up, this can be accomplished through 'detachment.' This reverses those very qualities of attachments that created our distinct personality but which now prevent us from rediscovering our most authentic self. Through releasing these attachments, through detaching from them, we can then experience the boundless freedom of our divine nature.

Q. Are there qualities in pure consciousness that are our origin and birthright?

R. The pure consciousness that marks our birth is inherently, simultaneously, and paradoxically eternal, infinite, courageous, open, free, trustful, wise, tranquil, creative, grateful, and more. These are not qualities we learn; they are re-cognized as they appear within ourselves, others, and the outer world. Wise guidance will, of course, encourage their development as they begin to appear and be recognized. Pure consciousness is a unity of distinguishable but nonspecific qualities because they are indivisibly in/as pure consciousness and reside there as pure potentiality. They manifest specifically as they emerge in the expanding awareness of the individual, and always in relationship to the changing, expanding milieu of the individual. Who we are and become is the result of the interaction between our Self, our unique self, and our environment.

Q. What is the difference between consciousness and 'pure' consciousness?

R. 'Pure' denotes something that is free of contamination. Awareness (consciousness) *as* awareness (consciousness) is not contaminated. We can be aware of contaminates, but our awareness itself is totally untouched by anything and everything that arises in it, and in that sense it is 'pure.'

If a person considers 'pure' as something that is unalloyed by anything else, they might conclude that 'pure consciousness' is made up of multiple qualities (love, happiness, etc.). It is only 'the thinking mind' that sees multiple qualities in and as 'pure consciousness,' for the 'thinking mind' must set up distinctions and differences. In a spiritual understanding of 'pure consciousness,' the words descriptive of its quality are found to be identical to the other fundamental and pure virtues. Any quality, when fully realized, will be found to incorporate the other qualities. They all integrate to constitute the original singularity of their pure status as potentiality, now manifested in time and space as us.

Q. What are some of the qualities that we commonly experience that are not inherent in our original Self?

R. Absent from our original Self are fear, anxiety, worry, impatience, hatred, dislike, judgment, boredom, and other undesirable qualities. These are entirely learned reactions to specific situations. When our natural and original nature is faulted or denigrated, negativity and suffering occur. This is what sets up the need – and opportunity – for detachment, by offering the prospect of rediscovering our original wholeness.

Q. When a person finally discovers the undesirability of the learned features of the self-sense and develops deeper and more spiritual aspirations, how do they release the ego properties that have defined them (and by which others know them)?

R. A vital part of the dis-identification process is the need to become aware of the unwanted aspects with unbiased objectivity, that is, with dispassionate neutrality – the simple recognition of them in one's conditioning and habitual patterns. One might begin by applying mild negativity to behavioral patterns that are annoying but not deeply ingrained in one's personality. This can be helpful with superficial, arbitrary habits, and at most would be a beginning, though not appropriate when facing more fundamental aspects of our self-image. The value of regarding behavioral changes like these with lightness lies in not needing to feel guilty or even embarrassed about them. They were habits taken on and now are habits undone.

When we face mental-emotional content with the same kind of neutrality, we are actually applying two of the most salient standards emphasized in the Buddha's experience and earliest teaching: to neither grasp nor resist, neither pull to oneself nor push away; instead to simply note, to be aware of, to acknowledge as now present. These two egoistic forces (the habituated reactions) that block our path to the realization of our true identity are the two forms that *dukkha* (suffering) takes in Buddhist teaching. Hinduism agrees: "Attraction and repulsion ... are seated in the senses. Let no one come under the control of these enemies" (*BG* 51). To accept reality fully as it is, as it presents itself, is to be free of both craving and rejecting. Note also how these polar opposites (wanting/not wanting) keep us trapped in the dualistic world, the world of either/or, and not the unitary world of both/and.

A third block to the realization of our true identity is ignorance (i.e., failure to understand how the world works, what reality actually is, in contrast to how we merely think it is). If we have a mistaken view of how life is, we can never harmonize with life as it actually is. We will always face disturbance and discord, suffering of one sort or another. A basic aspiration and prayer in Hinduism is: "Lead us from the unreal to the Real."

Chapter Two: Attachment: Why We Need It; Why We Don't

> Attachment is the great fabricator of illusions; reality can be obtained only by someone who is detached. (Simone Weil)

Attachment plays a dual role in our lives. On the one hand, it fulfills a necessary and crucial role in all human growth and development – individually, psychologically, religiously, and spiritually, as well as racially, socially, and culturally. On the other hand, if it becomes fixed and resistant to change, it undermines continued maturation. We need to know the pros and cons, the benefits and liabilities. We'll begin with the downside and discover the limitation and error in the most debilitating attachments. Then we'll consider the necessary but temporary role of indispensable attachments, the transient value of even useful attachments. Necessary, positive attachment fulfills a required function in the dynamic, perpetually changing and unfolding nature of life, both for individuals and humanity at large.

The full range of attachment constitutes a continuum: extending at one end from psychological illnesses, such as obsessive-compulsive behavior and addiction, through a middle range of extreme to moderate to mild so-called normal attachment, to the opposite end exemplified by indifference and unconcern. Curtailment of the natural unfolding of growth and development inheres in each of these attachment categories.

Strange as it may seem at first, indifference and unconcern are definitely forms of attachment. Those victimized by attachments like these are not free to respond appropriately in their interpersonal relations. They're attached to aloofness. Any attachment in the outer ranges, all of which impede natural or evolutionary growth, is undesirable. The limiting feature in the middle range (the range of so-called natural attachment) is conditionality (e.g., interpersonal relationships governed by a kind of economic expectation): if you'll do what I want, I'll do what you want. Unconditional love and compassion are absent. At best, wholehearted concern for the welfare of the other is dormant.

Let's clarify this continuum a bit further: addiction, an extreme and especially destructive form of attachment, hints at the subtle, hidden danger in all forms of attachment, namely, it inhibits full and appropriate participation because anyone attached is incapable of being fully present, fully aware. Addiction carried to the extreme objectifies this principle when it results in the loss of consciousness, as some forms do. The opposite extreme is indifference, unconcern, "couldn't care less," "they brought it on themselves," "it's their karma." Here the same inability prevails. The middle way includes forms of love that carry conditions, even within families and between friends. This becomes apparent when any difference between the parties disturbs the relationship, and is particularly blatant whenever "or else" becomes a threat.

Some believe that love always involves, even requires, attachment. Not true. The confusion here is due to not recognizing that the love of parents for their children, or the attitude of anyone responsible for them, entails standards and requires correction when these standards are not met. If instruction and guidance are offered with objective, non-emotionally-charged, matter-of-fact directives, those receiving it are likely to respond positively and with goodwill. Unfortunately, often in parental, instructive, and training contexts, attachment does occur and is handicapping to both parties: the leaders are disappointed and feel negatively toward their charges; those in the subordinate roles feel badly about themselves and their leaders.

Finally, the ideal, most effective attitude resides in the nonattachment of unconditional love, the love that resides at our core, well beyond emotion – a love that springs forth to instruct and guide the young, to face, ameliorate, and heal whenever suffering, pain, discord, consternation, injustice, prejudice, sorrow, etc., arise. Nonattachment means seeing the intrinsic worth of others – what is sometimes called their "Christ nature" – without any fixation on particular results, especially any of personal benefit. When this occurs, mutuality and compassion flow forth naturally and freely.

Part I: Agent of Identity and the Ego

Attachment is how we construct a personality and a character. It enables us to become one-of-a-kind. By means of attachment, we become recognizable as a distinct person with special abilities, with strengths and weaknesses, with likes and dislikes. Our attachments make us who we are and thereby fashion someone that others will want to be with – or otherwise. Our particular attachments build our identity and our ego. They attract some to us, turn others away, and leave others indifferent.

For most of us, the process of becoming a unique person is more automatic than deliberate; we probably don't even know what is taking place, how, or why. Looking back over my own childhood, adolescence, and early adulthood, I can identify now some of the assumed principles, concepts, and words that shaped who I became. I don't remember ever questioning what I was told or even heard from a relative, teacher, or admired adult. I met – unconsciously tried to meet – their expectations. One time as a teenager while driving with my dad and one of his best friends to go deer hunting, his friend, the head of the electrical utility company in our area, made a comment and I offered something different that I had learned in school; my comment was immediately discounted, and I felt diminished. While I've long since forgotten what I said, I've remembered the 'put-down' (now only an emotion-free memory). Incidents like these keep many of us confined within narrow worldviews – until we go to university and are encouraged to explore and think for ourselves and reach the rational stage of personal development.

We cannot avoid constructing an identity. Identity is established from the family into which we're born, our race, our nationality, where we live, the schools we attend, the activities we take up (I play a trumpet, I play football, I'm in drama), the religion we embrace or reject, our political views, our gender, our job or profession. These factors (and many others) make us who we are as social beings.

All of this is important but does not constitute the fullness of our identity. Prior to this and far more important is our humanity and its fundamental nature. Our *human* nature determines the basis on which our identity develops and becomes established. It takes precedence over all lifetime influences. This is where the divine integrates into the human and becomes our incarnational identity, the root on which all else occurring in time and space impacts us. Important as our social identity is, it becomes problematic when not seen to rest on our divine/human identity, as indicated in the first chapter.

* * * *

Another way of talking about identity is to see it in terms of the roles we fulfill in society. Some roles fall to us naturally; for example, the role of son or daughter is ours without choice since it is determined by our gender. Developed societies, with compulsory education, force us to become students – another unselected role. As we grow into adulthood, we pick our roles, often however with a lot of subtle and not so subtle influence from others. When we marry, we automatically become husband or wife, most often followed by father or mother. Again to a great extent, society sets how we're going to fill those roles. Additional roles derive from the job or profession we choose. A physician's life is very different from that of a carpenter.

The reason for this brief description of what is evident and undeniable is to show that these identities and roles are not fixed and unalterable. Even those identities that fall to us by right of birth can be changed in the way we occupy and fulfill them. Today, even gender identity can be changed. Other identities, those we've chosen and those taken on unconsciously, can be changed, though this may involve a great deal of difficulty for ourselves and others. Even when acknowledging the fact of perpetual change – in the universe at large, in human communal life, and in ourselves individually – many of us, perhaps most, are uncomfortable with change. It is rarely easy.

The most important benefit gained from recognizing and naming our identities and roles is the discovery that they *can* be changed. Not everyone, however, takes advantage of this possibility. At the local fitness center, I see a woman who may be the most unhappy, despondent, forlorn, downtrodden, and sour person I've ever met. I've learned enough from her to know that she sees herself as a helpless victim. Although she volunteers nothing, I have learned that she works constantly when at home. Her husband works too, but only enough to get discounts on what he wants for his hobbies; otherwise, he just sits. She comes to the fitness center every day at 3:00 or 3:30 a.m., works out about two hours, and then goes to a full-time job. When I've suggested the possibility of change to her, it seems to fall on deaf ears. It's sad to see a human life so painfully experienced and apparently squandered.

The process of changing our identities can become easier if our roles are likened to the clothes we wear. To a great extent, our dress reflects our roles, sometimes obviously as with the military, in the health profession, and in the uniforms required by some employment. My own dress was that of a professor when on campus, moderately casual with a sports coat and tie, which was entirely inappropriate at home (especially if I was in the barn feeding my cattle). This homespun comment is meant to underscore the looseness with which identities and roles rest on our essential nature (i.e., our pure consciousness, our spirituality, happiness, and love). Just as we have added the roles, we can change them or drop them.

A. What is the Ego? How Does It Operate?

Even as attachment builds identity, it builds, expands, and solidifies the ego. The ego is our sense of being a separate person, an individual standing apart from all others and everything else. In this sense, the ego has gotten a lot of bad press, frequently being considered entirely bad, something to be destroyed. Some Muslim mystics, for example, speak of annihilating the ego. The informed among them, however, are actually urging the annihilation of all sense of separation from God. These are Sufis who have come to the realization that everything is Divine. They interpret a Koranic verse (2:115), "Whithersoever you turn, there is the Face of God," to mean that "Thus, there is nothing in existence save only God," as interpreted by al-Ghazzali, one of Islam's most respected theologians and mystics (*HTM* 258f). These sages see the ego as God's protective presence necessary until a person has evolved enough to entertain the full magnificence of the Divine. Kahlil Gibran may have had something like this in mind when he penned the following:

> The veil that clouds your eyes shall be
> lifted by the hands that wove it.
> And the clay that fills your ears shall be
> pierced by those fingers that kneaded it.
> And you shall see. And you shall hear.
> Yet you shall not deplore having known blindness,
> nor regret having been deaf.
> For in that day you shall know
> the hidden purposes in all things.
> And you shall bless darkness as you would bless light.
> (*TP* 127)

Reflecting on the major times and issues in one's personal history often leads to discovering that even when the ego was most active, vital developments occurred that brought one to the present time and situation. Gibran's lines acknowledge this meaningful continuity.

Even while honoring its protective and guiding role, however, the ego must be tamed to avoid it creating untold suffering and damage to the self and to others. If the authentic ego is understood as the central organizing principle of waking life, with the limiting, destructive, and separative function simply added to it, the demand for its complete destruction becomes unnecessary. Since the ego is actually an assumption, a thought, and a way of acting, then once the mistaken, separative self-sense function is recognized, it can begin to be minimized and its operations eventually eliminated. While the achievement is rare, countless lives over time have shown themselves to be egoless in this sense.

Although the process of weakening the ego can be summarized in a sentence, it may be difficult to understand properly, and even more difficult to put into effect. With ongoing practice, even egoistic self-centeredness can be progressively reduced. Then we begin to feel less alone, less alienated, and less fearful. The best news is that the separative ego can be entirely eliminated. This happens when we feel at home no matter where we are, and happy no matter what conditions prevail.

If our essential nature harbors the qualities of love, happiness and tranquility, as set forth in the previous chapter, how did something so distorting as the ego arise to block this awareness? The fact that it is a universal feature of humanity suggests that it is necessary and inevitable. Why does it exist? How did it form? We've seen one religious perspective above, the Sufi. There are others, but they need not detain us since our objective here is to account for the ego from a more natural and universal standpoint, one that is less historically conditioned, less cultural, less religious. Fortunately, there is a way to account for this self-limiting 'handicap' in the context of how we evolve in the natural course of human life.

A newborn, a neonate, may be aware but not self-aware. Self-awareness arises as the infant experiences a need (something absent but wanted), for example, hunger. This automatically gives rise to discomfort and crying. When the need is met with feeding, satisfaction arises and contentment returns. But then disturbance returns when the food is processed and waste is expelled from the body. The latter may be a pleasant feeling initially but is not when its result is left unattended. So a sense of discomfort arises again, stimulating unpleasantness until intervention occurs.

In the first scenario, something is wanted; in the second, something is not wanted. This alternating pattern becomes embedded in the psyche and shapes the child's basic development throughout life. The oscillation between these poles is assumed to be normal, natural, and inevitable. Therefore, for the rest of our life, a feeling of subtle or extreme dissatisfaction orients us, even compulsively drives us, to be either grasping something wanted or pushing away something unwanted. This is the ego at work in its separative function, perpetually keeping us out of harmony with the flow of life, always wanting things to be different from the way they actually are at each unfolding moment. According to the analysis of the Buddha, this is suffering in its most subtle but comprehensive form.

* * * *

A little over 2500 years ago, the Buddha's investigation into the human situation produced a crystal clear understanding of this universal dynamic, a dynamic that activates one of the most powerful, often unrecognized sets of urges governing how we live our lives: preferences (likes and dislikes), judgments ("He's too fat; she's too skinny"), distinctions (friends and enemies), desires ("I want this, not that"), and on and on. The Buddha summarized his personal, experiential investigation into the human situation by identifying *dukkha* as the basic predicament with which we humans struggle, the inevitable affect of which is to feel separated from the whole, from the flow of life itself.

Dukkha is usually translated as "desire" but is more subtle and comprehensive than our common understanding of that term. Dukkha names any sense of discontent, dissatisfaction, or unease. It designates the feeling, often subtle and unrecognized, that this moment, this situation could be better if it were different. For example, if you assume you're going to be happier some time in the future than you are right now, you are experiencing dukkha. The Buddha then pointed out that dukkha derives from *tanha*, the desire that a given situation be otherwise than it is. So tanha is wanting this and not wanting that.

When discontent (subtle to extreme) and desire (for or against) occur simultaneously, which they do universally in humans, we have set up an inevitable contradiction: we are wanting something to be different that *could not possibly* be different – because the complex of conditions, causes, and choices that gave rise to it have *already* resulted in the situation we now want to be different. To expect any situation to be different from what it is at any specific time and place is to expect history to reverse itself and come back in the form of what we want. Not likely to happen! Based on the insight of the Buddha when he became enlightened, the analysis of this pervasive and persistent human condition remains, from my perspective, unchallenged.

Buddhism continues its clarification of our subtle, ever-present discontent by declaring that it derives from three interrelated factors: (1) ignorance, (2) wanting this, (3) not wanting that. Ignorance, most simply, is the failure to understand and correct the constant projection of our own likes and dislikes on the world. In the final analysis, ignorance is simply a personal expectation projected onto reality, the expectation that reality should conform to our particular likes and dislikes. Therefore (to describe the Buddhist analysis succinctly), we are always a little discontented because we're ignorant of how reality works: reality is what it is – and does not accommodate our particular desires (what we want and don't want). The three factors, therefore, reduce to one: ignorance. What could be more improbable – actually, impossible – than this, that reality should accommodate our whims? And yet this is what drives most of us, *unconsciously*.

All of this is true only of the ego as the separate-self-sense, living as a "skin-encapsulated ego," as Alan Watts in the last century aptly put it. If the ego is regarded as the central organizing principle that allows us to operate as an individual among other individuals, then it is not only useful but necessary. We cannot do without a comprehensive guidance system that enables us to move with some degree of ease within life, especially contemporary life with its increasing rapidity of change and complexity. For this we need the ego.

This dimension of the ego is also needed as we work for change in situations we accept or acknowledge as the necessary reality of the moment. To withhold our personal preferences, our individual likes and dislikes, is not to render us inactive or without values. In a word, there is no necessary conflict between acceptance of 'what is' and working to make the next 'what is' better.

What we need also, however, if our personal unfolding is to continue, is the skill to note when we are not feeling relaxed and content, when there is something amiss, something causing disruption of our well-being, maybe even strain or stress. When this occurs, we have an opportunity to look within to see if there is some form of attachment operating, some expectation foreign to the situation in itself. More pointedly, the question might be something like this: What is going on in me that could be causing or contributing to this disturbance? This is one of the most important ways to discover attachments, a constantly available principle in the ordinary affairs of life. No need to withdraw into solitude or join a monastery or convent.

* * * *

Even as we arrive on the planet in human form and are defenseless, the love embedded in the universe, in parents, in hospitals, and even dormant in us, nurtures and protects us as we begin our life journey. We also bring with us a yet-to-be-discovered wholeness. William Wordsworth seems to have recollected something like this when he wrote: "Trailing clouds of glory do we come / From God, who is our home" ("Intimations of Immortality from Recollections of Early Childhood"). Most humans never recognize wholeness, the state in which we are born.

Before the ego becomes operative, to actually permeate and structure our awareness by dualizing our experience, it rises out of and pulls away from this wholeness and obstructs the all-pervasive presence of our original nature. The ego is made of the same 'stuff' as consciousness. However, by extracting itself from its origin, it seems to stand apart from it. Thus, seemingly separate from the whole, it begins to function by seeing everything as other than itself. Now begins the usual life-long challenge of living in a dualistic world, one founded on the struggle between opposites and fortified by the thinking mind and its dualizing operation within a world fragmented into endless parts. Because we assume a world based on a me/not me dichotomy, we never find true rest or ease. Where there are opposites, fear arises. An ancient Sanskrit text affirms: "Where there is no other, there is no fear."

Now deprived of its former wholeness, the ego becomes permeated by a sense of insecurity and fear. It tends to automatically – even unconsciously – sense danger. In doing so, it constructs a variety of defenses to protect its imagined solitary confinement in the big and dangerous world. Because of its sensed fear, the ego concocts various stratagems to preserve its status as the controlling center of the conscious personality. Primary among these is judgment, the critical rejection of that which is believed to be other, different, and especially, threatening.

By means of judgment, the ego maintains it position and authority. It's as if it is saying to the larger self, the whole person: "See how I'm protecting you from danger, from all the many things in life that are scary and threatening. You need me." Actually, of course, it is only the ego that is threatened. More often than not, fear is not real but imagined.

There are endless ways of imagining and projecting fear. One of the most obvious ways of creating a nonexistent fear is to project it into the future. A great deal of life in all cultures and societies operates by means of this dynamic (e.g., insurance, in its many forms; military defense; borders, border walls, and check points; partisan politics and campaigning; conspiracy theories; fundamentalist religions; parental standards and restrictions, and more). Perhaps less obvious is the imagined and projected fear that often motivates the advertising that prompts buying: buy this and you'll be more attractive, better dressed, smell better, be more secure, more comfortable, etc.

Naming the fear inherent in the ego and its machinations does not mean we can dispense with caution and foresight; it means rather that we avoid letting fear govern our lives, that we recognize how it operates and do not become victimized by it. Fear itself melts in the company of trust and love.

Derived as it is from wholeness, the ego 'forgets' its origin, feels less than whole and attempts to fill the vacuum by adding more and more experiences, achievements, wealth, prestige, positions, acclaim, friends, on and on. The 'on and on' is a definitive feature of the ego because it is never satisfied. By right of its lack, it continually searches for fulfillment but always in directions and ways that can never really satisfy. Because the seeking is always for things that are themselves limited, the accumulation of 'stuff' can never contribute to completeness. Driven by a blind search for more and more, the ego can never find genuine satisfaction.

Admittedly, when something wanted is received, a sense of happiness and accomplishment usually exists, momentarily. This sense, however, derives from the temporary cessation of the ego's embedded sense of incompleteness and continual seeking. Because these gains are always short-lived, the pause from compulsive desiring proves temporary and inadequate. The brief satisfaction experienced from the desired gain, while temporary and partial, is nonetheless a hint of the wholeness timelessly abiding in our intrinsic nature. This fundamental and essential nature may be occluded, but it can never be destroyed.

* * * *

As we have seen, when we think of the ego as the separate-self-sense, it can eventually, after much 'grinding away,' be dropped. We continue, however, through most of our adult life to need the 'purified' ego in order to function in a useful and meaningful way. Finally, even this seemingly necessary role of the ego can be eliminated. If we regard it as *a role* we play in our journey through life, we can see clearly that it is not integral to the all-encompassing consciousness that we are fundamentally. It is superimposed. This claim needs further clarification.

As the central organizing principle, the ego is necessary only until we rest fully and unreservedly in our deep, unchanging Self as the divine in human dress. A person who has arrived at the post-integral stage – perhaps hardly imaginable for most – is totally unselfconscious as a separate being and therefore without any need for a central organizing system. Such a person lives nondualistically in the dualistic world. Each is a center without circumference, harmonizing in and as a Whole that is not different from the Self-sense. There is no longer a need to deliberate or make choices. This 'individual' is now so in tune with the unfolding of the universe that the implicit intelligence of the universe emerges in, through, and as him or her. This intelligence is what was embedded as everyone's original birthright, now re-cognized and restored.

Most conventionally religious people assume God's will to be what they've come to believe from their scripture and spiritual leaders. This works well enough in exoteric forms of religion. However from the less restricted mystical and non-dual esoteric religious view, God's will for an individual is to align and to act harmoniously out of a pure heart and mind with the unfolding and ever-changing reality of the here and now. This is what *A Course in Miracles* proclaims as: "My will and the Will of God are one" (*W* 54, 5:5). Six centuries earlier, Meister Eckhart taught that the will functions properly when there are no blocks around the human heart that may have accrued to keep it from being what it truly is. In other words, God's will is for perfect and appropriate alignment with what is, having fully released all personal (i.e., egoistic) projections (*WJ* 16).

In the wisdom traditions of the East, a person of this status has become *sahaja* (literally, 'natural'), one with All and living spontaneously. Sahaja also designates ultimate realization and thereby calls attention to coemergence with the universe *as* Universe, which means one is aware of being fully human and simultaneously linked intimately with and as Ultimacy. These states of realization, whether affirmed in the East or the West, come to fullness only through long and extraordinary detachment and letting be.

B. The Many Forms and Degrees of Attachment

One of the most remarkable Christian texts remains unknown to the vast majority of Christians. *The Gospel of Thomas* was discovered in the Egyptian desert in 1945 and is believed by many scholars to have been written even before the *Epistles of Paul* and the four *Gospels*. Its early date heightens its claim to authenticity. This brief text consists of 114 sayings of Jesus, at least thirty-three of which speak in various ways of non-attachment. In one of these sayings, Jesus declares: "If you do not fast from the world, you will not find the Kingdom." Fasting refers metaphorically to not getting caught up in the things of the world, to detaching from the world; it's a reminder to "be in but not of" the world. On another occasion, the disciples ask: "When will be the day that you appear to us? When will be the day of our vision?" and Jesus replies: "On the day when your are naked as newborn infants ... then you will see the Son of the Living One." "Naked" refers to detaching from all the identities (we've built) and the roles (we've taken on) that block the realization of our core spiritual nature. As we drop these identities and roles, we align with and take on the very mind of Christ.

Throughout Christian history, a specific promise and challenge (hardly conceivable in the modern age) is Jesus' assertion that his followers will be able to move mountains. This bold promise and challenge is found in Paul's letters, the canonical gospels, and *The Gospel of Thomas*; these multiple sources make it hard to overlook or even minimize the claim. Interpreting the meaning of these words, however, should take into consideration how translations of historical writings from one language to different language might 'tarnish' the original meaning. For example, few Christians are aware of the fact that Jesus spoke Aramaic, an Eastern language, and that the earliest translation of the *New Testament* was in Greek, a Western language. There were many idioms in Aramaic that had no equivalent in Greek. "Move mountains" is a case in point. In Aramaic, it means to remove obstacles, to remove that which blocks one's way, that which impedes progress. Therefore, moving mountains is a vivid metaphor for detachment.

A short but influential tract from China opens with the assertion: "The Great Way is not difficult for those who have no preferences." This bold claim is easily misunderstood if the word 'preferences' is not interpreted here in the sense of grasping and clinging, of needing something so desperately that if not secured, discomfort, anxiety, and loss arise. Rather than being handicapped by our preferences (our tendency to grasp and cling to perceived needs), we can learn to relax and feel our inherent wholeness. This is entirely possible as we release attachment to simple preferences.

I used to 'need' a bowl of ice cream covered with peanuts and chocolate every night before going to bed. With some slight but felt difficulty, years ago the habit began to be released; that particular attachment is now gone. In former years when I played marbles, table tennis, or nearly any other 'game,' I drove myself to win, or at least to be better than most. Noticing this, my wife once asked: "Why do you always needed to win when you play with the boys?" Today I'm happy to just enjoy the game, to share an activity while easefully participating; it doesn't matter who 'wins.' Formerly, I became extremely upset if my new car got scratched or dented; now it's just part of wear and tear.

Years ago, one of my female students would not appear out of her dormitory room without first putting on her customary makeup, which was elaborate and took considerable time. When I suggested that the habit was not essential, she gave it up and saved money, gained time, felt more confident, and was freer. Standards of home tidiness have lessened for many, certainly a sign of reduced attachment. We all used to get dressed up in our best clothes when going to church or any important function. Today this social expectation has eased enough so that almost any 'decent' apparel is fine.

During our lifetime, most of us have probably participated in some hobby, sporting event, or outdoor activity. These may continue for some. Those we performed well, we tended to develop and enjoy; with others, we lost interest and dropped them. We like the activities that we perform well and from which we get acclaim; we don't like those in which we don't do well, especially if it's also apparent to others. We attach to the first and detach from the latter. Both add to our identity: this is me, that is not me.

As spectators, we may also develop attachment to certain teams (often those closest to where we live) and not to others (their rivals). Watch any major sporting event today, professional or amateur, and we'll see tens of thousands roaring fans in the bleachers. University and professional football today is a business, an industry. If a team is winning, the coffers overflow and the university thrives, as do investors in the professional teams. Yes, it is a business, but the loyalty of the fans is directed to the teams and the players. Specific players (those who score often and are most skilled) get the greatest attention.

Picture a major university stadium on a fall Saturday afternoon: tens of thousands fill the seats; bands perform; cheerleaders cavort; vendors sell; players sprint onto the field; referees ready themselves; a coin is tossed; the teams align, and 'play' begins. Fans are on their feet yelling support: for the offense, for the defense, "run over them," "push them back," "heave it over their heads," "sack the quarterback." Why the shouted support and its opposite? Because of attachment, for and against.

When objectively analyzed, the fun is diminished if not destroyed. Does this suggest that we give up our interest and passion for sports? Definitely not. But it might suggest that we not identify so completely with a loss that it causes us to sink into sadness and despondency, or allow a victory to make us feel joyous, proud, and maybe even invincible.

Televised images of fans indicate that these reactions often occur. We see tears and elation. These are 'games,' and it's called 'playing.' These behaviors may reflect our social identity, but are a long way from our divine/human identity. These instances of fairly shallow attachment demonstrate that detachment can be fairly easy sometimes, especially when we get a clearer understanding of what's going on.

The attachment/detachment process is a dynamic one that occurs naturally in the course of a lifetime, in the ordinary span of maturation. The instances discussed above often occur spontaneously. This is not so with attachments that develop in the more central dimensions of our nature, that constitute our self-conscious identity and are held so tightly that if challenged, an automatic defense is activated.

* * * *

Attachment to features of our personality by which we are known and from which we gain attention, whether admiration and respect or rejection and judgment, are more central and much harder to change. These reflect our character and reputation. Reputation and character may not be clearly distinguished from each other in the popular mind, but are crucially different. I remember a federal committee hearing when a highly educated judge was being vetted to determine his competence for the US Supreme Court. A charge was brought against him that threatened his trustworthiness. In response to testimony that would seem to disqualify him, he replied: "You have destroyed my character." This would be utterly impossible. We know what our character is and it cannot be threatened by verbal attack. Our reputation, however, can be.

Reputation derives from our persona, our publicly displayed self. Reputation is how I'm perceived. From this, we need to detach. The central Hindu scripture, the *Bhagavad Gita*, asserts concerning reputation: "He who is thus indifferent to blame and praise, ... who is ... of steady mind – that man is dear to Me" (*BG* 105). Buddhism adds six more public assessments from which the truly wise will detach: loss and gain, pleasure and pain, dishonor and fame. To clarify when to do so is appropriate. Selfless intention may be appropriate for those truly detached from these traits.

Character, on the other hand, is who I am as a person. It includes the qualities and virtues that mark my identity as a human being within a specific society. Those taking the high moral and spiritual road will manifest and enhance their positive qualities while dispassionately undermining and releasing the negative qualities. We must detach from all of this in order to align fully with our deeper, divine identity, our abiding 'I am.' Unlike detachment from reputation, however, this detachment does not require elimination, but does require simple objective recognition, without a particle of pride, or sense of achievement, or need to defend. On the latter point, *A Course in Miracles* (*W* 284) proclaims: "In my defenselessness my safety lies." Character results from grace, life's greater intelligence that guides the entire evolving process of which each of us is an integral part contributing to the whole. If this is acknowledged, the need for defense or justification becomes irrelevant because we know within our heart of hearts that we are aligned with the Real.

Obviously, only the person attached can undo attachments. Fortunate is the person who discovers his or her attachments and acts to remove them, whether they are self-discovered or pointed out by a family member, friend, someone disliked, perhaps even an enemy. Quite likely in these cases, most egos will try to protect their status by automatically denying, justifying, defending, or excusing the action or statement in question. Egos rebel against being recognized. This is, however, an opportunity for significant change if one is honest and courageous enough to acknowledge the need for charge, to reflect on it, and if finding it accurate, to commit to detaching from it.

The ego can most effectively be undermined and eventually vanquished through admitting its presence – without defense. Calm, detached clarification may be in order if the critique is based on mistaken observation or voiced from a more limited evolutionary perspective. Otherwise, the most honest and effective response is defenselessness. More often than not, defending oneself only leads to back-and-forth argument and hard feelings. Even more important – from the standpoint of undermining the ego – is the fact that defensiveness is actually an act of the ego designed to make its action appear proper and therefore to substantiate its presence. Defending oneself strengthens the ego and reinforces the sense of disconnection and disharmony.

* * * *

As attachments increase, our identity is established. The process makes us who we become. We all begin life by attaching to mother, father, family, home, toys, visitors, and perhaps in this order. Somewhere along the span, we discover and attach to our body and become it. This becomes one of our assumed and fixed attachments, beginning to weaken only when we discover that we *have* a body but *are not* the body. Many, maybe most, never make this crucial distinction – crucial from the standpoint of countering a commercial culture that encourages fixation on the body in order to sell products, all the way from houses and cars to clothes and cosmetics.

To acknowledge that we *have* a body but *are not* the body is not to denigrated or lessen the importance of the body, not by any means. To see the body as a tool, an instrument, analogous to a car, requiring from time to time refueling and repair, is to see it properly and worthily. Our physical embodiment is always to be honored and respected. Without the body, we could not live the wonderful and ever-unfolding life we are given. Even as the world of nature would not exist without the planet, we would not exist in the fullness of our humanness without the body.

A further value of the body, even more rarely recognized, lies in the fact that it is always in the present – and only in the present. Human attention does not connect with the body as it was or as it will be but as it is, just now. Admittedly, we can recall something of how the body may have felt in the past, but that is the result of memory and not immediate awareness; also, we can imagine what it might feel like in the future. To tune into the body is to bring the focus of the mind out of the past or the future into this moment here and now. One would be hard-put to find a spiritual principle more often stressed than the ideal of living in the present. Bringing attention to the body begins the retraining.

* * * *

Neighborhoods add to our attachments and identity, as do schools and the grades we receive, the friends we have, the groups we join, the work we do. As children and teenagers, we have no idea how these connections lead to attachment and identity. We only know: "This is me and how I am." As we grow, we add more and more to "who I know myself to be." As a teenager, we may explore different ways of being 'me,' at one time wanting independence from the family, at another time withdrawing into the security and warmth of the family. If that environment is not available, retiring to one's bedroom or 'hiding' place, escaping to a friend's house, wandering the streets, or joining a gang may become substitutes. The options are many; we all need a sense of acceptance and belonging. We'll find it somewhere or sink into despair. Identity develops as an interaction between the distinctiveness of our nature and the particular features of our surroundings. We grow and mature in relationships. We are communal creatures who thrive in community. We don't do well if forced into isolation. We may choose solitude for a particular reason and for a period of time, but compelled apartness is punishment, as in the solitary confinement of prisons.

Interaction between oneself and one's environment inevitably gives rise to issues needing resolution. Teenagers are particularly vulnerable as they learn to be themselves, surrounded as they are by innumerable models and ways of being. Countless more options exist now than in previous times when culture was more uniform. Youth is a time of experimentation, of trial and error. Inner urges interact and frequently collide with outer expectations. What to do? Raised as I was in a family molded by conservative principles, I read books and pamphlets on proper behavior, dress, etiquette, and appearance. My home encouraged this, along with faithfulness to church standards. Everyone is subjected to particular influences. All home life shapes but it does not determine. All individual life continues to develop, either extending or contending the influences of the early years.

Irrespective of the particular home environment, everyone faces social and moral dilemmas. The question, "Who/how am I going to be?" has to be answered. If the intensity of the inner urge is greater than the restraint of the home, especially if support comes from the outside world, the urge may be secretly expressed outside the home. This may lead to inner dissonance and possible conflict. Often in this situation, the psyche will activate in the form of the Shadow; the particular issue (anger, fear, moral ambiguity, sexual frustration) will become repressed to such an extent that it disappears into unawareness. Psychology has demonstrated convincingly that repressed feelings and urges are always projected onto the outer world. Some contend that the projection of disowned feelings and urges are so assuredly going to occur that there are no exceptions. Those projections may even be seen in oneself in distorted forms. The stronger the emotion, the greater the likelihood that these disowned feelings and urges will be activated and seen as manifest in other people. Jesus asked: "Why do you see the speck in your neighbor's eye, but do not notice the log in your own eye?" (*Matthew* 7:3)

Some of our self-identities are obvious, others may be operative but rarely sensed, and still others may be totally absent from our awareness. Repressed content definitely contributes to identity and will eventually need to be faced if the fullness of life is to be known. All identities limiting the spontaneous manifestation of our core nature restrict our full engagement with life.

* * * *

We all begin with life itself, each of us constituted by a unique set of potential qualities and features but no identity other than human. All that we become is added to our core reality and constitutes our unique identity. We build this identity over time as experience extends, typically by adding more and more. To live well is to embrace life eagerly and open to each unfolding moment. T. S. Eliot rightly noted: "We shall never cease from exploring." A friend likes to ask a rhetorical, provocative question: "When did you decide to stop learning?" thereby pointedly affirming that it is best never to stop. We've seen above the advantage of continually opening to the evolutionary potential of unfolding reality.

This is exactly what Gautama Siddhartha did to become the Buddha. After his enlightening experience under the Bodhi tree, he moved from village to village in Northern India, sharing his insights into human nature along with his understanding of the basic human predicament and its resolution. These issues draw the attention and interest of those who met him. Devotees accompanied him. He moved with exceptional grace. He spoke knowingly with calm certitude, and many wanted to know who he was. When asked, he did not give his name, identify where he was from, reveal that he was the son of a king, declare that he had a wife and son, or name the disciplines he had practiced. He responded with the most important thing he had learned in his years of searching and practicing. He replied: "I'm awake," thereby getting the title "the Buddha" ("the awakened one"). He pointed to awareness, his crystal clear, undistorted consciousness. This was his true and essential identity – as it is ours.

The situation was similar for Jesus when he roamed the hills and valleys of Palestine. He too had a following of disciples. His teaching differed from tradition. He often began: "You have heard it said, but I say to you." He spoke not as the Scribes and Pharisees, but with an uncommon assurance, with a knowing that attracted attention and confidence. On at least one occasion, he asked his disciples: "Who do people say that I am?" They responded by naming well-known, respected persons, John the Baptist, Elijah, and Jeremiah. That question, however, was merely the prelude to the real question: "But who do you say that I am?" Peter answered: "You are the Christ, the Son of the Living God" (*Matthew* 16:13-16).

Gautama and Jesus formed their identities in exemplary fashion. They sought and questioned, refusing to take life in perfunctory ways. They were not content with mere tradition, with hearsay. They wanted truth and the real. They doubted, and tested, and experimented, satisfied only with what rang true and consistent with their inner knowing. Hearsay meant little; only what proved true in their life-experience mattered. Only this builds character and broad experience, thereby enabling one's word and example to be trustworthy.

※ ※ ※ ※

Every culture and religious tradition harbors views of human nature and historical 'fact' that may be widely assumed and taken for granted and propagated broadly as if they were undeniable, fixed, and unchangeable. These 'views' are commonly "taken for granted" and unquestioned. This holds true for Christianity as it propagates its worldview in the West and much of the world. Central to this worldview, whether openly affirmed or tacitly held, is Jesus the Christ as the perfect God-Man whose life and teachings set the ideal pattern for all men, women, and children. For believers, Jesus as the Christ holds this position because he was/is the incarnation of God, God in the form and nature of a human.

Drawing together several verses from the *New Testament*, theologians in the fourth century, acting under the authority of the Emperor Constantine, formulated the Nicene Creed. This creedal affirmation attests to Jesus the Christ as the one and only Son of God, begotten not made – and therefore qualitatively unlike all other humans. Discussion and debate continued in an effort to clarify what the incarnation meant. The main effect of the traditional understanding of the incarnation elevated Jesus to worship status; it put him "on a pedestal," thereby deifying him.

The groundwork enabling a markedly different interpretation of the incarnation has occurred over many years and has culminated in making a distinction between the Jesus of history and the Christ of faith. Scholars are now able to distinguish between the life and teachings of Jesus prior to the Easter story, and the interpretations of the teachings and events attributed to him that arose later. To summarize: (1) before his death, Jesus was a wandering teacher of extraordinary insight, a sage; (2) after his death, he was deified and made the God-Man by his church-oriented followers.

Though traditional Christianity claims that the incarnation of Jesus the Christ is unique, it is not. The prevailing culture in the first century and even earlier recognized other divine-human beings. Dying/rising gods were common in the Greco-Roman world and in Egypt. Among others, they include Osiris, Tammuz, Adonis, and Dionysus. Even the Hebrew religion, from which Jesus emerged, recognized humans as gods. The Psalmist (82:6), addressing fellow Hebrews, declares: "You are gods." The doctrinal and creedal claim of traditional Christianity is not unique at all. The history of religions provides many examples of new religions drawing from and interpreting their specific features according to the categories of other religions, both earlier and contemporary.

* * * *

A monumental conclusion can now be drawn: Every human being is an incarnation of God, not just Jesus the Christ. We are all born with a divine essence, conjoined to which is our human essence. This twofold nature will seem to separate as we grow and develop. With the inevitable emergence of the ego, the separate self-sense, we may seem to lose access to the divine quality. Most of us from now on will know ourselves only (and perhaps merely) as human. For those of traditional Christian heritage, Jesus will continue to be a friendly but removed God-Man whose life and teachings are so historically crucial, magnificent, and inspirational that he deserves to be worshipped. He is one of a kind, so claim most Christians. But no, absolutely no! That was believed by traditionalist to be the case, but need not be believed any longer.

We are all incarnations. Every human at birth is of the same nature as that attributed to Jesus: divine and human. His uniqueness lies in the thoroughness with which he integrated these two dimensions into one – into one way of being. Just as there was no discrepancy between his teaching and his behavior, so there was none between his divinity and his humanity. They were integral, distinguishable but not separate. He was one and single within himself and therefore could see the oneness of humanity without judging in terms of superior and inferior. All humans are worthy in the sight of God.

What could be more important than our identity? It is a 'fleshing out' of our 'I am,' our God-given essence, our unadulterated consciousness. Coming from a different background, Ramana Maharshi, Hindu sage/saint of the last century, summarized the entire religio-spiritual venture as enquiry into our identity, "Who am I?" He sometimes noted that pursuing the injunction in *Psalms* 46:10: "Be still, and know that I am God" would lead to the same realization (i.e., knowing ourselves as integrally divine/human). This view is wholly justifiable when understanding the "I" in the quotation to be a single reality embracing all of reality, including the divine and human. Muslim mystics know this to be true. Sufi Jalaladin ar-Rumi declared: "I searched for myself and found God; I searched for God and found myself." Jesus asserted: "The Father and I are one" (*John* 10:30).

* * * *

We've now distinguished between our human/divine identity and our social identity. We've also seen how our social identity is established by means of attachment, what we like and don't like, what we draw to ourselves and what we reject. Now we need to discover how this mechanism works over a lifetime. Is there a common pattern of human development from birth to death? Yes, in fact, there are many ways of depicting the unfolding of human development.

The patterns of personal evolution described below are among those I've found most helpful. They account for the most salient developments in my own life, and I've seen how well they account for growth in others. Finally, they are well documented in scholarly literature. Familiarity with these stages of personal development carries multiple benefits: (1) they authenticate one's own experience; (2) they encourage the release of critical judgment; and (3) they indicate why it is fool-hardy to judge others.

The specific patterns of growth, the values derived from them, and the last three points above come together in a poignant insight: each ascending stage in the hierarchies is not one of status – none is better than another – instead, each is more inclusive, more embracing than the earlier stages in this amazing journey as we integrate and harmonize with the all-inclusive universe. Even when terms like 'higher' and 'lower' are used, the reference is to scope of view, not to superior-inferior, much like our field of view expands as we ascend the top of a skyscraper, fly in an airplane, or see our planet from a satellite.

C. The Stages of Life's Journey

Reflection on patterns and stages of human development reach back to the classical period in Greece. In modern times, German-born Jean Gebser picked up the issue and outlined a pattern of the human developmental stages that has motivated other researchers also to take up the challenge. Toward the end of the last century, Ken Wilber was instrumental in founding the Integral Institute, a think-tank that attracted other researchers to map the evolutionary patterns of human consciousness. The stages have been extrapolated from the development seen in people whose lives have unfolded and grown over a lifetime. Therefore, they have been discovered in the real-life maturation processes of human beings just like ourselves. Having been empirically established, they carry scientific validity. Wilber's contribution, among others, lies in the discovery and emphasis on the increasing integration and inclusivity found in ongoing maturation. Life becomes bigger and bigger even while centering more and more in less and less. Our worldview expands as we discover life's unifying principles. Detachment is crucial to this process.

The stages of growth progress upward and outward through Archaic, Magic, Mythic, Rational, Pluralistic, and Integral. Every individual (and every culture) passes through these stages – if their development is not arrested. Unfortunately, most individuals and cultures do stop growing before reaching the higher stages. For our purposes, the identifying name of each stage is enough to suggest the scope of the outlook at that stage. We won't spell out the specific characteristics of the stages; to do so would lead too far from our focus.

The crucial fact for us to realize is that attachment and detachment are necessary steps in the growth process; attachment advances it, then thwarts it. Detachment is then required to clear the way for the next attachment, which, in the normal and healthful growth process, advances upward and outward to a fuller, freer, more pleasant life. Typically, when faced with any change, especially those pertaining to personal identity, fixed beliefs and lack of trust give rise to fear, anxiety, uncertainty, and hesitation. Capable of arising at each transition, attachment tends to forestall continuing growth. Ongoing transformation only occurs as one detaches from the limiting perspectives of each stage.

Examples of transition to a more evolved stage will demonstrate the need to detach from the earlier. One cannot move to the Rational Stage if one still believes in the traditional, particularly literal, interpretation of the stories that make up the Magic or Mythic Stage. To believe that the world was actually created in six days by command of a god is convincing evidence that reason has not been applied to personal belief. The same can be said of the view that the crucifixion of a man over 2000 years ago, extraordinary and inspiring as it may be, could – simply by believing in it – cause a cosmic, psychological, and spiritual change that would ensure freedom from all remorse and guilt that anyone might experience, regardless of the nature of the crimes and misdemeanors committed, and also assure eternal life in Heaven. This is not to claim that beneficial results cannot take place from belief in such an event, but only that a more rational interpretation, accompanied by changes in attitude and behavior, is essential for the traditional promises to actually and fully occur.

Wilber also groups the six stages of growth into three developmental groups: (1) pre-personal/pre-rational/pre-conventional characterizes the earlier stages; (2) personal/rational/conventional describes the middle range of growth; and (3) post-personal/post-rational/post-conventional indicates the later stages. Children and the earliest cultures represent pre-personal/pre-rational/pre-conventional. Most adults and world cultures are personal/ rational/conventional. However, a few adults and some subcultures have developed to the post-personal/post-rational/post-conventional levels.

At these later stages, we find features of maturation that are pluralistic, integral, and beyond. Those evolving to the Pluralistic stage realize that the different ways people understand and act are entirely appropriate for the stage of growth they've reached, thereby releasing the tendency to be critical of earlier ways of being (pre-conventional, for example). The Integral level recognizes that different views don't just stand side-by-side but express a unifying principle when seen from a deeper and more inclusive stance. For example, all of the gods, supreme beings, higher spirits, and absolute realities fall into Ultimacy; all are specific cultural forms of that which governs all and is itself beyond dualistic understanding (*HTM* 23-34). A post-integral stage designates continuing development beyond prior stages. It is not possible to postulate an end to human psychospiritual evolution.

Even though most of us locate at a specific stage, we also tend to flow back and forth, back to an earlier stance and forward to an emerging one. Once a transition is well underway, however, the new stage becomes our "center of gravity" where we're most stable and comfortable. Another evolutionary principle is summarized as "transcend and include": this indicates that we never discard entirely all the elements of earlier stages. We drop some completely and re-interpret others, incorporating them into the next stage. We transcend some by detaching entirely from them; re-evaluate others in light of our more inclusive understanding; and acknowledge still others as appropriate for those who hold them even if they no longer appeal to us.

A particularly valuable and insightful realization emerges from what Wilber calls "the pre-trans fallacy." Based on the three groupings above (early, middle, later), the pre-trans distinction (occurring before, occurring after) enables a clear understanding of why some evaluations of human experience are so mistaken. The fallacy occurs in two directions: when an advanced view is interpreted as an earlier one, and when an earlier view is understood as higher or latter. For example, Sigmund Freud reduced mystical experiences to instances of regression to the oceanic feelings he attributed to the newborn. His faulty reasoning was based on his view that because mystical experiences are not rational, they must be infantile. He could not envision the discovery of authentic insights beyond the range of rationality, a limitation that also prohibited him from seeing the value in Carl Jung's insights based on his exploration into the unconscious (which was not *inferior* to reason but *other than* reason, beyond reason and therefore transrational). Freud was so attached to reason – exceedingly valuable in itself – that he could not envision transrational awareness, even though it was authentic and undeniable to Jung, who clearly held a view of human nature more inclusive than Freud's.

Several decades ago, well before I had come to my view of Ultimacy, but when I was already struggling with the impossibility of adequately describing 'God,' I was in conversation with a niece, a thoughtful university graduate then in medical school. She wanted to know how I understood God. Her mother, a conventional Christian and staunchly devoted to her church, was not a part of the discussion but was sitting nearby. My response was careful and measured but with some hesitancy because it was not expressed in terms of traditional belief. Consequently, it was seen as faltering and heretical by my sister-in-law. With a tone of disgust and dismissal, she declared me ignorant of knowing who God is. Only later, after discovering integral thought and stages of growth, was I able to understand more fully my sister-in-law's reaction. I was trying to convey a transrational view to my niece and was heard by her mother from a pre-rational stance (i.e., conventional, permeated by mythic). My sister-in-law exhibited the pre-trans fallacy.

Misconstruing experiences of the young that are more commonly attested in older people is another example of the pre-trans fallacy. Children commonly feel a 'mystical' connection with the larger world, often coming forth with "Wows" as they discover something new and awe-inspiring in nature. Another example of authentic spirituality in children that adults typically have to cultivate lies in the apparent ease with which they 'forgive' wrongs committed against them. Additional instances of the spiritual precociousness of children will appear in subsequent chapters, notably the last, where we'll find extraordinary instances of what children claim to remember.

In a culture where reason and rational thinking are seen as the supreme achievement, someone who has not had transrational experiences, with their expanding awareness and liberating benefits, is likely to deny the very existence of the transrational. However, to be so attached to the dominant views of one's culture that other views are ruled out arbitrarily or distorted is to cut short the potential of one's own life experience and possible advancement.

* * * *

New perspectives and attitudes emerge as progression unfolds. One of the most important discoveries is an expanding inclusiveness, as we have seen. One's sense of what belongs to life broadens. Less and less is arbitrarily excluded, criticized, condemned, denied, or rejected. What might have been branded previously as satanic and evil is understood less pejoratively as one view among the many that humans devise as they negotiate life. One's own worldview becomes large enough to included beliefs and actions that, while anathema to oneself, are calmly acknowledged when held by others, even as one may work to offset them. Acceptance without condoning becomes natural.

Another personal discovery as growth occurs is an increase in concern and care for others. Compassion arises more naturally, easily, and genuinely. We empathize more readily with those less fortunate and those suffering. We eagerly do what we can to be helpful to others. These two features, broad inclusivity and compassionate action, demonstrate fundamental trans-formation in head and heart.

Related to these two developments is a third, introduced above but worthy of further unfolding. As we ascend/expand the developmental scale, we respond to life with an understanding and loving acceptance unavailable to us in earlier stages. We recognize the limitations inherent in the earlier stages because they remind us of our own earlier status and struggles. However, just the opposite is true when looking from an earlier stage to a later one. Those at the earlier stages of development cannot see the truth and value in the later. It is foreign to their experience. It may seem ill-founded and heretical, and will likely be openly and aggressively criticized, as was the case with my sister-in-law. Analogously, a high school student can understand primary school arithmetic, but a primary school student cannot understand high school calculus; a physician will be familiar with first aid, but a Boy Scout with a first aid merit badge will not be able to diagnose hepatitis.

The last pattern of life development we'll consider derives from a twofold analysis, expansion-consolidation. This too is one in which we all engage (as discussed earlier in terms of identity formation). The first and lengthy phase is one of constant expansion, continual addition of new information and experiences, encountering more and more. This phase is inevitably marked by fragmentation as additional boundaries are established when new experiences occur, one thing set apart and distinguished from other things. In both thinking and behavior, we eventually and inevitably face contrary and contradicting situations. Tension after tension and discomfort after discomfort arise in the sensitive person, some minimally disturbing, others more strident and not easily dismissed. This expansion is inevitable if we continually open to life in its unfolding as life expands to more and more and engages more and more. For some, the accompanying discomfort will prompt a reassessment, a re-evaluation of how one thinks and acts.

At this point, a reversal of the expanding, fragmenting character of life may be undertaken, and when we begin to seek indications of commonality within the complexities of life, then uniting principles expose underlying similarities and identities. For many, this shift will occur when approaching retirement. An urge to simplify and downside may emerge. A case in point: when retirement caused me to give up my campus office, I had eight to ten thousand books to reduce to a number that would fit into a much smaller home office. About ten years later, when moving from a rambling farmhouse to a cottage on Lake Erie, further cutbacks were required. More recently, when locating to a retirement community, a third reduction was necessary.

In addition to a reduction in book ownership, further downsizing took place when leaving a 44-acre farm with five outbuildings, and moving onto to a quarter acre lot with a smaller house and no garage. An eighteen-foot square building, well equipped as a workshop, eventually became reduced to a toolbox. This decrease in material possessions and accompanying responsibilities indicates the simplifying of life. Other simplifications included: (1) dropping involvement in activities no longer serving my best interests, and (2) discovering and applying the integral principles that were particularly relevant to my worldview. These principles are available to everyone and can be found with committed interest, good fortune, and a willingness to detach and move on.

Given the varied, contrasting, and contradictory beliefs, rituals, and practices of the world's religions, finding integrating principles is needed if we're going to make sense of religion. Knowing that religio-spiritual experience evolves through stages provides a meaningful integrative scheme, as we've seen. Here too an especially useful integral principle is available. There are three ways in which humans experience and express their religion, regardless of the particular tradition. Religion as we commonly know it is most easily recognized in the first category, the conventional or exoteric. This is the usual religion of church, synagogue, mosque, temple, etc.; it is the only religion most people know and practice; and it is the form most frequently criticized. The second form, mystical or esoteric religion, grows out of the former and centers in having a loving and harmonious connection with God, as well as having a living sense of God's presence everywhere all the time. The third form, nondual or metateric, transcends such polarities as sacred-profane, spiritual-material, and self-other. This is where the nonduality introduced in the first chapter comes into fullness. The metateric is an all-encompassing spirituality that recognizes the value of the two earlier stages for those who embrace them. A nondualist may participate in one or more of the customary forms of religion but need not and may not identify with any.

Locating religiospiritual experiences and expressions into three groups offers an integrative principle that neutralizes a great deal of doubt and confusion, and also provides a meaningful pattern of development allowing the endless number of religions to make sense (*HTM* 34-61).

Part II: The Liberating Power of Detachment

The liberating power of detachment is not easily won. The perverse and pervasive ego is uncannily adept at causing us to feel almost always separate, apart from all that is happening, occasionally even isolated. Sometimes it seems that multiple instances arise everyday that require a dressing down of the ego. These are among the most difficult and challenging confrontations we face. In most of us, our assumed identity is virtually equivalent to the ego; that is, who we think we are as a person is identical to what we are as an ego. When our sense of self is challenged, when we feel really confronted, we take it personally and react as if our very personhood is threatened. Does this not raise the question of whether or not there's any real difference between me as a person and me as an ego? Perhaps the question can only be answered experientially when all sense of separateness is gone and we're then able to know what remains, what or who we are without the ego.

In the meantime, what do we do about it? First, we need to discover the many ways in which the operation of the ego can be recognized. We'll do this by naming the opportunities for change, growth, and transcendence that frequently come to us. Unfortunately, these are too often unrecognized, ignored, resisted, or denied. Note that these are truly opportunities, even though they will seem challenging or even threatening. Among them are the following: doubt, fear, anger, anxiety, impatience, depression, disgust, pride, selfishness, and others. These arise because we have contracted from our original state of being, our 'I am.' Each of these deviates from our larger Self, our essential identity, to indicate that we've unwittingly fallen victim to the prevailing features of our culture at large and religion in particular. Each calls attention to the attachments that have occluded the divinity inherent in our humanity. Broadly speaking, among those engaged in the transformation activity, the undoing process, these attachments are regarded as negative and disturbing aspects of life. While normally seen as undesirable, the arousal of any one of them is simultaneously an opportunity for self-exploration, a chance to see the ego in action and to undermine the ego by means of detachment, at least enough detachment to see it objectively and take whatever measures are advisable to nullify it.

Without exception, each of the examples of attachment/detachment in this chapter and the next is a step (great or small) in progress toward reconciliation, harmony, and happiness. Without continuously detaching, however, no adherent of any religion is likely to fulfill the expectations of his or her professed tradition, much less progress from conventional (exoteric) to mystical (esoteric) to nondual (metateric) realization.

Most practitioners probably believe they are faithfully living the tenets of their faith. Friends and acquaintances, however, may see discrepancies between principles claimed and actions performed. "Walk the talk" and "practice what you preach" are well-worn reminders of the value placed on personal integrity, on conformity between profession and practice. Without integrity, personal tranquility and interpersonal harmony are impossible.

It may seem obvious that our religious and spiritual views are impacted by our conception of God and our desire to live up to the ideals we hold. Yes, it is obvious. But holding *uninvestigated* assumptions (as all assumptions tend to be) may prove unproductive, as we've seen in our discussion of the ego. Theologically, a contrast, even contradiction, may exist between what we think we believe and its reflection in daily life. Believers claim that God is omnipresent, existing everywhere always, but this seems to be a verbal declaration more than a lived reality. To take an obvious example, in formal worship and personal prayer, God is often invited to come and be present, as if he isn't already present.

Another unrecognized profession-to-practice disjunction occurs in those who believe that God's love is unconditional (i.e., extended equally to all) if this view is coupled to an anxious striving to be more spiritual. This is particularly evident if there's any sense of inadequacy in meeting God's expectations. If this leads to the feeling that God's love is not reaching them, the devoted may try harder and become even more stressed. Of course, none of this denies the value of intending to, and working to, remove impediments to wholeness. It's rather a reminder that fundamental change requires a great deal of deconditioning that is seldom accomplished instantaneous or without time and repetition. Patience with oneself is as crucial as patience with others. We don't want to become obsessed, discouraged, or stressed. I have personally benefited from a common maxim in India that states that God is not in a hurry.

Most Christians know that Jesus taught the Kingdom of God as both inner and outer, as now present and eventually fully to come. There are many 'faithful' churchgoers, however, who hold political views contrary to what Jesus taught, and who overlook his teaching that counters these views (See *Matthew* 25:31-45). For example, instead of supporting measures that serve the poor, the sick, the elderly, the marginalized, the imprisoned, the 'foreign' – broadly, the needy – many conservative Christians oppose health reform, aid for illegal aliens, minimum wage increase, social welfare, gun regulations, and other policies because they have been rejected by their political party, or because they might impact their personal income. Many of these same Christians maintain that America was founded as Christian nation, which would seem to make them supporters of the very causes they oppose. Even the view that America was founded as a Christian nation lacks historical validity. Substantial evidence indicates that our nation's Founding Fathers, while influenced principally by Christianity, officially upheld support for belief in a Supreme Being and not for a particular religion. A mistaken view on the part of many conservative Christians is their common unwillingness to acknowledge the value that lies in religions other than their own.

Whether or not these discrepancies between actual history and subjective interpretations of history are true for a particular person depends on a number of factors: the strength of their commitment to truth, the accuracy of their self-understanding, the resolute honesty with which they pursue this self-assessment, and their willingness to admit to themselves (and to others when appropriate) any and all that contradicts the values they uphold. This is a high standard. One of the dastardly skills of the ego … devious and wily … lies in hiding 'assumptions-taken-as-fact' in the mind. A specific instance of this occurs when the ego implants within itself the assumption (conscious or not) "I'm a spiritual person" when that may be more of an ideal and a commitment than a reality.

A conversation with an acquaintance indicated that his self-confessed practice of forgiveness fell short of what he believed to be true of himself. He spoke as if he had forgiven a longtime friend but continued to be guarded in his relations with that friend and to have reservations about that friend's sincerity. In Chapter Four, we will discover the perspectives and attitudes required for forgiveness to be real and effective.

Reality belies profession; actuality belies assumption; deed belies claim. We benefit from remembering that our self-understanding may include the unquestioned assumption that our integrity, our consistency, our upholding of the values we claim actually is as we believe it to be. But, we might benefit by remembering that this assumption may NOT be as we believe it to be as well. If a discrepancy is noted, sympathetic compassion is still in order – in light of the subtle and powerful trickery of the ego that plagues, or has plagued, all of us. Self-correction is always advisable; self-incrimination … never.

* * * *

Interlude: I want to depart from the thesis and sequence of the book for a moment to share a dream from last night that is strikingly relevant to the topics we're now considering: (1) the devious and wily ego; (2) attachment, its subtle and haunting effects; (3) detachment, its enlarging and releasing effects; (4) repeated occurrence of the same ego trait; and (5), a new topic, the wisdom hidden in dreams. Some of these points would ordinarily fit the next chapter on testimonials; but they're so pertinent here that I want to share them now.

The dream that stimulated this incursion into the continuity of the book follows: I'm scheduled to give a baccalaureate address on the West Coast. My wife is already there. For unknown reasons, I'm late in making travel plans. I don't even think of flying; I'm trying to get a train ticket. The setting is now India where I must travel to one station to get a ticket and another to catch the train. There's not enough time. By now the baccalaureate service has begun. I want to call my wife to let her and the audience know that I won't be there. I'm away from home and don't have a cell phone. I manage to borrow one but can't figure out how to use it, and there's no one to help. I borrow another and again can't make a call with no one to help. I try a third mobile with the same problem. I wake up feeling extremely frustrated.

My first but tentative interpretation of the dream is that I'm afraid I'm not going to live long enough to finish *Undoing*. It's a book that I definitely want to complete, publish, and share, but I certainly don't have any sense of imminent death; my health is good and, if anything, I'm more content and happy now than ever. I tell the dream to others in hopes of further insight. My daughter suggests that the dream might be addressing my lifelong sense of personal responsibility, not my current writing project. That rang a bell; I instantly resonated with the thought.

As the first-born male – like most first-born males – I was given a bit too much responsibility too soon. Even at five or six, when my parents went away for an afternoon or evening, I became "the man of the house." I became the protector and caregiver of my two younger brothers. An example from when I was nine or ten: one evening when mom and dad were gone, we were in bed and heard a noise in our big farmhouse. I got my 22-caliber rifle and, with my brothers on my heels, searched through the whole house from our bedroom on the second floor to the basement and finally the fruit cellar built under the cement floor of the back porch. In spite of our fear, we left no place unexplored where a person could hide. Even when back in our beds, I couldn't sleep until our parents came home. This same sense of responsibility inspired and drove me to get good grades in public school, become an eagle scout and a leader in youth organizations, take a young family across the planet, work diligently for my higher degrees, demonstrate competence in university teaching, more recently to finish a scholarly book twenty-seven years in the making, and finally to write another book.

The dream now makes sense and is, for me, a convincing reminder that the fullness of my life does not hinge on the publication of a book – or any particular achievement. Instead, it depends for me on the meaning and value I find in this human adventure, especially *knowing* the Real beyond the material and temporal, and on sharing this knowing in a realistic, balanced, and comprehensive way. More specifically, in addition to the spiritual, it means measured reading, writing, teaching, and time with family and friends.

The dream conveys the same correction to my 'hidden' self-sense and life pattern as one described in detail in the next chapter, a dream (involving my college ID card) that occurred in 1973, forty-seven years earlier. Both dreams depict the deeply buried sense of responsibility that infused itself in my conscious and subconscious mind, a sense of responsibility that enabled me to serve in a professional position – but one that also expanded to crowd out other legitimate dimensions of a well-rounded human life. In the older dream, responsibility focused on my teaching career, in the recent one, my writing career.

When interpreted properly, some dreams reveal a previously unrecognized, distorting pattern in one's life that limits the fullness that would be otherwise available in a comprehensive and balanced life. The emerging awareness stems from the still deeper wholeness of our origin, the 'knowingness' of the mind, what some might call intuition, an archetype, the Holy Spirit, God, or a greater intelligence that pervades the universe. Another marvel to note about this ingrained orientation toward balance and wholeness is its ability to know when and how to manifest itself. It seems to possess memory of the past along with present awareness of re-emerging and limiting patterns, thereby attesting to an inherent drive in human nature toward growth and full freedom.

Accurate interpretation of dreams can be an invaluable aid in discovering how we are actually living our lives and how we can make changes to live more fully and easefully. If not all dreams, at least some do express – by means of symbols, metaphors, and stories – central features of our deeper nature, even that of our birthright and divine origin (i.e., an orientation toward wholeness and balance). When life falls off center, signals rise from our essential nature that draw attention to the imbalance, thereby suggesting a needed correction – in the case of both dreams, a modification of my attachment to a social role, detachment from it, and recommitment to a fuller and balanced identity became clear.

Throughout the months I have been writing *Undoing,* I have not given a moment's attention to whether or not I am personally attached to anything. Without actually thinking about it, I've assumed that I'm living a relatively nonattached life, one that freely (i.e., without self-conscious oversight and control) expresses who I am. With the recent dream, I've discovered otherwise: the unquestioned assumption has been shown to be false. The ego had effectively worked one of its devious ploys in me – exactly when I was bringing attention to these tricks *in others*. Not only did I discover attachment in myself, I also discovered I was projecting attachment onto others. Alas, for a time I was attached and projecting while assuming I was doing neither.

When an attachment pattern is discovered and seemingly released, another trick of the wily ego often appears in the assumption that victory has been achieved, that is, an easy attitude of, "Well, that takes care of that." Most often, attachments don't disappear so quickly. When a habitual pattern becomes ingrained in one's personality in early family life and reinforced along the way, it probably will reappear, even after awareness and 'fixing'. We saw this in the two dreams reported above. The thrust toward wholeness and harmony embedded in our innermost divinity does not give up – as long as our deepest commitment is to discover and live the truth of our incarnation. Wisdom suggests that we welcome our dreams as messages from Beyond, certainly beyond our immediate sense of who we are.

To summarize the interlude: Two dreams, widely separated in time, have shown how I have been operating from a longstanding, unacknowledged *attachment* (to 'responsibility') in myself while addressing attachment (as an essentially human problem) in others. In the dreams and their interpretation, we have seen also how the ego used *projection* to keep my focus on transformative principles in the abstract (in me) while addressing a major transformative limitation (in others). The ego has been protecting its domain in me by keeping me blind to my own shortcomings, attachment and projection. How subtle is this devious monster!

But all is not lost. As we've seen by means of the dream interpretations, that the deeper Self, where wholeness lies, broke through with awareness of what the ego was doing by means of hiding attachment and using projection, two of its favorite tools. If commitment is genuine and persistent enough, our occluded, divine nature will work its timeless ways over time. Patience on this side of life (the human and temporal) mirrors the other side (the divine and eternal).

* * * *

A common form of attachment – attachment to the results of action – often goes unrecognized in the West but is addressed directly in the East. In the earliest spiritual traditions of India and China, the practice of nonattachment to results, of actionless action, is emphasized. The Hindu scripture, the *Bhagavad Gita*, reports Krishna, the god-man sage, saying: "He who sees inaction in action and action in inaction, he is wise." This special kind of action occurs when one does what is appropriate in each situation – with no expectation in the outcome. The principle is violated if any result is expected: "I'll get a reward"; "I'll convince him I'm right"; "They won't do that again"; "If I wear this dress and smile, I'll get the job"; "If I'm friendly and kind, I'll be liked." On and on it goes: desires, intentions, hopes, cravings, gripes, and fears become motivating attachments.

Our behavior is informed by an endless flow of preferred outcomes, of what we hope will be in the next bit of time. Krishna asserted: "Actions do not stain me: for I have no longing for their fruits" (*BG* IV: 18, 14). This is a hard truth; at the outset, it is truly difficult to apply, but it then becomes increasingly effective as we release more and more of our personal objectives.

The *Tao Te Ching* advocates the same principle with the expression "wu wei" (non-doing). The sage is one who knows that "the Tao never does a thing, yet there is nothing it doesn't do." He is also one who "performs effortless deeds." Building on these and other verses, Wu Ch'eng (1249-1333) concludes: "The sage's inaction is inaction that is not inaction" (*LT* 74, 4, 117). Additional perspectives follow from this basic idea of the Tao, living with non-interference, without imposition, according to the rhythm of the natural world. Wanting the Tao – the natural way of the universe and humankind – to be other than it is (i.e., as *we* want life to be) only causes us to feel out of harmony with it. This is the root of our suffering, discontent, and difficulties. Private, personal objectives contrary to the Tao result in disruptive disharmony within us. To expect anything from one's endeavors is to be attached, and indicative of the ego's deception. Tao, Brahman, God, the Holy Spirit, Universe, Greater Intelligence, Natural Law, Ultimacy – these underwrite All. To harmonize with the Great Harmony: give up, let go, be with, flow. Do what is appropriate in the situation and release the outcome to be what it will be. This too is an exceptionally high standard, not easily understood by those early in the rediscovery of their fundamental spiritual Self. Yet, it is a realizable goal when you are ready for it!

* * * *

As we've seen, one of the most devious tricks in the ego's repertoire lies quietly in the assumption that we're so committed to the spiritual path that nothing could sway us from it, least of all the critical opinion of others. The more solidly this conviction is held, the more disguised and subtle are the ego's tactics to keep it in place. Any defense against someone pointing out a shortcoming confirms the ego's success. When a personal shortcoming is made known to us, we have an opportunity for inner clearing, growth, and a chance to weaken the ego. The healthful response is appreciation and the expression of gratitude to those who are helping us.

The opportunity "to grind away at the ego" is lost if there is any defense, any attempt to justify, to "save face". This may be true even if the defense is based on the key principle in *A Course in Miracles* that one's safety lies in defenselessness. So-called defenselessness can itself be a defense (and even a form of passive-aggression) – if the defender says: "Well, I've seen you do the same"; walks away without a word; is to any degree smug; points out his/her non-defense; feels at all superior to the other party. The defender in her or his heart of hearts will know (or maybe only suspect) if their 'defenselessness' has served as an ego weapon. Any response other than calm listening with love suggests the ego's success. If the charge is legitimate, acceptance with thankfulness is not only in order but also further undermines the ego. If one honestly finds no legitimacy, further consideration may still be in order.

Restraint from self-defense is a lofty and difficult endeavor that is not likely to appeal to any but those who have already dissolved a good deal of their ego. To expect too much too quickly can only lead to discouragement. Charity and patience are in order, for ourselves as well as for others.

Part III: Nonattachment and its Benefits

The central aim of this book is to set forth and to clarify the principles and practices that enable us to rediscover and manifest our original, natural identity, the Self which has always existed but which has been hidden beneath the socially conditioned self-sense accumulated over the years. Undoing or detaching is the means to this end. At the same time, it is well to realize that our undoing, our detaching, does not do what we may think it does.

When we attach to anything and it thereby becomes a feature of our identity, we are definitely 'doing' the attaching. We can't blame this on anyone else. Strictly speaking, however, when we properly detach there's nothing actually done comparable to the 'doing' that created the attachment. It's analogous to the actionless action discussed above. We're no longer doing what we've been doing; we're no longer holding ourselves to a particular identity, role, viewpoint, stance, belief, alliance, etc. However, our penchant for defending ourselves when criticized or misunderstood proves that we are still attached. What could this be but evidence of attachment to who or what we think we are? Why would we defend except to justify?

On the other hand, if a situation has been misunderstood (e.g., due to an observer not being familiar with certain factors), an explanation in order to clarify would be quite different than defending. An explanation to help someone understand factors that may not have been apparent, factors that shed a different light on an incident, might be appropriate. Even here, however, the ego stands in the wings in hope of a chance to spring again into action. The distinction between defending and clarifying is itself a subtle and crucial one that puts the ego in a position to be under-minded or to assert itself.

When we detach or 'undo,' we are letting go. This releasing is more a *ceasing* to do than a *doing*. There is simply a shift within oneself of no longer attributing value to something that had been consciously or unconsciously valued. Detachment withdraws the psychic energy that supported the mistaken image concealing our original, actual identity. We are engaging the same emptying process that characterized Jesus of Nazareth and enabled him to align with Abba (Aramaic for "Father"), his preferred name for God. In fact, this self-emptying enabled every religious founder, sage, and saint to become as they became. *Have This Mind* is based on the validity and universal practice of this emptying, releasing, detaching, undoing, deconditioning process. By means of it, we rediscover the qualities embedded in our original nature as spelled out in Chapter One of this book.

This clarification of undoing as something we do not actually *do* is crucial. If we had something specific in mind that we wanted when we let go of who/what we've been, in all probability we'd simply be taking on another self-limiting, temporary, partial identity. Authentic detachment, on the other hand, opens into the wholeness we actually are, the all-inclusiveness of pure, objectless consciousness, with expectancy but without expectation. Accordingly, that which is 'built in,' or natural, is more likely to emerge.

The detachment process is a natural activity if we engage it, if we consciously take it on. It becomes an adventure in re-cognizing – knowing once again – and restoring the pristine qualities implanted in our essential spirituality, qualities inherently pure in their potentiality which have become distorted when manifesting in culturalized life. By means of undoing, we become as we've always been beyond the attachments, and simultaneously extend outwardly what has become translucent to us, in us, and as us.

* * * *

Many years ago, one of my teenage sons asked how he would know if he were detaching, what his inner awareness would register. I suggested that he clench his fist tightly, note the tension in his forearm, throughout his body, in his overall inwardness; hold it a half-minute or so, then relax and note that feeling. I added that he might also recall what it's like to carry a heavy load and then set it down. The vanishing of effort or stress is reminiscent of what it's like when we detach. We sense a letting go, releasing, no-longer holding. Other examples include: letting go after holding one's bladder too long; relief from a headache; the feeling when antacids begin to work after over-eating; the relaxation that comes when laying down to sleep after a busy day. I suspect that mothers have a similar sense of relief when holding their baby after the contractions and pushing of childbirth.

We have all experienced physical pain to one degree or another. Sometimes it's so excruciating that it dominates our attention and becomes so overwhelmingly intense that it is seemingly unbearable. This can constitute suffering to the extreme – an abscessed tooth, burst appendix, migraine headache, broken ribs. The natural reaction is always to resist the pain, to push against it, to want it gone. This habitual reaction actually intensifies the pain and contributes to suffering. Buddhists note this distinction between pain and suffering. Pain is inevitable as long as we have bodies. Suffering is voluntary since it is caused by resistance to something natural, something that cannot be avoided if there is a problem in our physical body. To the extent that we can detach, back up from, and simply note *the fact* that we are at the moment experiencing pain, rather than trying to resist it, the suffering will diminish, probably not disappear, but ease a little. The distinction here is between the physiological pain and the psychological suffering, a distinction that I believe is entirely valid and useful. Those I know who accept their pain with choiceless awareness attest to the effectiveness of the distinction and the practice.

Outside the physical realm, the feeling of detaching is analogous to being informed by a professor that the multiple-choice exam you failed, that caused you so much consternation, had been machine-corrected erroneously; you actually got an A. It's like the change to elation following the disappointment felt by a team and its fans when an umpire's on-the-field call is reversed after watching the instant-playback camera. If insulted by a workmate with whom you regularly have lunch, you're quite likely to feel hurt and confused. If the friend, with genuine sorrow, apologies and explains that the charge was based on mistaken information, the unpleasant feelings will vanish. It's like being in debt and finding money, suffering from unemployment and getting a job, being abandoned by a friend and finding a better one, losing something valuable and then locating it.

Detachment constitutes a return to a more whole, natural, and beneficial state, finding what was lost, restoring what's right and proper. In the physical or body-based examples above, we are returning to a more healthful state. In the examples dealing with loss, we are restoring contentment and happy states of being. With a reversal of a mistaken judgment or view, that which was wrong becomes right. All of this authenticates detachment as a return to and rediscovery of our truest nature. When abandoning the incorrect and limiting, we are restored. Undoing – a fundamental principle of life – opens life to its fullness.

None of the examples mentioned or even the references to 'likely feelings' will indicate accurately what anyone will necessarily experience when detaching. At best, these are analogies, similitudes, parallels; none is a true likeness since that word suggests too much commonality. Also, because of our distinct individuality, one person's experience of detachment may be different from another's. An additional variable lies in the particular attachment, how long it has existed, the extent of impact, and its intensity. Certain, however, in every actual detachment will be relief and release, increased freedom, expanded inclusiveness, and an improved ability to express unconditional love.

The most convincing evidence of detachment bar none arises when we look back over our lives and see how we've changed.

* * * *

We have now investigated attachment and found it to be crucial for creating an identity and for maturation to occur, especially spiritual maturation. We've also seen that these attachments can become burdensome and restrictive to further psychospiritual growth and may require detachment. It's an ongoing, cycling 'outward' and 'upward' journey with no final stopping, not even when merging into the eternal and infinite. A final, mundane example from childhood illustrates the process.

As a child, I developed a special appetite for cookies, all kinds of cookies, but especially peanut butter. Whenever I got a chance, I would snatch one or two or more. Limitations were placed, but I did my best to circumvent them, usually secretly. The fondness continued through my teens, early adult years, and into middle age. I married a woman who became an excellent cook and her favorite item to bake was cookies. (I firmly believe this alone proves that marriages are made in heaven.) I gained the playful title 'cookie monster.' Eventually and reluctantly, I discovered I was gaining weight, getting an oversize belly, and eating too much sugar. With little enthusiasm, I cut back on my cookie consumption and nearly gave it all up. A new identity based on detachment arose to replace the longstanding attachment to cookies. This new identity includes better health, a trimmer waistline, and only an occasional cookie.

For those who have not stopped learning and exploring – whether by negligence, necessity, or free choice – the alternating attachment-detachment pattern continues throughout life. But it does require a willingness at times to give up immediate gratification or satisfaction for a greater or more worthy objective, as illustrated above. Some lower primates don't seem able to do this.

Some monkeys lose their freedom to be monkeys, to join with other monkeys and roam the jungles and abandoned temples in India, all because of their 'love' for bananas (perhaps much like my former 'love' for cookies). If a dried coconut shell with a small opening is stuffed with chunks of banana and secured near them, they will squeeze their hand through the hole and grab a handful of the fruit. They are trapped when they won't let go. Their refusal to give up the banana binds them to the spot – a frightening analogy for those so bound to their usual ways and desires (from which they won't detach) who won't let go of the familiar even to regain their wholeness and birthright freedom.

* * * *

In this chapter, we've discovered a number of benefits from practicing detachment: it fosters a sense of expanded identity, an increased confidence that the life being lived is my life, an increased freedom, a felicity in life's routines, and a relaxed confidence, to name just a few. As we continue to make detachment our ongoing practice, the discovery of additional benefits will occur. The next chapter reveals additional benefits gained by fellow humans who have detached and continue to evolve.

Chapter Three: Testimonials: Attachment and Detachment

> The essence of the Way is detachment.
> (Bodhidharma)

The following testimonials have been offered by persons whose lives demonstrate the joy, inner peacefulness, contentment, and interpersonal ease that comes with detaching from a belief or practice that has become constraining. The accounts are living proof that the practice of 'undoing' carries benefits for self and others.

Nonattachment in University Sports

One of the longest running and most intense rivalries in collegiate football is between the Wolverines of University of Michigan and the Spartans of Michigan State. The Wolverines hold the better overall record, which only serves to drive the Spartans even harder in each annual contest. In the 2015 game, with ten seconds left to play and ahead by a score of 23-21, Michigan elected to punt on the fourth down. Uncharacteristically, the punter fumbled. A State player scooped up the ball and ran thirty-eight yards for the win. In an interview about the event, the punter, a foreign student from Australia, responded with admirable maturity. Acknowledging the support he'd received from State fans and many from back home, he reflected with apparent detachment: "You learn so you can do better. You pick yourself up, dust yourself off and move on." (*DFP*)

Detaching from a Family Tradition

As a boy I had great admiration for my dad, an admiration that has deepened and expanded now that he is gone; whatever he did I wanted to do. He was an outdoorsman and avid hunter who, with his friends, hunted every year both small game, rabbits, pheasants, squirrels, and big game, deer, moose, and bear. I wanted to be like him and could hardly wait until I was old enough to go hunting with him. I had my own guns, regularly read the hunting magazines, and joyfully help take care of the hunting dogs we always owned. The biggest events every fall and winter were hunting adventures. Sometimes hunting for me depended on getting at least a B+ average in my high school classes. But another year, I had to finish the requirements to become an Eagle Scout. Once in college, I hunted with some of my classmates in four different states. When living in Kenya, I hunted regularly, partly to supply meat to the students at the theological school where I taught. I collected mounted heads and tanned skins of trophies and displayed them in my home with a sense of real accomplishment. Though completely unrecognized by me, I was deeply attached to hunting. Hunting was a big part of my identity.

One weekend in graduate school, my wife and I put on a party for our closest friends. When two of them entered our apartment, they spotted the trophies and began asking questions I'd never considered: "Why do you hunt? Do you like killing animals?" They were clearly unimpressed. One friend crawled under a zebra skin and began crawling around the living room. For the first time in my life, I realized I didn't have to go hunting; I didn't have to kill these beautiful animals. Hunting was something that had been added by family tradition but was now no longer necessary or even desirable. I gave away my guns and trophies and never owned a hunting dog again. My identity and life experiences expanded when I ceased to be a hunter. (Jim Royster)

Detaching from Religion Itself

I grew up in a committed, conservative Protestant family. We went to church several times a week: on every 'Lord's Day' to Sunday school, morning worship, afternoon youth meeting, and evening service; during the week to Wednesday night prayer meeting, Thursday evening choir practice, and often a young peoples' party on Friday. I belonged to the church's Boy Scout troop, went to the church college and graduate school, was ordained, and served five years abroad as a missionary.

Looking back on my life, I realize that during my high school days, I unconsciously held myself apart from my fellow students. I was different because I attended a church that taught 'the truth' of the Bible and I tried to practice that truth faithfully. I was something of an outsider and didn't 'fit in' quite like the other students. When I went to the church college, however, I suddenly did belong. I felt at home and among friends. I was attached to my church.

In spite of that attachment, I began even during college days to wonder about certain biblical interpretations and doctrinal claims. I was most disturbed by the exclusive teachings and practices. In theological school, I became committed to the ecumenical movement. In college and graduate school, I encountered the world religions and was profoundly impressed with the truth I discovered there. As I became acquainted with more religions and their myriad of practices, I realized that they all give sufficient direction to their members for them to attain a reliable sense of the divine, and for their adherents to have meaningful experiences and life guidance.

Though it took many years to feel entirely free from my earlier religious heritage, it has occurred. I am no longer attached to a particular religious view or practice. I now see religion, when authentic, as a useful guide for discovering and living a meaningful human life – as I also see many other systems of belief and practice. I don't any longer feel attached to any particular religion, to religion itself, or any single way of being human. At the same time, I fully realize the extent to which I have benefited from the teachings and practices of the world's religions, especially their philosophical, mystical, nondual, and wisdom traditions. Deep appreciation does not require attachment. (Jim Royster)

Nonattachment Under a Different Heading

In a psychology of religion class in graduate school, the professor began a class by asking: "When do you feel most free?" We all sensed that to be a profound question, and we began to ponder it. There was a long silence. Eventually, one student said, "When I left home for college." Another indicated it was when he quit a job he didn't like. A female student said it was when her parents raised her curfew by an hour. The professor, Dr. McCutcheon, clarified: "I want a comprehensive principle, something that always occurs no matter what the specific circumstance." We were dumbfounded, unable to meet his request. Mercifully, he finally declared: "We feel most free when we realize how we have not been free." He then went on to talk further about this valuable insight. For our purposes: the feeling of freedom always accompanies genuine detachment. Attachment, whether imposed on oneself, on others, or by others, always limits. (Jim Royster)

Healthy, Natural Detachment

I have attached and detached inconspicuously from my childhood, teen, and adult years. I got past the attachment to my teddy bear, homes and neighborhoods, grades, high school, nurses training, jobs and careers, parents, sibling, children. Most of these ongoing processes leave me with good memories and seemed natural as I matured and moved on in the years of my life. (Sally Bard)

Transcending Distorted 'Love'

Recently, I was freed from my distorted 'understanding' of what love is. My early experience consisted of punishment given 'in love' by parents, seeing the abuse of women by their husbands who claimed to 'love' them, school teachers who loved selectively, and many other manipulative expressions of love by family and friends.

Now, I am relieved to know that love is inherent in me, a divine quality. Those early experiences caused me to withhold and not express that of which I am. I choked to say, "I love you," or even to receive another's expression of love. Hugging was very difficult. Now my eyes are open to the beauty of love all around me, like the song, "I can see clearly now, the blocks are gone." The obstacles are cleared away. I see bright sunshiny days as I choose love over fear and hatred, an act of willingness in answer to the world's call for love. My attachment to a distorted view has been replaced by true understanding. Now I can give and receive love freely. (Alma Hamblin)

Helping Others Inspired by Nonattachment

In the summer of 1996, I was told I had prostate cancer. How could this happen? I was only fifty-five and too young to die! I was fearful and attached to my cancer for ten years, going through various treatments to fight the disease.

I stopped treatment about eight years ago and started helping other men who had prostate cancer. Like I had, many of them thought their lives were over. I began studying prostate cancer treatments and procedures to slow the growth. I became a trained prostate cancer advocate and facilitator, able to support and educate others about the disease. Now I facilitate monthly meetings in my retirement center where up to seventy-five men and women come to hear guest speakers and receive support from each other. My objective is to help these people reduce their fear of the disease, and learn about their options.

I went from being afraid of death and attached to my cancer to learning all I could about it and sharing what I had learned with others. I remain with a positive diagnosis; my PSA continues to rise slowly. I'm on a monitoring program called Active Surveillance. If my condition gets worse, I will seek further treatment. I remain optimistic and am not letting the disease ruin the rest of my life. (Dan Bard)

Nonattachment Pithily Stated

Haiku is a popular form of Japanese poetry usually presented in English in three lines of five, seven, and five syllables for a total of seventeen syllables. There may be variations in length but haiku are always short. They often contain a reference to nature and are intended to convey an attitude or state of mind considered commendable. The following examples speak to nonattachment.

Haiku offered by Joti Royster:
    Dew evaporates
    and all our world is dew
    So dear, so fresh, so fleeting.
    (Issa on the death of his young child)

    The thief left it behind:
    the moon
    At my window.
    (Ryokan after a thief stole away with his clothes one

night).

Barn's burnt down:
Now
I can see the moon.
(Masahide who was poor and without regret).

"I Don't Mind What Happens"

Krishnamurti (1895-1986) had been 'discovered' at the age of fourteen and underwent extensive training to become *the* World Teacher of the Theosophical Society. However, he unexpectedly and publicly disavowed the position at a world meeting of the Society by claiming, "truth is a pathless land." He was thirty-four at the time, and went on to teach that truth cannot be realized through "any organization, through any creed, through any dogma, priest or ritual, not through any philosophical knowledge or psychological technique."

The truth that frees comes only through understanding the content of one's own mind. This content makes one different from others in observable characteristics but not unique. The uniqueness of the individual lies in "total freedom from the content of consciousness." Krishnamurti explained further: "Total negation is the essence of the positive. When there is negation of all those things which are not love – desire, pleasure – then love *is*, with its compassion and intelligence."

Krishnamurti showed how he had internalized his teaching when giving a lecture in California in 1977. Part way through the talk, he paused, and then asked, "Do you want to know what my secret is?" The audience leaned forward in rapt attention; here about to be revealed would be the secret to Krishnamurti's inner life, the reason for his inherent contentment and freedom. He quietly said, "You see, I don't mind what happens." Krishnamurti was living a nonattached life. (G/USE)

Detaching from the Need to Convince Others

As a result of my deep appreciation for the world's religious and spiritual traditions – and the liberating expansion they've had on my life – I wanted the same broadening and deepening experience for those still practicing religion conventionally. When covering Christianity in the classroom, my personal spiritual growth led me to criticize some of its key features. I remember to this day when one of my students told me after a class that she had gained a lot of appreciations for the world's religions, but had been hurt by some of the things I said about her personal faith.

It seems strange to me now that this denigrating practice of mine relative to Christianity alone was not softened by my early acquaintance with the sages and saints, for many of them accepted that whatever others thought could not have been otherwise given their past teachings and their level of maturity. For example, Junayd, a Muslim saint, was able to perceive God in every form of belief.

When teaching in the classroom or talking one on one, why did I continue pointing out the 'shortcomings' in perspectives I once held myself and even preached? Why did I want others to 'upgrade' their beliefs? If there are answers to these questions, it might be as simple as the power of habit, or that I was not yet fully convinced of the validity of such broad and uncritical acceptance, or that the perspective was not deeply enough embedded in my own understanding (i.e., in my heart as well as my mind).

I am pleased to affirm that this longstanding, unquestioned practice has disappeared. I'm now content with what others believe and practice from their religious outlook. Just recently, my wife and I met some friends from our college days over sixty years ago. He was a retired clergyman and she was a teacher; the religious beliefs they held in the early 1950s had not changed. I was entirely content on discovering this and felt no desire at all for them to change. I matter-of-factly shared a little of my perspectives, with no sense of my view being superior or more advanced. I carried away from that shared luncheon a real appreciation for the lives they have lived, and now feel a deeper love for them than ever before. How magnificent that life provides opportunity for such meaningful change.

[I trust that those reading my personal confessions will sense the spirit from which I write them – objectively, matter-of-factly, absolutely without any sense of 'better than.'] (Jim Royster)

Detaching from the Loss of a Recent Purchase

It happened just today, something that can happen to anyone at any time. It's a small matter that seemed big at first. There's a saying, "The little foxes spoil the vine," which I take to mean that we often lose our inner peace over the small things that come up in our everyday life's journey.

I had gone into McDonalds to have lunch with a friend and brought my fairly new Kindle e-reader, along with some papers that I planned to discuss. When we finished lunch, I absentmindedly walked away and left my Kindle on the table. When I arrived home about an hour later, I discovered what I had done and called McDonald's. But no luck: my second Kindle in recent months was also gone. My next thought was to check the car, which also produced no luck. Then I began to think more calmly and clearly: "Give thanks in all things, and in all things give thanks."

Problem solved: let go of the attachment to my e-reader and move on.

Another aphorism came to mind: "The goose is in the bottle, the goose is out of the bottle." Life moves this way and that; sometimes we have something and then we don't. So buy another Kindle, my third one. Even though it's a refurbished Kindle, it has features my earlier ones did not, like a keyboard that makes it more useful than the others. The losses have taught me to be more careful about where I leave things, to be more aware. (Ernie Riedel)

Detaching from the Rationally Incompatible

A dear friend has developed the gift of connecting on a spiritual level with those in the spiritual world. She somehow 'sees' and 'hears' loved ones who have passed the veil of human death, and captures evidence for clients who come to her, often grieving over the loss of their loved one. In her private meditations, she 'receives' uplifting messages and shares them daily through electronic posts to a wide audience. In public gatherings, she channels a variety of entities by transcending to higher levels of consciousness. She then speaks and gestures – clearly different from her usual patterns – on a wide variety of subjects, many of which are new even to her.

Having personally witnessed hundreds of these events over eight years, I continue to be baffled. My mind cannot logically conclude that this is really happening. At the same time, I am unable to deny that these events are real, and thus the paradox.

When one comes to the awareness that a situation like this is paradox, one has a choice to either continue to be challenged by it, or to detach from it. It is what it is. Having detached, the paradox is transcended, and my life has become more harmonious. (Connie England)

Letting go of the Need to be Right

A number of factors – each one, actually, a conditioning – came together and 'caused' me to feel that I had to be right. These included being: the oldest of three, a son (i.e., male), a good student who got top grades, a graduate with honors, a devout member of my church, a model Eagle Boy Scout, a clergyman, a professor. I was so thoroughly identified with 'being right' that I didn't even recognize this arbitrary feature of my self-sense, arbitrary because it was something subtly learned over time, the result of the blind conditioning that I now understand was totally inappropriate. Needless to say, the assumption that I had to be right led to arguments, discord, and bad feelings.

The habit began to weaken when I started to ask myself what my role was in these unpleasant encounters, how I contributed to them. It wasn't long before the answer emerged within myself, helped along as others pointed it out – and finally admitted to myself. But the tendency didn't disappear easily. I consciously had to stop asserting my viewpoint. The habit weakened a bit when I began to realize and acknowledge that others have a full right to hold their personal views until their experience of life leads them to change. I can offer my view, but I don't need to argue it, to insist on it being the way things are. The need rarely arises anymore. When it does, the liberating practice of detachment is activated and applied. (Jim Royster)

Learning Detachment when Driving a Car

As a young driver, I was always finding fault with other drivers. I eventually realized that this was causing me to be continuously upset. When I began thinking more about this, I considered that maybe there was a reason others were speeding, maybe they were rushing to something very important. Then I began to rationalize their behavior as the result of their genetics or upbringing. But I was still judging them.

The change I have discovered in myself since those days is remarkable. When I notice illegal, dangerous, or erratic driving now, there is no emotional reaction. It doesn't bother me. I don't have to make an excuse for them. It's a nonissue. I don't know what would happen if the action injured me, a family member, or a friend. Hopefully I won't need to find out. I do feel, however, that the reaction will be under control.

The change that has taken place in me when driving has permeated my entire life. There is much less need now to dwell on the actions of others or things that are actually insignificant. (Ron Strong)

Abrupt Stop and Great Gain

I started smoking in high school. At that time, a pack of cigarettes cost twenty-five cents. It was the 'cool' thing to do. A pack of cigarettes under your rolled up tee shirt! How 'cool' is that. I continued through college, smoking a pack a day. I sometimes smoked a pipe (another 'cool' thing). As I'm writing this, I'm realizing the enormous influence of my ego in these 'cool' decisions.

In the Air Force, all the vices were really inexpensive. A carton of cigarettes only cost one dollar, that's ten cents a pack. Alcohol also was cheap. I've always wondered why the military made it so easy to abuse one's body while in the Service. I smoked cigars, a pipe, but always came back to cigarettes.

One night, I was awakened by uncontrolled coughing: I couldn't catch my breath. I seriously couldn't catch my breath. I don't remember now whether I had a cold or an allergy was involved. What I do know is that when I had that coughing/choking attack in my mid-twenties, my desire for smoking ended abruptly, and I haven't had a cigarette since. My intent to live a meaningful life must have over-ridden what I knew to be a superficial and dangerous habit. (Ron Strong)

Detaching from a Loved Profession

I had always wanted to be a teacher. My two sons were on their own, my daughter was in middle school, and I went to college. A dream came true when I became a first grade teacher. It was a job I loved. It became a part of me.

At the beginning of the school year, I had the students write and draw about something they liked to do. At the end of the year they did the same thing. It was astonishing to see the progress. By using various activities, greetings, songs, and games, students develop oral language skills, self-control, and problem solving abilities. We had a lot of fun while learning! There were consequences, not punishments. Kindness toward others was important. My school recognized the strong link between academic success and social emotional skills and that a high quality education is built on a safe and joyful learning community.

One of our links between school and home was evident in Grandparent's Day. Grandpa and grandma enjoyed the children's songs and other activities. We made words with letter tiles, which enhanced phonics and spelling for the children. It was a fun activity enjoyed by the grandparents and students. One grandpa remarked that school was never this much fun when he went!

Then it was time to retire. I was devastated. All I could think of was all the years I had spent learning how to be a better teacher. I had many games, activities and songs that I had accumulated. I had a large collection of books I shared with the students. I had many files I created to support the curriculum. None of this would be used by me anymore. I would miss the students. It was like 'cutting off my arm.'

Some of the mothers had a surprise party for me at a teahouse to show their appreciation. I had the traditional retirement party with my colleagues. I cleaned out my 'stuff.' We sold our house and moved to Florida.

It took time to adjust. I read a book that said "what we do" and "who we are" are not the same. I had not looked at it that way. I had to let go of thinking of myself only as a teacher. I realized that teaching was what I did, not who I am. I realized how blessed I was to have had a job that I loved to the very last day. I cherish my memories.

I now live in a retirement community, with more time to do the things that are hard to fit in when working. I have time to read, travel, attend study groups, go to movies, and much more. My husband and I have made many new friends. He had been busy with his career too, so the best part is being able to spend more time with him. Life is good! (Judy Lapham)

Releasing a Son into the World

Our fifty-four-year-old son was diagnosed as bi-polar about ten years ago. He has a history of drug and alcohol addiction, is a smoker, and asthmatic. Since his early teens, he has been troubled with himself, his family, and society. Were we 'shitty' parents that we lost him so long ago? Maybe so, but we tried hard to make up for the deficiencies of being too young, naïve, and inconsistent with our parenting skills. We tried everything we could think of to heal the tensions in our family, the hurt and angry feelings between our troubled son and his two brothers and sister. They pulled away from their brother, which was, of course, upsetting to us. In spite of our efforts to create harmony in the family, alienation occurred, and communication became difficult, if not impossible.

My husband and I have now decided there is no way any longer for us to influence his life patterns and decisions. No more rescues, interventions, coaching, or suggestions. We, of course, love him dearly. How could we not – his hugs, sense of humor, and wit? He is more than sufficiently of age to be on his own in the world, and we want nothing but the best for him, with no strings or attachment from us. (Sally Bard)

Detaching from an Addiction

I grew up in rural New York near the Canadian border. The population was mainly Irish and French with a culture of alcohol use. I had seen a good deal of damage done by alcohol in my own family and with acquaintances at school. I vowed to never drink alcohol.

At age seventeen, I took a drink with friends and was astounded by the good feeling. I immediately decided I had been wrong in my opinion about alcohol use.

Over time, I became a daily, heavy, barroom drinker. I became increasingly self-centered and got in a lot of trouble, including barroom fights, car wrecks, DWI citations, and an arrest for public intoxication. At the same time, I was considered a good worker, intelligent and was well liked. I denied that I had any problem with alcohol; I told myself I simply drank because I enjoyed it.

My drinking caused increased problems with my wife. Also, I was no longer getting relief or good feelings from drinking. I started to attend AA and did not drink for one year. Life was good. Problems faded away and I believed that it was safe for me to drink again. In a very short time, all the trouble returned, and it became apparent that I was indeed an alcoholic and powerless over alcohol.

I prayed to God for relief even though I had no real belief in the divine. I stayed sober on my own for two and a half years. I had come to believe that for me to drink would be fatal, though I wanted to drink on a daily basis. I was restless, irritable and discontented. I decided to return to AA and to work the program the way it was suggested. I accepted my alcoholism, decided to trust God, did an honest and thorough moral inventory and shared it with another person. I looked at the damage I had caused myself and others, and made amends to those that I had harmed. Relationships were restored by making amends and living in a responsible way. With the passage of time, I was able to forgive myself by seeing my faults and shortcomings, attempting to live a sober and sane life, helping others, and realizing that I was forgiven by my Higher Power, by God. The proof of forgiveness for me is that I continue to remain sober. I have not consumed alcohol in nearly thirty-nine years.

Many other attachments have been let go of over the years. The process seems to be that the attachment causes pain and suffering that becomes unbearable. I then recognize and identify the attachment and become willing to let it go. I deny the attachment until forced to recognize it by pain. I have been able to forgive others by looking at my own life and seeing the damage I caused others and for which I have been forgiven. I realize that others may also suffer from the spiritual malady of extreme self-centeredness. (Don L.)

Detachment Leads to Academic Achievement

During my early childhood, I missed a lot of school because of epilepsy and deafness. By the time I was eight years old, these issues had been resolved by surgery. But I had missed a lot of foundational learning. Due to the bullying I faced in secular schools, my parents decided to place me in an alternative school where I received more individual help. When high school rolled around, I was still far behind. Besides feeling that I didn't fit in, and failing a few of my classes the first year, I did manage to be advanced. My math, reading, writing, and spelling skills were years behind my peers. At the end of the first year in high school, after working really hard to improve, I came to the conclusion that I just didn't have the intelligence to get a high mark.

Life went on, and I gradually grew into an average to high achieving student but never reached excellence – until the middle of grade ten. When I was leaving the classroom after a difficult exam, my teacher asked me if I'd like to see my grade. He handed me my paper and I saw a big "A" in red at the top of the page. At that moment, the idea I had about my capacity dissolved instantly. I thought to myself, "Wow, I can actually do this."

The next semester and every semester after that I worked hard toward my goal of improving my personal best. My confidence grew as I ascended the academic ladder. By the end of high school, I was in the top ten percent of my class. I am now halfway through medical school. (Hannah Grace Royster)

Detaching from Social Protocol

I was sitting next to Dr. Royster during one of the discussion group sessions when his cell phone vibrated on the table. He picked it up and recognized the caller's name on the ID. Then he immediately passed the phone to me, asking me to take the call for him. The elderly gentleman calling, known to each of us, explained that he was late for the meeting. I said quietly that it was OK, and that he could just come along even though he was late. Class discussion group continued.

I instantly felt I must call the gentleman back, to be sure that he knew the way; he had never attended the group at this location, and I felt that I must catch him before he ventured on an unnecessary journey. I thought he might have confused in his days of the week thinking it was Saturday, a day he and Jim regularly meet for coffee. I got up, went to an adjoining room, called him back, and sure enough, he had confused the days. I returned to the room and took my seat.

The discussion was about detachment, and the incident with the phone seemed to reflect that very subject. I had given no thought to whether or not leaving the room was within social protocol. It was just appropriate, with no conscious deliberation. On returning to the class, I offered the event as one that was 'from within the moment' or 'in the now,' the evidence for this being in the action 'beyond thought.'

A participant in the group suggested that there might have been a different way to respond: let the Holy Spirit function, through grace. Jim explained that that was precisely what had happened. The participant questioned whether or not I had thought about letting Grace take care of things. I responded that if I had thought about letting Grace take care of the matter, I would have been functioning from my human thought system. What had happened instead was a spontaneous action originating in and from Spirit. Jim too had responded spontaneously when he passed the phone to me. Each of us responded from Spirit. By not being limited by social expectation, we were able to act spontaneously and without deliberation. Jim said actions of this type are rare but wonderful when they occur. (Connie England)

Transcending Anger

My dad really struggled with anger, as had his dad, my paternal grandfather. As a child and teenager, I often saw my dad 'lose his temper.' My brothers and I also frequently got mad at each other. Fights were common. My mother had little success in reducing these eruptions.

Even as a young adult, I occasionally lost control. When home from college for Christmas, I felt my younger brother was not showing proper respect to my parents. On the front porch, I hit him in the face, knocking him to the ground. The hurt, sorrow, and disbelief on his face when he turned to me 'broke' my heart. I knew my anger was out of control. When playing on the college golf team I went out to practice one afternoon and took my girlfriend along. I missed a putt, lost self-control, swung my putter into the grass, and tore up a huge piece of turf – on the green. Then I was doubly mad and threw my putter as far as I could. Unaccustomed to outburst of anger, my girlfriend said, "If you do that again, I won't ever play golf with you." I mustered some control.

There were other instances, however. I started a fight with a man so drunk that he fell down when swinging at me. I argued heatedly against beliefs contrary to my own. I became frustrated – a milder form of anger – when I couldn't get my farm animals to do what I wanted. Once, when I was trying to repair my tractor, even though I almost never swore, I began cussing loudly. A friend suddenly approached, heard me cussing, and calmly reminded me that such behavior never helps. After a long and hot bus ride coming down from the Himalayas in India, I desperately needed water. A local fellow was selling it for about a penny (or less in Indian currency) per tiny plastic cup. I drank a couple of cups but didn't have any more small change and figured the water vendor wouldn't have change for bigger bills. I was about to re-board a waiting bus for another long, hot ride. I grabbed a couple of the cups, rushed to the bus with the vendor hollering at the top of his voice. My thirst and anger overrode social decency.

One of the most serious breaches of calmness and self-control occurred when I was a father correcting (punishing) my children. I over-reacted when I saw one son purposely destroy the other son's toy. Only Grace, coupled with their commitment to personal growth, enabled my children to become the happy, mature, and responsible adults that they are today.

Early in my teaching career, I carefully studied an advanced Tibetan Buddhist text for those wanting to purify their habitual attitudes. Each chapter focused on a particular human attribute. When I read the chapter on anger, I found only counsel on how to develop patience. Wow! What an insight! Impatience is a form of anger. Impatience was another bane of life for me. I took these teachings to heart and began slowing down and relaxing when noting the old patterns becoming activated. Over the years it has helped immensely.

Yes, most of us do become less prone to anger as we age. This is certainly an important and happy development. But given my heritage, my genetic and early paternal example, my years of expressed anger, even more years of somewhat-controlled anger, I find my current state nothing short of 'miraculous.'

There are still occasional mild and quickly recognized instances of impatience, but they are rare now. One of the most telling bits of evidence occurs when driving. I now easily and without reactive emotion respond to the careless and risky antics of other drivers by making the necessary shift in my driving to give them the room they need or want.

In conclusion, the first step in overcoming my outbursts of anger was to admit and fully acknowledge the anger, that it was a habit pattern that could be changed, and, importantly, was not a quality of my deeper, essential, natural, or God-given nature. It was a feature of 'me' but not of 'I'. As this anger was something added, it was therefore something that could be subtracted through the steady ameliorating process of long-term development of patience. I believe this had a huge neutralizing impact on the deeper sources of anger embedded in my psyche. Along with this, I tried to decipher each situation in which I became angry in order to find the precipitating factors. When I discovered that expectations lay behind my anger, I could then make changes within myself; I began to be more aware of my expectations (of others and myself), became increasingly able to drop them, and found my anger diminishing. Throughout these many years, I was also reading widely in personal transformational literature, attending related events, and committing myself to *actually practicing* the principles advocated by the world's spiritual and wisdom traditions.

I can't imagine becoming angry anymore. This is not to say, however, that I now ignore or tolerate injustice. Rather, I can face the many inequities and injustices in this country and the world with an open heart and mind. For example: While acknowledging the pain and suffering of victims caused by such horrendous acts as rape, murder, torture, and terrorism, I now acknowledge as well the suffering and psychic confusion and turmoil experienced by the perpetrators, and their sense of social isolation and alienation. My perspective on antisocial and criminal behavior in no way means I am condoning these behaviors, nor does it weaken the necessity for prosecution and punishment. (Jim Royster)

Life Throws a Curve Ball

A year ago, at the age of sixty-one my life seemed tidy and I was beginning to think in more concrete terms about a future that included retirement, travel, time with my family and grandkids, and all the things I had not had time for during the decades of parenting and making a living. I was somewhat disconnected from my spiritual self and my true north was located outside of me. Nonetheless, I had patted myself on the back more than once that my world in the illusory realm was admirable. My children seemed happy and were excelling in their careers. I had beautiful and healthy grandkids. I was formulating a vision for the next phase of my life that would be full of bliss, or so I thought.

The universe it turns out had other plans. A year ago the cracks in my son's marriage began to show: his wife, who is unstable, decided he no longer loved her and if she could not have him no one would. She proceeded with a scorched earth strategy that cost him his job, landed him in jail, destroyed their family, and separated him from his children for an extensive period of time. For me, all of this meant that I lost my grandkids.

The past year has brought so many challenges that as I write this I wonder how I survived. The best answer I have for that question is that, with a lot of effort and help from the divine, I learned how to detach. First and foremost I had to detach from hating my son's wife, and oh how I hated her. I took it to an art form, spending every waking minute hating her. Only with time did I come to understand and accept that not forgiving her only served to keep me mired in my pain. The pure logic of that recognition is what allowed me to detach. I had to detach from my cherished role as an active participant in the lives of my grandchildren, and I had to watch the pain my grandkids suffered from losing me and a father whom they adore. To detach, I mentally placed them in the hands of God, and I learned to accept and trust that their happiness does not depend on me.

I saw my son's life destroyed and watched as he lost every material thing. His heart broke in unspeakable ways. Eventually I came to see myself as separate from my son and learned to detach from his journey. I remembered that Khalil Gibran had said that our children don't belong to us but are gifts from life itself. I learned to honor my son's path and trust that he is a child of God with a Spirit in him that will see him through. He is reaching for this Spirit and I am certain he will find it. I have learned that the options available to me are to love him and set an example of forgiveness and the benefits of peace and serenity.

I had to detach from concepts that included a perfect family and perfect life. I had to accept that my grand design was never so perfect or grand after all. Much of this came from recognizing that the building blocks for my grand design were illusory and temporal, like all things in the worldly realm. I gained more than I lost this past year. I can only say that now, sitting on this side of it. One of the healthiest detachments I made was from the illusion that I ever had any control over the insanity anyway. What I can control is which path I choose, how I react to insanity, and how I prioritize my peace. (Anonymous)

Attachment Notice Given in a Dream

My first college professorship was at Western College in Oxford, Ohio. I had just finished a PhD in world religions and was eager to begin my career. As students were leaving for the summer at the end of my third year, the entire faculty and staff was called into a closed meeting and informed that the school would not open in the fall if funds did not become available. We were shocked. Everyone was urged to begin efforts to relocate. Happily, an arrangement with Miami University was negotiated that allowed one more year of operation.

I was unable to find a permanent position during that last year at Western College because higher education in the US was hit hard with financial cutbacks and virtually no hiring was taking place. During this final year (1973-74), however, I did manage to put together short-term teaching contracts in three different colleges. One of these required me to leave my family in Ohio and travel to Minnesota. I found a room in a farmhouse a few miles from the campus and went there only to sleep. On campus, I was either in the classroom teaching, in the library doing research, or in my office meeting students, preparing lectures, or applying for permanent teaching posts in other colleges and universities. I was under a lot of pressure to find another job.

During this time, I had a dream that I immediately understood. In the dream itself (not in the morning but in the dream), I wake up from a night's sleep and find my eyes matted shut as if I have a really bad cold. I can't open them, so I stumble to the sink, splash water on one eye, spread it open with my fingers, and looking back at me from the mirror is my faculty ID card. My eye is my ID card, which is me, my identification, who I have become, "I". More succinctly: eye = ID = I = who/what I've become = me = what my current life has become.

I had been so totally focused on become a good professor, finding another teaching position, thereby able to support my family, that the breadth of my humanness has been reduced to my job. I had, out of a sense of responsibility, become attached to my profession. Detachment became necessary: I accepted invitations to dinner with fellow faculty, went to sporting events, relaxed more, and continued my professional involvements but with ease and trust. This was truly a vital and revelatory dream that enabled me to get more on track as a well-rounded human being. (Jim Royster)

Detaching from Depression

Fifty years ago I was depressed and unhappy in many, many ways. I often thought of taking my life. About this time, I met some very wise men, not just smart with lots of information, but wise, truly wise; they understood Truth. These men led me into a spiritual movement that helped me change my consciousness and thought patterns. I paid close attention to their teachings and began to apply them in my daily life. My entire outlook changed from one of a hellish experience to a heavenly life. Nothing changed in the outer circumstances of my life; I was in the same situation as ever, but now my outlook was different. Before, I was controlled by outer circumstances and impulsively reacted to them. After my awareness changed, I found I was in control of the former harmful feelings when they arose. I didn't react out of those feelings but was able to express love and truth. I became able to remain in a steady state of love. Feelings of depression gradually waned and eventually disappeared. It was sort of like breaking an old, destructive habit, such as smoking. When the habitual urge came up, I consciously chose the new response. In time, with patience, the undesirable reaction dropped away and was replaced by the beneficial attitude and behavior. (Ernie Riedel)

Detaching from the need to Control

"My sister's friend, Sasha, and I both like to go to church. My sister, Alice, doesn't. I was serving one evening at church and Sasha planned to come and wanted Alice's company. Sasha and I pleaded with Alice to join us. It was a battle all the way from the house to the car to the street to the church. Alice was not keen on the idea even though she enjoyed the music and people. I had a deep feeling of urgency about getting her there. When we arrived at the meeting, a friend asked me why I seemed stressed. I told her what had happened and that Alice and Sasha were outside waiting for the service to begin. My friend said to me, "Hannah, you are so tight-fisted about everything. Don't you know that God loves your sister way more than you do, or ever could; open your hand, let her go. Trust her to God." And so I closed my eyes and opened my hand. God has her covered." (Hannah Grace Royster)

Releasing False Role Expectation

A woman entered marriage with the belief that her duty as a wife was to 'take care of things' for her husband, to neutralize any weakness or need he might exhibit, and to keep him happy and contented. He took for granted her role in the marriage, never acknowledging her needs that went unheeded and unmet for many years. She eventually gained enough understanding to realize that she was actually enabling his neediness, was able to let go of the intervention, and even forgave herself for her 'mistake.' (SM)

Releasing a Bit of Self-consciousness

In grade ten when I was fifteen years old, I stood with two of my peers in a science lab. We were inspecting the equipment for our practical lesson that day. I picked up a bottle of blue fluid and read the ingredients out loud. Instead of reading: "Not safe for consumption by underwater organisms," I read: "Not safe for consumption by underwater *orgasms*." My classmates burst out laughing, almost falling over themselves. I began to feel embarrassed. Their laughter hurt, and I started to feel the age-old wound of not being able to read or spell very well. Instead, however, I took hold of myself and burst out laughing too. That day I learned a great lesson: I found the freedom that comes from being able to laugh at myself. (Hannah Grace Royster)

Letting Go of Control and Anxiety

I was nine weeks into my fourth year of medicine when it became evident that I was burned out. I had been running the academic excellence marathon for over five years and had just ended a long, unbeneficial relationship. I deferred my exams and took a year to rejuvenate. In the latter half of the year, I enrolled in a Christian leadership course. I felt really stretched but loved the growth. In one session, we read about the gifts of the Spirit. Adam, our leader, asked each of us to choose two spiritual gifts. I chose healing and faith. Each person stood in the center of the room surrounded by those who prayed that we would receive our chosen gifts. When my turn came, I moved forward and was prayed for. Adam asked, "Why do you want faith?" and I said I needed it to be able to finish my final three years of medicine.

When we prayed, I could feel the Holy Spirit in the room, my skin tingled up and down my body, and waves of warm and cool flowed through me. My body began to sway and I was held steady by the praying hands that were laid on me. Then I fell backward without the feeling of falling, more like lightness, embraced by strength and gentleness. I seemed to drift to the floor, lightly bumping into those behind me. There was no anxiety or fear, only peace. I was barely connected to my body. I felt embraced by God. As I lay on the floor, I sensed Him say, "Lie Down."

That evening, Adam said to me: "I think God wants you to surrender medicine to him." That struck a chord of truth in my heart; I spent the next few weeks praying that God would show me how to release medicine to Him, which I now believe I have done. Instead of being anxious about my need to perform and achieve, I am now filled with peace. Of course, I still have to study and work hard, but I know that God's got me covered. I know that this is His path for me. I am confident of God's continual presence and guidance for my life and chosen career. (Hannah Grace Royster)

Detaching from a Painful Past

When I was thirty-two, I met Mary Beth, and she was perfect. I had been struggling for six years in a failing marriage. In Mary Beth, I found hope. She completed me, I thought. We ended our marriage after thirty-five years. She left for a variety of reasons. I now understand that our relationship had quickly fallen into co-dependency. I thought that our individual strengths were shared and filled our separate weaknesses. Somewhere in the journey, I lost myself, and began working to become what she wanted. She seemed to need to control everything in the relationship. The real issue, as I saw it, was that her model for a husband was her father, how he acted, how he dressed, how he was respected, and his success in business. As it turned out, each step I took to be like her father was praised, and each wrong step led to distance between us.

Now that I am divorced, the ability to detach from my need for approval has become a daily, haunting ghost. After my wife left in 2012, I felt lonely, abandoned, betrayed, and lost. I turned to alcohol to numb the pain of the loss and the inability to live without her. Since the divorce, I have had five six-week rehabilitation sessions, three DUI convictions, nine weeks in jail, and one year in a halfway house with much younger alcoholics and drug addicts.

Since moving to a retirement community, I have been actively searching for purpose and meaning in my life. I participate in several spiritual groups and clubs, in AA, in church and in Bible study. I sit with Alzheimer patients. I counsel in the Stephen Ministry, and try to keep my mind sharp and active with thinking games. These involvements help me detach from my painful past. I continue to have unanswered questions (why my former wife refused marriage counseling with me). I realize that detachment and healing is an on-going commitment. (Tom Alles)

Reluctant Detachment

I've had a long and happy cycling life. I got a tricycle well before kindergarten and my first bicycle years before the neighborhood streets got paved. It was used, had fat tires (they all did back then), and was really special because it had springs between the frame and the front wheel. This was supposed to give a softer ride but actually made the bike harder to peddle. I got my favorite bike as a teenager after we moved to the country. It had skinny tires. Every spring, I took it completely apart, soaked the greasy parts in gasoline, re-lubricated, occasionally sanded the paint off the frame and repainted the whole bike, and then put it all together again – without the fenders. I wanted it light enough that I could lift it head high with one hand. Why? Because that also made it fast!

In those days, I was a Boy Scout and earned the bicycling merit badge, which required a fifty-mile cycling trip. I also had a daily paper route, eleven customers, and raced about three miles to deliver the papers. The country roads were paved; I could go really fast and get back home to listen to "The Lone Ranger." My high school was in the city about twelve miles away. My parents usually drove me, but once in a while I rode my bike. There were two advantages to it: being light, it was fast; and being old and stripped down, no one else wanted it, so it was relatively safe and I didn't have to fuss with a lock (honesty was more common in those days). Fond memories, all of them!

Recently, now in my mid-eighties, I decided to ride a bike I was storing in my garage to the nearby postboxes for the day's mail. We all know the common saying, "You never forget how to ride a bike." Well, it's not true. I couldn't stay balanced. I swerved from side to side and finally fell, getting three bleeding gashes on my leg. Fortunately, there was help at home to clean the wounds and bandage my leg.

The moral of the story: in spite of my desire to someday get a new, modern bike with multiple speeds and go on biking trips, I've decided to detach from cycling. In itself, this is not the kind of detachment that opens to a fuller life but one that does forestall the likelihood of serious self-damage. Therefore, it is simply prudent and not liberating. I would still like to make short biking trips, but common sense takes preference over an activity that might be fun. (Jim Royster)

Detachment Leads to a New Life

Years ago when I was training as a counseling psychologist, a woman was referred to me by the county court. She had been placed on probation for assault and battery. In our first session, she was reluctant to share much information other than being mad about the referral by the court. However, she did cooperate because she wanted to be released from probation in order to resume her life. She finally revealed that her anger came from the fact that her husband had an affair and moved in with his girlfriend. She felt betrayed, angry, and vengeful, so she took a baseball bat, went to the girlfriend's house, and broke windows out of her husband's car parked in the driveway. She was arrested, faced trial, and was put on probation with mandatory counseling.

In the counseling sessions, we discussed at length her relationship with her husband, her feelings about marriage, her betrayal, and what she wanted to get out of life. It was apparent that she had been the primary breadwinner in the family and made most of the decisions in the home. At the end of one session, I asked, "Why do you need your husband?" She looked startled for a minute, was contemplative, and finally responded. "I don't! I can take care of myself and the children." When she left the office, she scheduled another appointment for the next week, but did not show up. I called the probation officer who said, "I don't know all that happened, but she filed for divorce, paid restitution, applied for an education grant, and was the happiest that I have ever seen her." We can't know the extent of her inner detachment, but it's obvious that she detached from a life situation that was not working, thereby benefiting her children and herself. (Jerry Lapham)

Detachment and Change in Professions

In 1957, I passed the Ohio Bar examinations with the intention to practice law. The GI Bill, following military service from 1946 to 1948, enabled my four years of undergraduate education at Mt. Union University where a Bachelors of Arts degree was earned, followed by a four-year plus Doctor of Law degree from Youngstown State University.

Unknown to me at the time, my educational pursuits were far from over. Let me explain. After a brief practice as a lawyer, I experienced a tremendous undoing of my thought processes. I came to understand that I had chosen law simply because it would provide prestige and a comfortable life. I did not realize that in choosing law I was electing conflict and confrontation. Had I not enough of that in post-war Europe?

This led to the radical decision of entering the Augustana Theological Seminary in Rock Island, Illinois, for four additional years to become an ordained Lutheran pastor in 1962 with a Masters of Divinity degree. Although being a minister should remove one from conflict, guess what? It didn't! The undoing process eventually led to divorce and a painful breakup of my marriage. This occurred in the early seventies and resulted in a return to the practice of law. Fortunately, my added experiences as a minister led me to a more compassionate understanding as a criminal defense lawyer. How? My clients and I, upon deciding an eventual strategy (i.e., whether to go to trial or plea bargain) developed a trust relationship beyond all ethical and moral considerations. I also call this an undoing.

Eventually, I returned to the ministry and retired in 2002 as a Presbyterian minister (PCUSA). My love for teaching included *A Course in Miracles* as well as historical studies about the man we know as Jesus, whom I consider the world's most advanced Teacher in and for undoing our conflicted minds. (Howard Westin)

When Detachment is Required from a Worthy Objective

Up to a million protestors, most of them university students, occupied Tiananmen Square in 1989 in support of a popular human-rights reformer who had recently died. At the time of this event and for about forty years previously, the Dalai Lama had been working toward dialogue with the Chinese in hope of gaining recognition of Tibet as an autonomous region within China. He had resolutely avoided any policy that would damage relations between the Chinese and the Tibetan government in exile (then in India, as it is even now over half a century later). The Dalai Lama's position is reminiscent of Mahatma Gandhi who, in his lengthy, non-violent campaign to win Indian independence from England, refused to take up any position or action that would jeopardize eventual good relations with England.

Representatives of the Dalai Lama had been making real progress with the Chinese toward negotiation when Tiananmen erupted into massive demonstrations. It became clear that if the Dalai Lama backed the protestors, the negotiations would most certainly be aborted. Even though it was unnecessary, the Tibetan foreign minister reminded the Dalai Lama that the chance for talks might well be ended. The foreign minister reported that the Dalai Lama's energy became "like that of a tiger. He said: 'Yes, it's true. But if I do not speak out now, I have no moral right to ever speak out for freedom and democracy. These young people are asking for nothing more, nothing less than what I have been asking for. And if I can't speak for them, I'll be ashamed to ever talk about freedom and democracy.'" The prospect for negotiation was shattered – and has not occurred to date. The Dalai Lama's commitment to freedom and democracy took precedent over his concern for Tibetan culture. The Dalai Lama had to detach from the political objective for his people in order to uphold his moral stance for all humanity. (*WF* 78-81)

Detachment Exemplified in Public Meeting

When teaching at Cleveland State University, I had the privilege of moderating the biannual meetings of the Cleveland Conference of Religions. These citywide gatherings brought together members of the many religions and churches that made up Greater Cleveland. A typical session had three periods: a panel composed of a Hindu, Muslim, Buddhist, Baha'i, Jain, Sikh, Jew, Protestant, Catholic, and occasionally, a Native American, each of whom addressed a pre-set topic from the perspective of their tradition; second, a luncheon was provided by the participants from one of the faiths; and finally, the group reconvened for the audience to direct questions to the speakers.

At one of the earlier meetings, a Sikh newcomer from India angrily confronted the Hindu speaker by accusing his tradition of waging war against the Sikh religion. The Hindu, with calm respect, tried to appease the challenger, but without apparent effect. As moderator, I noted that the events that enflamed the newcomer had taken place centuries earlier, that they were perpetrated by no one now living and certainly not in Cleveland, Ohio, and that the intent of the symposium was to build respect, harmony, and cooperation among the religions. I invited the disgruntled gentleman to respond to what he heard from the Hindu and myself. He did so but with no sign of any softening in his viewpoint. When I asked the Hindu if wanted to say anything further, he calmly declined. The Sikh, a recalcitrant fellow who appeared nervous and distraught, had refused to forgive and thereby continued to suffer personally as he persisted in injecting alienation between communities when none was any longer relevant. (Jim Royster)

Detachment from Family, Country, Culture, and Faith

The strong Christian foundation that had been established in my childhood was less of a focal point when raising my children, but those roots certainly informed my worldview as an adult. However, many church doctrines kept grating against a deeper knowing that felt truer to my heart. Church attendance stopped. The time came when my children were older and my marriage was stable and comfortable. Life seemed perfect. Yet there was an underlying sense that something was missing, something was not quite right. It seemed time to head back to college to finish degree work that had been put on hold to raise a family.

A class on Hinduism was being offered. It was scheduled at a convenient time and would fulfill a degree requirement. Little did I know, as class began that first day, that my life would be forever changed and my worldview radically altered. That day, the foundation for my pilgrimage toward the One Truth that has many names was laid. The class brought light on a deep inner knowing and an inexplicable strong bond to India and her ancient wisdom. What I thought I knew and who I thought 'I' was was remolded and thoroughly re-envisioned. I had a repeated dream that I was perched upon a precarious precipice starring out into a mysteriously, scary dark void. I sat there with a chilled heart in my throat, clinging tightly to a pillar of black stone. The pillar, which I somehow knew was all that had been stable and solid in my life, turned to smoke and the inner voice said, "Let go and jump." Although terrified, I did just that. The free fall into the open arms of that One Truth has continued to uphold me on my journey.

Family as I knew it has changed. I am not the Betty Crocker wife and mother I thought I would be, not the mom-grandma living just around the corner, baking cookies, ever-ready for the kids to drop by. And there is no husband-dad-grandpa by my side. Our marriage slowly dissolved. I finished my degree and after the children began their own families, I moved several times around the country, studying and teaching yoga as a life-style. Eventually, I moved to India and continued studying there.

There have been many painful and confusing times for my family and me. At the same time, there continues a shared, underlying knowing that there is a rightness to it all. Although time spent with family is far less than I ever imagined, we do share deep love and connection. When I leave after each visit, it is bittersweet. Thanks to the wonders of video calling, we're enabled to stay in contact over the many miles. (Indukanta Udasin, formerly Jackie Papeleo)

* * * *

As Dr. James Royster, professor of the course on Hinduism mentioned by Indukanta, I'd like to add a few features about her transforming process that authenticate it even while adding to the mystery. After I assigned the reading of the *Bhagavad Gita*, Hinduism's most prominent scripture, Jackie didn't appear in class for a couple of weeks, strikingly unlike her regular attendance. When I inquired, she replied that when reading the *Gita* – for the first time ever – she had the sense that she knew the text well. This caused profound confusion in my mind, and I wondered about her background and how she came to have this sense of 'knowing.'

One day after class, she mentioned that her sleep pattern had changed; she began to wake up about four a.m., wander around the house feeling like there was something she should be doing but could not discover what it might be. I informed her that four in morning is the customary time to begin meditating in India. That made sense to her and ended the perplexity.

When the entire class came to the Royster home for an all-day meeting, we ended the session with group meditation. When that was over, the students retrieved their personal items, got a final bite to eat, said their farewells, and left – all this while Indukanta continued, undisturbed, to meditate. After she ended her meditation, it took sometime longer before I was sure that she had returned sufficiently to daily consciousness to drive safely home.

Jackie did not need to detach from these unusual developments; they had become core features of her emerging personhood and character. Given the depth of these experiences, the honesty and courage of her acknowledgement of them, her full incorporation and integration was the appropriate response. She could, of course, have decided differently, but her testimonial above attests to the correctness of the decision for her. (Jim Royster)

Healthy Love Through Detachment

My husband and I have an adopted son who made his appearance in our lives at the tender age of five weeks. He was always, from day one, a significant challenge to us, his new parents. He was very fussy and demanded what seemed like constant attention as an infant. His behavior became oppositional and defiant as he got older. I was an at-home-mom, so raising and disciplining him were largely left to me. I was committed to being a good mother and, therefore, sought all manner of help in my struggle with the parenting of our wayward child.

When our son was about ten years old, I attended an Al-Anon meeting with a dear friend whose husband was an alcoholic. I heard about 'letting go and letting God' and realized that was what I needed to do with our son. I knew I had become enmeshed in his behavior and his emotions, which wasn't working well for either one of us. I was exhausted.

The 'letting go' process felt unfamiliar and caused me to feel like I didn't love him. I discovered that I had previously loved through attachment; I was too enmeshed in his life. An 'attached' love was all I had previously known. However, I gradually practiced and learned to detach and foster a healthy love, with clearer boundaries for him and for me.

He is now forty years old and I am seventy-five, and we have a wonderful relationship. My moving from attachment to detachment was a critical step in the evolution of our healthy and loving mother-son relationship. (KS)

Outgrowing Formal Religion

During the process of dealing with my son's addiction, I began to question my Catholic religion. In the twenty-five years of spiritual reading prompted by the addiction problem, I came to know a different God, a more compassionate, loving, forgiving, and inclusive God. I am comfortable and at one with this God.

The break came slowly and with much consternation. Having been raised and educated all the way through college as Catholic, an Irish Catholic is who I was. The time came, however, when sitting in church during services I found myself saying, "Jesus wouldn't have said that." I knew it was time to follow my heart. It wasn't easy, but it became easier as my spiritual readings outside of Catholicism and even Christianity resonated and excited me deep in my heart and soul.

I've come to honor my spiritual journey, where it began and where it has brought me. I now have a daily, spiritual practice that keeps me grounded in the conscious living of my life. I now show up each day and engage life with more awareness. I am the one who determines how I live, not a set of remote beliefs and practices. (MK)

From Great Loss to Great Gain

My life began as a Catholic. My dad took my brother and me to church every Sunday. But we never spoke of religion and didn't have a Bible at home. When in college, I stopped going to church. Then, after getting married and having children, we choose to join the First Presbyterian Church. I found this to be more of a social gathering. Then, I became aware of my wife having an inappropriate relationship with a church elder. Needless to say, I found this to be a very difficult and irreligious situation.

One night I went to an event and met a friend for conversation. On my way home, I was involved in a terrible car accident. I suffered many major injuries: a dislocated hip, a broken arm, and traumatic brain injury. I was in a coma for over three weeks, in the hospital for more than three months, and in rehabilitation for over ten years. My memory was damaged; there are years in my past that I can't remember. My sense of balance is not good. During this time, my wife left me. I was left with the challenge of rehabilitation and looking after two school-age kids.

As I made progress in my recovery, I began to wonder about how to approach my new life. First, I found a guided meditation group and discovered the value of meditation. My son was also moving in a spiritual direction. He recommended Eckhart Tolle and *The Power of Now,* which opened another door for me. I began reading many spiritual authors: Deepak Chopra, Wayne Dyer, Sylvia Boorstein, Susan Jeffers, Peter Russell, and others. Then I found the School of Practical Philosophy in Rochester, NY. It was the answer to what I had been seeking. I met like-minded people, more advanced than I was, and found a "Spiritual Home." We met weekly; I learned a lot. Especially helpful were books of conversations with enlightened gurus such as His Holiness Shantanand Saraswati and Sri Nisargadatta Maharaj. Then I got the opportunity to be inducted into the practice of Transcendental Meditation. That was another huge step. I gained the ability to enter into a 'silent space' which offered wonderful peace.

These experiences opened my eyes and enabled me to rise above the meaningless frustrations of human existence. I discovered True Reality, which is a Single Reality that appears to most people as an ongoing battle between this and that, between one thing and another. In reality, we and life are One. By detaching from the heartache of abandonment and all sense of 'poor me,' I've been able to discover deep meaning and joy in life. Events that could have destroyed me are now seen as my path to profound realization. Detachment and forgiveness have facilitated this remarkable transformation. (Anonymous)

Detaching from Alienation

When I was a boy, my family avoided my paternal grandmother, who had separated from my grandfather years earlier. Grandma Grace left him, we were told, because he was "mean and cruel." Some of the stories I heard about how he treated my dad confirmed this. Grandma Grace took her three sons and a daughter with her when she left Grandpa Jesse. The divorce settlement required the two oldest boys, my dad and an uncle, to return to the father and the two younger ones to stay with their mother. She married Syd, and it seemed to me at that time that he was particularly disliked by my dad. And it also seemed that Syd was the 'cause' of the tension and avoidance between the families.

Since I was still very young, I didn't get to know Grandpa Jesse very well before he died following a bad automobile accident. My memories from the little contact I had with him were fine. He was kind and generous with a sense of good humor. I liked him and witnessed no harshness. By this time, he may have mellowed. However, we still had only cool and perfunctory relations with Grandma Grace; even though our families lived in the same neighborhood, we never got together.

Miracle of miracles! I know nothing of the specifics that led to reconciliation, but by the time I was a young adult, our families related to each other warmly and appreciatively. The grace of Grandma Grace became evident. In spite of the great distance between Michigan, where the Roysters lived, and Florida, the new home of Grandma, Syd and family, we got together and enjoyed each other's company whenever possible. Most surprising, Dad and Syd became close boating and fishing friends. My dad's earlier anger toward Syd changed to valued friendship. Attachment to a negative emotion disappeared and was replaced by a new joy and expanded life. (Jim Royster)

Chapter Four: Forgiveness: Neutralizing Grudges and Grievances

> The practice of forgiveness is our most important contribution to the healing of the world. (Marianne Williamson)

Part I. Unforgiveness – Its Power Undermined

Before searching the many dimensions of forgiveness and its benefits, we need briefly to identify the victimizing power of its diametrical opposite, unforgiveness. We can begin by noting Abraham Maslow's "Hierarchy of Needs," which is widely recognized as valid and helpful but is rarely used in reference to forgiveness. Its relevance for seeing the destructive effect of unforgiveness is astounding. Briefly stated, the hierarchy begins with our physical needs, moves through the need for security, love and belonging, self-esteem, and finally, to self-actualization. Unforgiveness impacts every level, even the physical.

The refusal or inability to forgive imprisons one in the past, a no-longer-existent past and therefore unreal. And yet, while it is historically past, its effects and affects continue into the present and future of the victim as long as the grievance is not resolved. To carry a grudge is to be bound to the past by a chain and hook that unknowingly works its wiles in the unconscious.

Unfortunately, the attachment to the grievance doesn't rest quietly or disappear in the unconscious. It's as if the memory of the hurt and the grudge is just waiting and watching for an opportunity to disguise itself slightly and burst into action, action that will repeat the discord and damage that happened before. Grudges inevitably and unexpectedly rise from time to time into awareness, distorting clear seeing and actions, thereby bringing varying degrees of hurt and damage. Lest we think we can avoid this course, note that this psychospiritual dynamic operates according to the universal law of cause and effect, a law recognized timelessly in every culture of the world. Some psychotherapists claim that projection ('seeing' in others what is 'hidden' in ourselves) is a one hundred percent, airtight rule.

Throughout the East, the law is labeled karma and identified as the driving power in samsara, the endless coming and going that marks all dimensions of the universe and that names the condition from which humans try to escape. In the West, we acknowledge it and then more or less nonchalantly ignore its operation. More often than not, we go about our activities without much thought being given to how our beliefs and actions will impact others and ourselves in the course of coming days.

Nonetheless, it is a law.

Few have taken this law more robustly and stated it more poetically than Ralph Waldo Emerson: "Punishment is a fruit that unsuspected ripens within the flower of the pleasure which concealed it. Cause and effect, means and ends, seed and fruit, cannot be severed; for the effect already blooms in the cause, the end preexists in the means, the fruit in the seed" (*TD* 40f).

Emerson's contribution notwithstanding, we don't yet have an entirely accurate view of how the law actually works. There is no 'passage of time' required between cause and effect. Cause and effect are simultaneous. Every effect is cause – at the same time. However, our minds operate necessarily in a linear fashion, one thing following another. The mind cannot do otherwise. But we can begin to soften this sequential requirement of thinking by acknowledging the validity of paradoxes (i.e., two equally undeniable factors that seem contradictory). A paradox signifies that the mind has reached the end of its abilities; it cannot reconcile opposites of this nature. The comfortable acceptance of paradox is essential to increasing insight into spirituality. This is done by means of symbols, myths, and nondual insight – and is unavailable to thought alone (see above on myth and stages of growth). Only rational thought requires continuity between cause and effect. Even the formulation 'cause/effect' is not entirely accurate; better would be each word coalescing into the other as a single word, thereby indicating their inseparability (which is, of course, impossible given the linear requirement of thought and language).

Why this departure from forgiveness – and laboring on the unthinkable? To answer this question, we must return to the traditional understanding of cause and effect, particularly the inevitable connection between a cause and its effects in the context of time. We noted above that every grievance continues to have its effects, apparent and devious, on into the future. The initiating cause keeps causing effects long into the future.

Fortunately, the effects of a cause can be neutralized, stopped. Karma, cause and effect, end with forgiveness. Forgiveness dissolves the otherwise inevitable effects of insults and injuries, recent or long ago. With forgiveness, the pain of the past, whether inflicted by another or oneself, vanishes. In this sense, forgiveness as a psychospiritual process vaporizes history.

Part II. Three Dimensions of Forgiveness

Forgiveness offered to others and to oneself is undeniably beneficial to both based as it is on the deep commonality linking all humans. Forgiveness abides in the 'best interest' of each, so it is not something to be minimized or ignored. Without forgiving others and oneself, spiritual growth is stymied. This may seem a bold assertion, but it is profoundly true. Indeed, forgiveness is the *sine qua non* of spiritual maturation.

As a specific case of detachment, forgiveness warrants special consideration, thus this chapter. As one detaches from past damage to oneself or someone else, an undeniable sense of release and relief, lightness, happiness, and peacefulness arises.

Traditionally, forgiveness falls into three distinguishable categories: 1. asking forgiveness from another for our injury to them; 2. forgiving ourselves for the injury to another; and 3. asking someone whom we feel has injured us to apologize and perhaps make restitution.

1. Ordinarily, if we injure or violate a fellow human, we need to apologize and ask for forgiveness. If we don't do so, a disturbance is registered in our conscience that may be denied, repressed, and ignored but that will nonetheless take the form of dis-ease and nullify contentment and well-being. Therefore, we need to feel genuinely sorry, to openly acknowledge the wrong, to accept responsibility, and to request forgiveness from the person wronged. Restitution may also be appropriate. If we are forgiven, the psychospiritual disturbance *may* lessen; while the injured person's forgiveness is desirable, it is not essential. Self-analysis might well continue with such question as, "What in me gave rise to injuring another?" and "How can my spiritual growth continue whether or not forgiveness is extended to me?"

* * * *

> *There are many ways that I have hurt and harmed others,*
> *Have betrayed or abandoned them, caused them suffering,*
> *Knowingly or unknowingly, out of my pain, fear, anger,*
> *and confusion.*
> *I ask for your forgiveness.*
> *I ask for your forgiveness.*
>
> (*AFLP* 49-51, *modified by the author*)

* * * *

2. Perhaps the most difficult part of forgiveness is to forgive oneself. This may be the most subtle and essential aspect of forgiveness. Why? Because the difficulty resides in the ego ... the sense I have that I am not the kind of person who would slight, insult, or injure another. Beyond the action might well be the assumption (held with conviction), "Certainly I would do nothing like that."

In another instance, we might recognize our outrage over the unconscionable actions of someone, and justify our stance as righteous indignation. We would do well to look inward and note our harsh judgment without having all the facts, especially the knowledge concerning prior conditioning of the perpetrator's life. But regardless of how an individual might look at his own behavior, he/she would benefit from further self-analysis that would provide an opportunity to grind away at the ego (sometimes manifested as spiritual pride, an elusive trick of the ego that some have called 'spiritual materialism'). Self-justification for our indignation might also call for self-forgiveness.

If we look openly and deeply into the question of why we might have injured someone, perhaps even a family member or friend, we will probably discover events, attitudes, or behaviors directed to us in the past, especially childhood, that were severely painful. Remember, psychologists have shown conclusively that if we were hurt as a child, as an adult we will inevitably hurt others, and probably a child, even (and most likely) our own. Our unintended actions likely stem from repressed and therefore projected, unconscious motivations, which explains why they are contrary to our self-understanding and self-image. In the context of this kind of personal reflection leading to understanding, we can begin to develop compassion for ourselves, a compassion that enables us to forgive ourselves.

A further benefit of self-forgiveness is that it makes forgiving others much easier. Compassion and understanding for ourselves enhances the ability to love and understand others. This is true because the need and the capacity for self-forgiveness derive from our deep oneness with all humans. We humans are so interconnected, even intermeshed, that the power of forgiveness, however and whenever realized, extends in all directions, comprehensively within (self-forgiveness), outwardly directed (forgiving another), and inwardly received (being forgiven).

Still another and quite different perspective on forgiveness for ourselves pertains to times and situations when we hurt ourselves, knowingly or unknowingly. For example, a poor self-image is definitely self-damaging and worthy of self-forgiveness. The same is true for the propensity to become unduly fearful, aggressive, overbearing, indecisive, judgmental, complaining, or any other 'complaint' we may have about our self. Self-forgiveness, a value in itself, will also facilitate the weakening and elimination of these attachments.

Self-forgiveness may also be in order if we happen to feel that life is offering more than our share of obstacles, setbacks, frightening situations, temptations, dangers, anything and all things unwanted. In our more relaxed and reasonable moments, we might not have such feelings and thoughts, but if we are tired, overly busy, or for any reason somewhat 'out-of-sorts,' such thoughts may surface. The first thing to note is that difficulties offer us opportunities to change and thereby to discover more peace and freedom within ourselves. If we acknowledge and investigate these kinds of feelings and thinking, we have an opportunity to forgive ourselves for them, including accepting their potential for self-improvement.

* * * *

> *I openly acknowledge to my self and others, that I have offended, injured, and mistreated others, unintentionally and intentionally due to ignorance, fear, anger, or impatience, and purposely in hope of gaining some advantage.*
>
> *For these unacceptable and indefensible words and actions,*
> *I am deeply sorry and fully admit my mistake and error,*
> *while hoping and trusting that the forgiveness offered by others will be as fully received by me, as I know it is desired and appreciated.*
>
> *Similarly, there are many ways that I have hurt and harmed myself.*
> *I have betrayed or abandoned myself many times*
> *in thought, word, or deed, knowingly or unknowingly.*
>
> *For the ways I have hurt myself through action or inaction, out of fear, pain, or confusion, I now extend a full and heartfelt forgiveness.*
>
> *I forgive myself.*
> *I forgive myself.*
>
> (*AFLP* 49-51, *modified by the author*)

* * * *

3. If we're on the other end of discord and feel wronged, we can approach the other party, mention the cause and how we feel about it. Clarification and/or apology may be forthcoming. Ideally, this will enable us to work through the process of feeling genuinely forgiving and let it go. If this does not happen, however, the grievance may develop, persist and seriously distort any further relationship with the person in question, to say nothing of the on-going and possibly hidden disturbance that inevitably accompanies an unaddressed grudge. Holding onto grudges can intensify anger and lead to depression and anxiety.

A rare and exceptionally advanced understanding of forgiveness recognizes that what others do to us may have little to do with us and be mainly or totally their issue. This view can be held, however, only after one has accurately and honestly considered one's own feelings, thinking, and behavior, and are convinced that no offense was given. What a person said or did may have seemed to them – for whatever conscious or unconscious reason – to be natural and appropriate, perhaps even seeing it as the only thing they could do. If another action had occurred to them, they might have acted differently. In such situations, our task is to not take anything personally, to know that we're free to see so-called wrong as simply a mistake from which the other party can hopefully learn and not keep making. But that's their work, not ours. Our job is to not judge, to let the matter go and move on – lovingly. This doesn't mean we forget, approve, or condone the action, but only that we don't condemn and hold a grudge. If we hold onto grievances, we continue to suffer. It's like taking poison and expecting the other party to suffer the effects.

* * * *

There are many ways I have been harmed by others,
abused or abandoned, knowingly or unknowingly, in
thought, word, or deed.

I remember the many ways others have hurt,
wounded, or harmed me, out of fear, pain, confusion, and
anger.
I have carried this pain in my heart long enough.

To the extent that I am able, I offer you forgiveness.
To those who have caused me harm,
I offer my forgiveness. I forgive you.

(*AFLP* 49-51, *modified by the author*)

* * * *

Is your forgiveness deep and full enough to allow you to forgive someone who isn't sorry? As we spiritually mature, there may come a time when there is no need for apology or forgiveness. The mature will relate to everyone with a truly loving, accepting, and inclusive understanding. At this stage, we've learned to not take things personally ourselves, and to not assume personal intention on the part of others. We realize that although the issue seems to belong to the other party, they too are acting out of instinct and conditioning. *If they could have acted differently, they would have, or might have.* At most, the "offending act" will be seen as only a mistake or misunderstanding.

In spite of the benefits already shown for forgiveness, some cynics may claim that it is, after all, entirely a matter of self-interest. The 'entirely' proposition is certainly mistaken, particularly since we have shown already that those other than oneself do benefit. Richard Smoley in *The Deal* asserts that forgiveness is "the best deal that anyone will offer ... at any time ... past or present or future" (*TD* 2). To construe forgiveness, however, as always and solely done out of self-interest would require a lot of argument and clarification to show just how this is the case. If the intent is to gain some advantage over others, then it is clearly an unacceptable form of self-interest. If, however, its intent and effect is to create more love and harmony, forgiveness is far, far indeed from selfish.

Part III: Forgiveness in the World Religions

The historical origin of the great religions occurred in what is often called the Axial Age, roughly from 900 to 200 BCE, when such intellectual and religious giants as the Buddha, Socrates, Confucius, Lao Tzu, Jeremiah, and the early Hindu mystics appeared with their fresh insights into philosophy, religion, and spirituality. Each of these founders and innovators arose at a time of unprecedented social disruption and violence. Their teaching and personal example introduced powerful new ways of being individually human and in relating to others. These new perspectives, moral systems, and practices included forgiveness.

In the absence of forgiveness, any number of interpersonal problems are likely to occur. Unforgiving attitudes promote discord among people and in the end lead to the disintegration of society. For any society and the religions in it, some means of reconciling interpersonal conflicts must be employed for social cohesion and harmony to occur. The means typically engaged include mores and morality, education, a police force, law, and prisons, to name the most obvious. To the extent that each of these operates as *a strictly civil or secular force*, they are likely to invoke and implement such principles as corrective retribution or just punishment to rectify conflicts. Violators must be punished because they 'deserve' it, and, as many believe, the punishment will deter other potential violators.

When religions function according to the values of their founders, the guiding prescriptions not only impact each of the social factors noted above, but set an even higher and more inclusive principle that adds to their effectiveness, namely love and forgiveness. Forgiveness without love would amount to a commercial exchange and have limited (or even no) impact on the inner make-up of an individual, the psyche, soul, or self-sense of the person. So-called violators might feel unduly punished, or even abused and violated themselves. Therefore, justice is most effective when tempered with mercy – an express purpose of authentic religion as demonstrated in the next chapter.

A. Western Religions

JUDAISM

Forgiveness figures prominently in the three Western world religions, Judaism, Christianity, and Islam. As the historic foundation for the development of the other two traditions, the centrality of forgiveness in Judaism extends to the others.

The eighty-six references to forgiveness in *Tanakh* (the Jewish Bible, what Christians call *The Old Testament*) culminate on the holiest day of the year in the Jewish calendar, Yom Kippur, the Day of Atonement. This is a time of fasting, repenting, and praying for forgiveness. In Judaism, forgiveness is a divine command.

The *Torah* (the first five books of the Bible, and also for the entire *Tanakh*) expressly forbids taking revenge and holding grudges. If you refuse a friend who asks to borrow something from you because he once refused you, this would be a case of holding a grudge and taking revenge. Rabbis and Jewish elders recommend several ways to learn forgiveness. For example, don't give in to the desire for revenge, but do ignore the perceived offense, and do relate to the other as if nothing has changed. Over time, the tendency and desire to strike back will weaken. Another approach is to think differently about the interaction. If life is a learning journey and God is guiding, then whatever happens is an opportunity for growth, something for which to be grateful and from which to benefit.

A sterling exemplar of forgiveness is Joseph, whose older brothers threw him into a desert pit and then sold him into slavery in Egypt. There he languished in prison because of false accusations. Against all odds, he eventually became the viceroy of Egypt. When his brothers came to Egypt after the death of their father, they naturally feared Joseph's revenge in light of the power he held. But Joseph surprised them by asserting that everything that had happened did so because of God's will. Joseph assured them they had nothing to fear because they were simply God's instruments.

Repentance and restitution are seen as essential in Judaism. If one has wronged another, it is proper and fitting that one offer to the wronged a verbal apology and then attempt to restore the formerly friendly relationship by making an honest attempt to correct the wrong. Naturally, the nature of the incursion will suggest the nature of the correction. If one has lied, offer the truth. If one has stolen, return the item, its equivalent, or more.

Since an offense requiring forgiveness is one perpetrated against a fellow human and also against the conditions stipulated by God for his people, forgiveness from God is also desirable. How can one know if

God's forgiveness has been given? One can be assured of God's forgiveness, rabbis and elders note, to the extent of one's sincerity in making amends and in one's approach to the divine.

CHRISTIANITY

Jesus was never a Christian. He was a Jewish sage who interpreted and applied the Judaism of his day. Similarly, his teaching and example were interpreted and applied by his followers, with some of this recorded in the *New Testament* that eventually became foundational Christianity. Quite naturally, much of Christianity reflects the main principles and practices found in Judaism. Among these is forgiveness.

When Peter asked Jesus how many times he should forgive someone who "sinned against him," and suggested that seven times might be enough, Jesus answered: "Not seven times but ... seventy times seven" (*Matthew* 18:22). Jesus was neither fastidious nor a moralist, so he surely didn't mean four hundred and ninety times. Forgiveness is a spiritual *quality* and cannot be quantified. Jesus taught that no limit can be placed on forgiving others.

Some of Jesus' most effective teaching came in the form of parables, that is, stories that hint at truth or give examples without pedantic literality. Those without adequate interest or maturity will not understand the teaching; those ready for it will. One of these, the parable of the Prodigal Son, treats forgiveness and demonstrates the effective impact a parable can have. A wealthy farmer had two sons. The younger, eager to explore the world, asked his father for his inheritance and received it. After he had squandered his wealth for many years in decadent living, a famine hit and he became destitute. Finally realizing how foolish he had been, he returned home repentant and apologetic. Without a moment's hesitation, the father accepted him lovingly and ordered a welcoming celebration in his young son's honor. When the elder brother learned of this, he was troubled and complained to his father, who pointed out to the older son that his brother had been regarded as "dead and has come to life; he was lost and has been found" (*Luke* 15:11-32). A compassionate heart finds no condemnation. Humble acknowledgement of personal error is enough to elicit full forgiveness.

The Lord's Prayer (*Matthew* 6:9-13), the most frequently recited personal and congregational prayer, seems to assume a different standard: "Forgive us our debts, as we also have forgiven our debtors." In other translations, forgiveness is asked for "transgressions," "trespasses," "offenses," "short-comings," even "sins." The prayer seems to make one's forgiveness by God dependent on the petitioner's previous forgiving of those who have been indebted to him or her, suggesting that if one has not been willing to forgive others, one is not going to be forgiven by God. The equal exchange feature is actually stressed in a version that reads: "to the extent that we forgive." Does this reduce religion to an economic scale, tit for tat, you get what you gave? Such an interpretation would certainly overlook love and grace, key features of Christianity. The import of this particular wording in the prayer is more likely meant to indicate that one who willingly forgives others is thereby more open to receiving forgiveness. In the context of the teaching and example of Jesus' life, and the *New Testament* as a whole, there are no grounds for reducing forgiveness to an 'economic' exchange. The love that Jesus exhibited reflects the total absence of any expectations or conditions. Unconditional love extends unconditional forgiveness, exemplified when Jesus was being crucified and appealed to God on behalf of those in his presence: "Father forgive them; for they do not know what they are doing" (*Luke* 23:34).

Most humans take personal freedom for granted, believing they deliberately choose their beliefs, attitudes, and actions. Sometimes, accompanying this conviction is the assumption that they also have the right to express themselves more or less without restriction. This overly simplified view, however, hides the fact that we can never know all the factors, all the causes and conditions that enter into any single situation and event. Beyond the range of our immediate self-awareness, there are subtle factors contributing to whatever is present in our conscious mind. In much the same way, in every situation and event there are manifold, unapparent but relevant factors that simply cannot be taken into consideration due to being unrecognized. This universal complex substantiates Jesus' prayer: "Father forgive them; for they do not know what they are doing." It is literally true: We never know exhaustively and accurately why or how any event takes place, either those in which we have input and those we don't. This perspective suggests a life that is broadly and willingly forgiving, one that easefully accepts whatever is arising.

This insight into the breadth of forgiveness allows us to interpret more accurately another parable of Jesus, the one set at the end of time when the Son of Man will make final judgments which relegate the goats (the wicked) to hell and the sheep (the righteous) to heaven. Happily, prevailing views in Christianity today (except for extreme exoteric forms) are entirely and radically different from the views and assumptions prevailing in Jesus' day. Still, we can extract a valuable principle from this parable. The story depicts those worthy of heaven as having lived a life of service to the poor, the sick, the hungry and thirsty, the marginalized, those in prison. The unworthy didn't serve the needy. Then Jesus announced that the service rendered to others was actually given to him, while that not given was withheld from him. He then reaffirmed his assertion by saying: "Just as you did [or did not do] it to one of the least of these ... you did [or did not do] it to me" (*Matthew* 25:31-45).

But how can we interpret this passage today, that is, from the standpoint of deeper and more inclusive perspectives unbound to first century views? One approach is to interpret the judge not as Jesus, a first century Galilean, but as an embodiment of Christ Consciousness, as one who exemplifies unconditional love. The literal judging in the parable refers to each person's ability to distinguish within himself or herself the worthy from the unworthy, the good from the bad, and to embody this distinction in her or his day-by-day life. So-called final judgment is an immediate, on-going process of choosing the high road over options that reduce or demean life. Mother Teresa made this her personal understanding and lived its literal meaning also as she served the destitute and dying in Calcutta, seeing them as "Christ, in his distressing disguises" (*WC* I 370).

A Course in Miracles (claimed to be a continuation of Jesus' teaching) builds further on these perspectives by helping us understand why we don't easily see the divinity in others, and why we get so caught up in their personalities and actions and assume that is who they are. In sum, it's because we see without forgiveness in our hearts and minds. We look at the world with a critical judgment that divides people, behavior, and ideas into acceptable and unacceptable, into moral or sinful, and oftentimes with no more backing than, "I like this and don't like that." Though the relation between the two may be seldom acknowledged, a little reflection shows that the refusal to forgive derives from a critical mind. An attitude of forgiveness – flowing from love and not judgment – allows us to see the true and authentic human beyond the particulars of his or her personality, beliefs, and actions. *ACIM* maintains: "Forgiveness ... [lifts the veil] that hides the face of Christ from those who look with unforgiving eyes upon the world" (*W* 122 3:1, 4).

Reinforcing and broadening this perspective, the text refers to the development of an awareness that enables us to "see the changeless in the heart of change." What might this "changeless" be? The injunction becomes clear in reference to what we discussed in Chapter One, where we discovered that our essential, God-given nature is pure consciousness, pure spirituality, which serves as the base and foundation on which we build our respective identities as human beings. Our physical sight becomes vision and in-sight when we rediscover that we are all, every last one of us, simultaneously changeless consciousness – from which, upon which, and by means of which we add all the events of our inner and outer lives. Permanently changeless and always changing; this both/and perspective names our nature, divine and human.

A Course in Miracles underscores, reinterprets, and extends the meaning, nature, and practice of forgiveness beyond any other source with which I'm familiar. It presents itself as a new curriculum based on the latest teaching of Jesus and asserts: "Forgiveness is the final goal of the curriculum, ... [and] is its single aim, at which all learning ultimately converges" (*MT* 16). The critical importance of forgiveness compared to other features of Christianity is clearly stressed in this quotation. The *ACIM* text requires study, and benefits greatly from instruction, discussion, and practice of its teaching toward that ultimate goal.

The first and arguably most important new perspective on forgiveness set forth in the *Course* is its denial of the reality of sin. So-called sin loses its pejorative nature. It becomes simply a mistake or error. Sin is typically thought of as an act that causes estrangement, alienation, and undesirable separation from others. It is seen as a product of the ego, the sense of being an individual separate from the world out there. But according to the *Course*, separation is impossible: to even think one sees separation is illusory. Thus, the underlying assumption that forgiveness for sin is necessary is demolished.

A common reaction to the sense of being wronged, of being victimized by action that usually calls for apology and forgiveness, is also to feel the need for some sort of defense to avoid it happening again. In contrast, *A Course in Miracles* instructs practitioners, as we've seen, to not defend themselves: "In my defenselessness my safety lies" (*W* 284). To defend oneself is to perpetuate separation, to act out of the ego. By not defending oneself, one is countering the habitual pattern of the ego to defend itself, thereby weakening it. The refusal to defend can be seen as a 'softened' application of Jesus' injunction "to offer the other also" if someone hits you on the cheek (*Luke* 6:29).

These 'upgraded' perspectives on forgiveness, along with corollary reinterpretations of traditional Christian views, add up to a radically new and comprehensive understanding. Forgiveness becomes totally unnecessary. There was only a mistake that gives no cause for retaliation. Since no real damage was done, at most the exchange between the two parties simply offers an opportunity for two-fold learning: for one party, "I made a mistake," and for the other, "No offense taken." When love is brought into the picture, the absence of any real offense is even more clearly seen. As set forth in the first chapter of *Undoing* and also taught by the *Course*, love is not something learned but something discovered to be already existing within us, as part of our birthright. Given the universality of love, the perception of any need for forgiveness is mistaken. Unconditional love makes so-called sin simply a mistake and so-called forgiveness entirely irrelevant since they never truly existed in the first place.

A number of different approaches to forgiveness are given in the *Course,* each offering a perspective designed to provide additional insight that enables practitioners to envision the absence of any real separation and therefore the illegitimacy of the notion of sin or estrangement (*W* 54, 5:5). It notes that forgiveness is an acquired or learned quality rooted in our essential nature as love. Just as we were taught about sin and now discover that it is non-existent, we can discover that forgiveness, while perhaps useful in the past, is 'beside-the-point' for the spiritually mature.

These upgraded perspectives on forgiveness and defenselessness call for further comment. The challenges they entail may seem extreme enough to alienate some and end further communication. Such a reaction would be unfortunate because these ideas are not suitable for everyone, anymore than the performance of heart surgery would be suitable for a Boy Scout with a first aid merit badge. We have already established the fact of human evolution through stages of development and seen the necessity of appropriate progression. Preparatory experience at each stage is essential before moving to the next. Indicators of one's own readiness to move forward would include: a mind/heart desire to do so; recognition of the personal benefits; awareness of the gains for others; and one's insight that this type of growth is a contribution to the slow development of human accord broadly.

ISLAM

As the third and most recent of the Western religions, Islam inherited much of its understanding of forgiveness from its predecessors. The *Koran* reiterates, in its own language, the scriptural teaching of the two previous monotheistic faiths by affirming that "Allah is Ever-Pardoning, Ever-Forgiving." Many Muslims memorize and recite devotionally the Ninety-Nine Beautiful Names of Allah, two of which are "The Forgiver" and "The Forgiving." Of the one hundred and fourteen chapters that make up the *Koran,* only one begins without the declaration, "Allah, the Merciful, the Compassionate" (and even here, the affirmation occurs within the chapter). Both the *Koran* (regarded by Muslims as a record of the very Speech of Allah) and the *Hadith* (the traditions of the Prophet, what he said and did) set the standard for forgiveness in Islam. Muslims cite many examples of how Muhammad forgave his enemies – even when some of his followers preferred revenge.

Forgiveness is important in Islam for several reasons, two of which are that forgiveness heals relationships and brings happiness, and that apologizing and seeking forgiveness *signifies* humility, while at the same time *granting* forgiveness indicates magnanimity. Muhammad indicated the extent to which forgiveness nullifies wrongdoing when he said: "One who repents from sin is like one without sin."

Forgiveness requires proper intention and sincerity as it is expressed in different situations. An offense may be directed toward individuals, society at large, even the natural order (willfully destroying a tree, for example). An offender is expected to admit the wrong and to promise not to do it again. When Muhammad was asked how many times a servant should be forgiven, he stipulated seventy times a day – giving such an exaggerated number to make it obvious that counting is irrelevant. Requesting forgiveness from the offended party is necessary, as is rectification to the extent possible. Because all offenses are against God, forgiveness from Him must be asked also.

As in the earlier religions, reciprocity in forgiveness also carries weight in Islam. A Prophetic tradition affirms: "Whoever does not show mercy will not receive mercy. Whoever does not forgive others will not be forgiven." The charitable outlook of the Prophet is seen also in his contention that a good leader will risk making a mistake by forgiving a criminal rather than possibly punishing someone who is innocent.

Forgiveness plays an important role in the Islamic debate on predestination and freewill. Advocates of the former believe that God predetermines everything that happens, thereby ruling out freewill. They cite the *Koran*: "He forgives whoever He wills and He punishes whoever He wills." These Muslims maintain that certain beliefs and actions are so absolutely forbidden in Islam that they can never be forgiven; they are so contrary to the omnipotence of God that even holding them constitutes an unforgiveable, heretical belief. Giving God an associate, a partner, falls into this category. Even here, however, those holding to freewill argue that *if* belief in other gods is dropped, one is no longer in the 'unforgiveable' category.

Muslims who support freewill point out that the denial of freewill undermines personal responsibility, upon which the whole issue of right and wrong, obedience and disobedience, depends. However, beliefs and actions that have been dictated do not allow a Muslim freewill – the right to do otherwise. Some Muslims believe that in the execution of His judgment, Allah balances freewill and determination. He modifies His infinite power (that controls and determines all things) when He invokes and applies His justice (i.e., He moderates His power as He executes His justice), and that He does this by means of His mercy. From this perspective, Allah is merciful as He judges according to His justice.

Knowledgeable Muslims are well aware that not all questions that can be raised can be answered. Muslims acknowledge their inability to know

God as He is in Himself by means of the principle of *bela kaif* (literally, "without how"), that is, God is so totally beyond we humans that our minds are incapable of knowing and understanding Him fully. Some aspects of God always remain a mystery.

The several contrasting perspectives mentioned above demonstrate that Islam is not a monolithic tradition forcing a single view on its members, which is a common misunderstanding among unsympathetic outsiders. As a world religion, Islam includes many features today from the various traditions that have contributed to its formation, features not recorded in the *Koran* (even though the *Koran* remains its foundational source). These include some of the social practices of that historical period, the formal traditions of the Prophet (his *hadith*), that of some of earliest followers, even some sayings from Allah not recorded in the *Koran* known as *hadith qudsi* (holy sayings). One of the latter announces: "Difference of opinion in my community is a token of divine mercy." The declaration asserts that differences of understanding within the Muslim community are themselves evidence of divine mercy. Ibn al-Arabi, one of Islam's most influential mystic philosophers, cites another extra-Koranic tradition expressed in the words of God: "I conform to the opinion that my faithful has of Me."

The interpretation of Islam given here pertains more to the trans-traditional than to the exoteric forms that tend to be more commonly stressed in the world at large. In other words, the views expressed above relate to the esoteric/mystical and metateric/nondual. In terms of world population, the latter are far less numerous than the former, as is true in all religious traditions. The picture of Islam given here modifies the one-sided portrayal found more widely and, from the overall perspective of the author and the contentions of this book, indicates the probable evolutionary direction of Islam's on-going development.

Finally, Ali, Muhammad's cousin and successor in the Shi'ite branch of Islam, is credited with declaring that to forgive someone who has injured you is like a flower that emits a fragrance when crushed underfoot (i.e., instead of retaliating, thereby perpetuating discord, extend a blessing and thereby break the cycle of discord).

B. Eastern Religions

HINDUISM

Forgiveness is recognized and valued in Hinduism, in part due to the declaration of Krishna in the *Bhagavad Gita* (Hinduism's most widely read scripture) that forgiveness is a divine characteristic embedded in humans. Mahatma Gandhi is a sterling example of the Hindu spirit of forgiveness, a forgiveness extended not only to individuals but also to an entire imperial government.

The views on forgiveness in theistic Hinduism are founded in basic human nature, including interpersonal relations, in much the same way as those shared by the Western religious traditions. Tukaram, a highly respected devotee in God-centered devotional Hinduism, represents the theistic expressions of the tradition in his heartfelt confession and plea for help:
> No deeds I've done nor thoughts I've thought;
> Save as Thy servant, I am nought.
> Ah, do not, do not cast on me the guilt of mine iniquity.
> My countless sins, I, Tuka, say, upon Thy loving heart I lay
> A beggar at thy door, pleading I stand.
> Give me alms, O God, love from thy loving hand.
> (*HTM* 114)

That Tukaram felt himself fully forgiven by God is apparent in this paean of praise and confession of redemption.
> Evil has itself been transformed into the highest good,
> Blessedness beyond compare!
> My emotions have been unified in God, as the rivers in an ocean.
> We, who are mad after God, are sunk in blessedness.
> My doubts and delirium are at an end.
> My exterior and interior are filled with divine bliss.
> (*HTM* 117f)

* * * *

Non-theistic or nondual Hinduism presents a different picture that harbors a further benefit. While the law of cause and effect (*karma*) operates here as in theistic forms of Hinduism, forgiveness now carries an additional positive force that (along with moderating, even nullifying, the negative karma of the offending action) opens the door to deepened insight and personal clearing. Following the sorrow, apology, and recompense (as appropriate) of offenders, the forgiveness extended by the injured enables healing and harmony to be restored, both for the others and themselves, all within the mysterious domain of karma. Advaita Vedanta, the major philosophy and practice of nondual Hinduism, treats karma traditionally – and then adds that forgiveness is less relevant than another issue at hand. More relevant is the realization that whatever happens in the ordinary course of events is the result of the specific beliefs and actions of the individual parties involved in each particular situation. As a consequence, each party in a dispute carries responsibility for personal reflection and evaluation that may foster liberating insight. In a word, disharmony and suffering offer the opportunity to learn and gain clarity and freedom. If one person inflicts harm, his task centers in himself, just as the injured party's focus is properly on himself. This additional perspective in nondual Hinduism denotes a striking similarity to the view outlined above from *A Course in Miracles*, namely that traditional so-called sins are actually mistakes offering an opportunity for psychospiritual enhancement.

* * * *

Some Hindus have discovered the intimate link between compassion and forgiveness, acknowledging that compassion fosters forgiveness and is itself enriched by forgiveness. The integration of the two motivates the intent to relate harmoniously with others and becomes the means to do so, thus inspiring a reciprocating response. The essential identity of the two serves as both method and end; the compassionate forgiveness of one person elicits a compassionate response that facilitates still further forgiveness – as applicable situations and opportunities arise. This realization is strengthened as one becomes able to recognize the divine in everyone and everyone in the divine, which is, of course, realization from the stance of nonduality, whatever historic form it might assume.

BUDDHISM

The *Dhammapada*, an early text setting forth the teachings of the Buddha, opens by affirming the centrality of the mind and thinking for human wellbeing. It then immediately illustrates with a common grievance (held, of course, in the mind): "'He reviled me; he injured me; he defeated me; he deprived me.' In those who harbor such grudges, hatred never ceases ... In those who do not harbor such grudges, hatred will cease" (*D* 8). Forgiveness is signaled out early in this basic text because of its essential role in the liberating objective of Buddhism. Without forgiveness, the development of inner tranquility and harmony is impossible. Similarly, these qualities are impossible as well in interpersonal relations. Human welfare, individually and comprehensively, depends on forgiveness.

Forgiveness derives from and depends on compassion, which, together with wisdom, constitutes the epitome of human realization, what Buddhist call enlightenment. Wisdom and compassion are so mutually essential that either one without the other is not truly itself. This understanding is apparent in the Buddhist perspective that in cases of forgiveness, the transgressor, more than the victim, stands in the greatest danger. This perspective encourages compassion on the part of the wronged for the one who perpetrated the injury. Ideally, compassion flows in both directions, from the victimizer repenting of the injury caused, and from the victim feeling the sorrow of the offender. This mutual acknowledgement of compassion expresses Buddhist nonduality, the inherent and intimate interconnectedness of the human heart and of reality itself.

Equally affirming the role of cause and effect, Buddhism and Hinduism also share the view that enlightenment and liberation require insight into the causes of confusion and discomfort in order to dissolve and transcend the forces that imprisons within the samsaric process (the endless repetition of the dualistic world). A basic and central cause is unforgiveness – if we don't forgive, we will continually build a false identity based on ignorance and suffering that will perpetuate ongoing difficulties and unhappiness in this life, plus initiate rebirth into further rounds of ignorant and painful lives.

Forgiveness itself offers a mini-experience of liberation. Coupled with other transformative principles and practices, the liberation path advances.

C. Far Eastern Religions

CONFUCIANISM

On forgiveness, Confucianism presents a somewhat different understanding than we've found in the other religions, mainly because Confucius did not found a religion so much, but taught a structured way of organizing society and government. In this sense, Confucianism is a system of customs, mores, rules, regulations, and ethical standards designed to foster well-being and accord among its followers . Within this framework, two inter-related principles operate: first, each person has the right to protect his/her self-respect, and second, if their self-respect is offended, they have the right of resentment toward the offender. Therefore, of paramount importance is the preservation of one's social position and ethical qualities and the right to demand compensation if they are violated. The difference between this compensatory view of interpersonal injury and forgiveness as seen in other traditions is evident. Nonetheless, the teachings of Confucius did inspire a religion and here we do find forgiveness in more traditional terms. A disciple once asked the Master if there was a single principle that would serve him until his death. Confucius reportedly replied in the affirmative by indicating reciprocity (*shu,* also translated "forgive," "pardon," "excuse") and then explained: "What you do not wish [for] yourself, do not [do] unto others." The similarity to the Golden Rule is obvious. Minimizing this statement, as some have done, by stressing its negative formulation is improper, ill founded, and clearly prejudicial.

Finally, Confucius himself may have opened the door to each of these ways of mending interpersonal breaches, thus granting individuals the option of proceeding according to personal inclination, for he says: "Recompense injury with justice, and recompense kindness with kindness." At the same time, he seems to give preference to forgiveness when he declares: "Those who cannot forgive others break the bridge over which they themselves must pass."

TAOISM

A novice, Anne, once accidentally broke a valuable glass lamp that had been a special gift to her Taoist teacher and was held with high regard. Anne felt deeply remorseful and sincerely apologized. Acknowledging the special significance of the lamp and the probable difficulty the disciple would have to actually feel forgiven, the teacher laid out a staunch program of repentance, one that would likely demonstrate sorrow and develop a propensity to feel forgiven. The student was required to keep track of her good deeds, list them in a notebook, and report them each week to the teacher. The teacher would give points for the good deeds and declared that ten thousand points would be required. When the student exclaimed in surprise that that was a lot of points, she heard a somber reply about how special lamp was.

During the week, Anne worked with special diligence, preparing vegetables for meals, polishing faucets, cleaning windows, sweeping floors, planting and weeding in the garden. When she reported her week's activities, the head monk commended her and recorded one point for the week's work. Anne was heartbroken, only one point. She went to bed that night, hardly sleeping, believing that she'd need to work nine thousand nine hundred and ninety-nine more weeks at least as diligently.

Much the same occurred in the following weeks. Anne worked faithfully and earned one point. Then one week when she went to report her deeds, she discovered she had forgotten to record them. She had been so focused and involved in the work that she hadn't remembered to write in the notebook. When she stood before the head monk and confessed her oversight, her mentor smiled broadly and said, "That's ten thousand points." This story aptly illustrates the Taoist principle of *wu-wei*, actionless action, doing what is proper or required without thought of personal gain.

Another Taoist teaching story is about a novice who inquired about forgiveness and was advised by his teacher to get a bag of potatoes, write the name of someone who had insulted or hurt him in any way on one of the potatoes, carry the bag over his shoulder as long as he could, then come back for the next instruction. Before the second week was over, the bag had become too heavy, too smelly, and too mushy to tolerate any longer. On returning, his teacher simply reminded him of what he had already learned: to not forgive only brings discomfort and pain on oneself.

Taoists principles, whether by self-discovery or direct teaching, aim to develop a mind of detachment and forgiveness, a free, open, and receptive mind that appreciates without reaction, a mind of nonattachment.

D. Smaller Religions of Exceptional Influence

JAINISM, SIKHISM, SHINTO, BAHA'I

Each of these traditions honors forgiveness and recognizes it as a vital process for the restoration of justice and well-being in interpersonal relations when lapses occur. We can safely conclude our foray through the world religions, knowing that forgiveness is championed as the principal way by which disruptions in the otherwise cohesive and harmonious relationships of humans can be resolved for all concerned. Throughout all of humanity, forgiveness is promoted to restore accord and peace within and among us.

Part IV. Forgiveness Outside Formal Religion

Healing the fabric of our mutuality when disrupted is essentially a human activity co-opted, interpreted, and formalized by the religions. The following programs are examples of forgiveness in secularized form (i.e., forgiveness in nonsectarian expressions).

Alcoholics Anonymous

Without forgiveness, A.A. would not be effective. Forgiveness from God and one's fellow man are essential, as is self-forgiveness. Bill Wilson and his co-founder, an alcoholic surgeon named Bob Smith, testified to this claim themselves. Both came to realize, after countless failed attempts, that they could not stop drinking without outside help. Together they formulated the twelve steps of a detoxing program and founded A.A. in 1935.

The foundational text, *Alcoholics Anonymous*, better known as the Big Book, outlines the regimen of recovery. The following descriptions are the most important of the rehabilitating steps. Participants must: admit their own powerlessness to overcome alcoholism, followed by calling on and surrendering to a Higher Power, however they may envision this Power; make an unedited, searching list of their character weaknesses and lapses; personally confess this to their Higher Power and to another person (who may become a sponsor and support); open their heart to the Higher Power and humbly ask for help; create a list of persons hurt and attempt to make amends; continue to search for personal shortcomings and wrongs and remedy them when possible; engage in ongoing spiritual development; and finally, share their life story and try to help others who might benefit.

An estimated twenty-three million people struggle with severe alcoholism and debilitating drug dependency. A.A. has proven effective in freeing countless millions from addiction to alcohol and drugs, but the regimen doesn't work for everyone. Study of the program's success and failures continues in hope of making improvements. The one feature well established is the need for and value of forgiveness: from the Higher Power, from those harmed, and from oneself. Without these, there would be no likelihood of release from the addiction.

Ho'oponopono

Originating in the native cultures of the Pacific Islands, this modality is currently practiced and expanding in the West. As a process of forgiveness and healing that typically occurs in a family setting, it honors the interpersonal or relational effect of violations of basic morality, a morality that may or may not be founded in the divine order. Because of the communal impact of 'individual' wrongs, a ritual may be employed to deal with the offense that has disrupted personal and family harmony. These rituals, conducted by a senior family member or a priest, typically include prayer, discussion, confession, repentance, restitution, and forgiveness.

In its adaptation to modern Western culture, Ho'oponopono focuses on four brief declarations: "I love you. I'm sorry. Please forgive me. Thank you." The interpersonal nature of specific, individual violations continues to be recognized in the contemporary applications. Clinical psychologist Dr. Stanley Hew Len, for example, claims to have fostered the cure of mentally ill criminals at the Hawaii State Hospital more that thirty years ago. This was done by repeating the four statements while focusing on the medical records of the patients, who he never actually saw in person (*ZL* passim). At the present time, Ho'oponopono is equally practiced within as well as outside of formal religions, by both individuals and small groups.

Tribal Life: American and African

In present times, the practices of the past have changed, and are no longer common in many American tribal communities perhaps because of the erosion of identity due to alcoholism, drug dependence, political issues, etc. The same may be true for the African societies of today.

Forgiveness and communal responsibility were nowhere demonstrated more poignantly than in some American Indian tribes: when one member violated the moral code, the entire family gathered in the local lodge to address the issue. A large circle was made up of elders, grandparents, mother and father, siblings, uncles and aunts, cousins, and of course the violator. The offender was required to confess the specific violation he committed or injury he inflicted: property destruction, physical attack, stealing, lying, or whatever it might have been. The somber mood created was apparent. The most unusual and exceptional phase occurred next when members of the extended family, one after the other, confessed the personal role he or she had played in the violation committed by their relative. The gradually emerging, heartfelt and tearful atmosphere created an undeniable sense of tribal interconnection and empathy, and feelings of compassion and forgiveness. It would be hard to imagine more striking evidence of human mutuality within the setting of family life, a powerful and challenge possibility for other groups that value interpersonal harmony.

In the Babemba tribe of South Africa, when a member violates social expectation (behaving irresponsibly, for example) or the moral code, he is brought to the center of the village and required to remain there unshackled. Village activities come to a standstill and everyone, men, women, and children, gather in a large circle around the accused. Each person then addresses the individual directly by reminding or informing him of all the good things he has done during the time they have known him. Every recalled incident or occasion is recited with as much detail and accuracy as possible. All his positive characteristics and strengths are announced, along with his acts of kindness and good deeds, all stated carefully and at length. The ceremony may last for several days. At its conclusion, before the assembly disperses, a joyful celebration takes place.

Not only does this event acknowledge full forgiveness, it serves also as a symbolic and actual welcoming of the individual back into the shared harmony of the tribe (*FLP* 42).

Part V. Science Investigates Forgiveness

Science today, for many if not most people, takes on an authority nearly unrivaled by other sources of truth and reliability. Knowing this, a number of scientific disciplines have addressed specific forms of religion and spirituality, including: psychology, sociology, anthropology, and phenomenology (the so-called soft or humanitarian sciences), and biology, psychiatry, neurology, and genetics (the hard sciences). Hundreds of formal studies on forgiveness are underway in universities around the world. While forgiveness plays a crucial role in all forms of interpersonal relations, probably nowhere is the subject actually studied more assiduously than in the health sciences.

A search of the archives of the Mayo Clinic in 2016 turned up one hundred and forty-five articles dealing with forgiveness. Among these was one entitled "12 Habits of Highly Healthy People" where forgiveness is listed second, right after physical activity. Supportive studies at Mayo Clinic name specific health-related benefits: (1) reduced stress, anxiety and hostility, (2) lower blood pressure and heart rate, (3) improved interpersonal relationships, (4) lower risk of substance abuse, (5) stronger immune system, (6) reduced depression and chronic pain, (7) enhanced psychological well-being, and (8) higher self-esteem. Other studies indicate that forgiveness enhances hopefulness and self-confidences; adds to the length and quality of sleep; reduces the number of medications needed; and contributes to relief from back pain. The health benefits of forgiveness are undeniable.

A recent study in the *Journal of Health Psychology* reveals an even more striking relationship between forgiveness and stress than reported above by the Mayo Clinic; forgiveness eliminates stress. The author of the study connects stress to mental illness itself and makes an even further claim, namely that forgiveness removes the connection between stress and mental illness by reducing it to zero. Forgiveness excludes stress as a possible cause of mental illness (*Time*, 4.16.2016).

If we shift to the hard sciences, we discover that evolutionary biologists argue that we are hardwired to retaliate when hurt, and to seek revenge. In the earliest centuries of human evolution, this may have been true, given the ever-present dangers impending on life. Even then, however, some would have discovered the advantage of cooperation and the value of human accord. From this, the evolutionary imprint may have shifted to forgiveness and reconnection. Thus, both tendencies may exist. Prevailing at any historic period in human evolution will be the one stressed most in family, religious, and societal evolution, with individual choice always playing a crucial role.

Among the hard sciences currently addressing the subject of forgiveness, brain investigation has gained considerable attention and impacted the popular mind as well. While most of these studies have been directed to the effects of meditation and compassion on well-being, some have focused on forgiveness. These show that forgiveness activates the limbic region at the base of the brain stem where emotional and empathetic centers are located. To this extent, the studies show overlapping evidence with neurological investigations of compassion and meditation. Thus, the same part of the brain, the limbic region, is activated when meditation, compassion, and forgiveness are activated in the heart/mind. Each of these 'feeling states' is a form of empathy indicating interconnection, harmony, and oneness.

The opposite state, of course, is also possible. Those who find it difficult or impossible to forgive, show brain activity associated with stress. Stress is known to activate the neuro-hormone cortisol, associated with negative forms of psychological, emotional, and spiritual well-being. An unforgiving attitude is likely to stem from and produce further anger and bitterness, contribute to depression, cause difficulty establishing new relationships, diminish the sense of life's value, meaning, and purpose, and forfeit enriching connection with fellow humans, perhaps (if particularly severe) even with pets. As we saw above, forgiveness is capable of removing the connection between stress and these problems.

Science leaves no doubt: forgiveness and its ensuing benefits enhance human life.

Part VI: How to Develop Forgiveness

Guidance from the Dalai Lama

When the Dalai Lama was asked how to grow forgiveness, he drew from his personal experience and shared several ideas to consider. The first thing is to be aware of others and not to think only or mainly of yourself. Remind yourself that others are human too, even so-called enemies. They want to avoid suffering and experience happiness as well. Also, enemies can be your best teachers; they give you an opportunity to practice your values.

A second thing to notice is that your future is connected with that of others. Everyone depends on others to one extent or another. If I relate to another happily, they are likely to respond similarly. If I'm distant or disagreeable, they will probably respond accordingly. If I'm friendly and smile, they will likely respond similarly (unless they're disturbed for some unapparent reason). When we get to really know individual persons, we often discover that they are dealing with some difficult issue or another. If we have some degree of empathy, we will note their confusion and suffering and be more understanding and compassionate.

It's useful to acknowledge that our own happiness and peace of mind depend on how we relate to others and how they relate to us. We are not likely to be content if we isolate ourselves. At times, it may seem that others only disturb our contentment and joy. But most of us benefit from and truly enjoy social interaction. A lot of evidence indicates that we are most happy and even healthier when we have positive interaction with other people. This idea may be difficult to understand. It is based on a central perspective emphasized in Buddhism, but is one that is universally applicable. This is the truth of the interconnectedness of all things: nothing exists in isolation from other factors (those in its immediate surroundings, those that brought it into existence, those that sustain it, and those that will contribute to its disappearance). This is frequently stated in this manner: when that arises, this arises; when that ceases, this ceases. In its most far-reaching formulation, it could be stated that everything is connected to everything else. The net of Indra, a Buddhist metaphor for the inseparability that pervades the cosmos, illustrates this view. A massive net surrounds everything that is. At every knot where the strands come together, there is a diamond. Every diamond reflects ever other diamond; everything contains everything else, and the net stretches infinitely in all directions.

The Dalai Lama points out that we also need to forgive the perpetrators of horrendous acts. This is obviously much harder than many acts of forgiveness. When we first hear about atrocities, it is quite natural to be shocked and to feel anger, perhaps even hatred, toward those acting so cruelly. But if we are committed to working toward a peaceful world, we must learn to allow our higher thinking to replace our natural inclinations.

In no way does this stance suggest that we are condoning horrendous actions. We can condemn and reject the action, the deed, with the full strength of our moral and compassionate commitment. Crucial, however, is the distinction we make between the person, the one who is as human as we are, and the action. We need not feel guilty because of our initial reaction to the culprit, but rather separate in our thinking the human from the action, and then modify our reaction. Certain realizations can help with this. Even cruel behavior is the result of conditioning. The perpetrator may well have been himself subjected to cruelty. Also, we must recognize the extent to which we are all bombarded by propaganda. In the case of those acting cruelly, this propaganda is often highly inflammatory and grossly negative. In light of the 'blinding' power of conditioning, it becomes all too easy to cease thinking for oneself, and fail to assess matters objectively from a position of human decency. Unconditional compassion leads us to avoid harshness and judgment.

I'm reluctant to share a personal account here because it will be so easy to misconstrue implications that might be drawn from it. However, I will share it. Following the tragedy of the two airplanes that flew into the Twin Towers, I did not hear of anyone else who felt sorrow and forgiveness for the perpetrators who had also lost their lives, who died in the process of acting on their personal beliefs, as horrendous and mistaken as they were. I'm not suggesting that there were no others of similar outlook, only that I haven't come to know about them. Nor should this confession be understood to suggest that I feel in any way more advanced that others, only that I personally found it natural, right, and proper to feel as I did. At the same time, I readily acknowledge that I have lots of personal undoing to 'do.'

Finally, be patient with yourself. All of us have been conditioned by innumerable factors. We need to attempt consistently to undo anything that sets up barriers between ourselves and others.

Richard Smoley: Steps to Contemplate Forgiveness

Smoley is the author of ten books, most of which feature esoteric religion. The following suggestions are drawn from his recent book, *The Deal: A Guide to Radical and Complete Forgiveness,* with modest adaption.

Development of the inner spirit of forgiveness that reinforces its actual practice can be enhanced by ongoing reflection coupled with a meditative discipline. Even though a special time and place might be set aside for the consideration of forgiveness, anytime is a good time if circumstances permit. If the question of forgiveness suddenly arises without apparent provocation, something relevant may be signaling from one's subconscious or even from an environmental setting. If possible, reflect a bit on what the germane factor might be. If not convenient under the circumstances, note as much as you can and return to your recollection when next it is possible.

When an isolated, focused opportunity arises without pressure of time, calmly center yourself in a reflective and meditative mood, releasing all care about the past and future, even the present except for the person relevant to forgiveness. Recall that forgiveness is a special opportunity to detach from something not yet fully released from your otherwise *natural state* of inner peace which is permeated by unrestrained love. This, of course, is the ultimate objective of all undoing. Release whatever is in your mind and heart, much as you might gently open your hand and release a bird from your palm. Practice without the slightest hint of negativity, discord, or recrimination. Psychospiritual cleansing occurs easily and naturally when unnatural and ineffective sensations abate.

If any sense other than contentment and fullness arises, and time permits, repeat the entire process, perhaps after a brief interval to breathe deeply, stretch, or do what's necessary without breaking the calm and centered state. Then resume the same focus and process – until a different inclination comes to the fore. This is your life and you decide how it is to be lived.

This might be a good time to recall and recite the italicized formulations given near the beginning of the chapter under the heading, "Three Dimensions of Forgiveness." You might want to refresh your memory by turning to those pages now, or photocopy them for later use. As you use them, do so with concentration on the relevant person and/or issue, with an open and loving heart. It virtually goes without saying that at any time during a forgiveness process, whether offering or seeking, one may appeal to whatever Higher Power one ordinarily recognizes. While this Reality is never absent, remembrance of this fact is always in order.

A sincere and concerted effort to make amends when possible is always in order. To take this finalizing action is to fulfill, confirm, and consummate forgiveness, to make it real for both the other and oneself. Smoley concludes his remarks on doing *the deal* by noting that it "is a major achievement," one worthy of humble self-commendation. He also suggests that forgiveness holds prospects beyond what might even be expected.

In the next chapter, we move beyond reflection about forgiveness to the discovery of its extraordinary power to transform the lives of all who avail themselves of it.

Chapter Five: Forgiveness Testimonials

Life is an Adventure in Forgiveness.
(Norman Cousins)

Actual accounts from fellow humans who have offered forgiveness to others, been forgiven by others, and have forgiven themselves can prove suggestive, instructive, and inspiring. The extent to which forgiveness is applicable and beneficial in interpersonal life, national life, and even the natural world, is impressive and amazing.

Forgiveness in a Business Betrayal

I was an aspiring thirty-five-year-old chef who bought a restaurant business. I teamed up with my landlord and helped develop a veggie burger called "Bocca Burger." It sold exceptionally well in almost every supermarket and health food store in the country, including some abroad. The business was thriving when, after three years, I received a telephone call from a Chicago investment company indicating that they had bought the Bocca Burger business for three million dollars. Unfairly, my partner had devalued the stock secretly prior to the sale, and it was worth nothing. Legal action produced disappointingly little.

My anger mounted and began to gnaw away at my usual happy and upbeat attitude. I eventually realized that only forgiving my former partner would reduce my disturbed state. By appealing to the Holy Spirit and repeating affirmations, my anger began to diminish and my sentiment about life and work started to improve.

About five years later, the Chicago company was sold for thirty-five million dollars. If I had held onto the devalued stock, I would have benefited greatly from this much larger sale. My triumph over my previous grievance served me well a second time. I stepped up my affirmations: "I have absolute faith that the divine spirit of God within me will help me forgive myself and all those who have brought me unhappiness in the past, whether they meant to or not." I've tailored the affirmations to particular situations and recited them for nearly fifty years. At eighty-four, I attest that the affirmations have become confirmed in my life. I also declare that my life, perhaps because of my trials, has been blessed beyond measure.
(Ron Raben)

Forgiveness Springs from the Heart

In 1991, Vanessa Kehde was twenty-one years old, a Mt. Holyoke exchange student studying in Italy, and staying in the bedroom and home of an Italian classmate back home. All was going well – until she passed out one day and was taken to the hospital. Pills were found in the bedroom and authorities concluded that she had overdosed. The pills, however, were for her long-standing struggle with a bi-polar condition. Assumptions were made without further investigation and Vanessa was released from the hospital with an entirely erroneous diagnosis.

On another occasion, Vanessa's boyfriend was waiting for her in her apartment when he too passed out. It turned out that there had been earlier occupants of the bedroom who also had fainting spells. Finally, Vanessa herself passed out again and this time could not be revived. She died of carbon monoxide poisoning. The bedroom and adjoining bath had been remodeled and a gas heater installed in the bathroom. The gas heater had been improperly vented.

Karl and Judy Kehde, the parents of Vanessa, were a more or less typical, middle aged couple with three young-adult children. Given the common regard of many mothers, Judy was apprehensive about her daughter going so far away and opposed the study abroad. Karl was enthusiastically supportive. Tension developed between the parents following Vanessa's death to such an extent that they eventually separated and finally divorced. Judy continued to blame Karl for their daughter's death and could not reconcile herself to the death. She died three years later.

Karl's response was remarkably different. His grief at the loss was deep and intense. Alongside that, he felt a strong urge to go to Italy, to visit the site of his daughter's death, and to meet her surrogate parents and Italian landlords. When Karl got there and laid down on what had been his daughter's bed, he began to weep with a broken heart like he had never known. The sense of loss and grief were beyond control and beyond words. Karl's host, the Italian representative of the foreign student program, later told Karl that he was either crying or laughing most of the visit, both entirely healthful ways of dealing with such a tragedy.

When Karl asked his host to arrange for him to meet the owners of the apartment, he was opposed and deeply apprehensive, not knowing what might transpire. Would there be unbridled blaming and intense anger? As it turned out, there would not be. Karl greeted the apartment owners with compassion and forgiveness. Full reconciliation came about. No blaming; no recrimination, just expressions of love and concern. (Karl H. Kehde)

Amish Forgive Murderer of School Children

Nine years earlier, the wife of milk-truck-driver, Charlie Roberts, lost a daughter in childbirth. He never forgave God and planned to get revenge someday. On a quiet morning in rural Pennsylvania, he entered an Amish one-room schoolhouse, barricaded its doors, and began his attack. One of the oldest girls offered to be shot first. She was, followed by continued shooting. By the time the local police were able to break into the school, ten girls had been shot, aged six to thirteen, five died. Then the shooter turned the gun on himself. Suicide notes he had left for his family told of his decades of inner anguish over unresolved sexual issues.

In the immediate aftermath of the shooting, the grandfather of one of the murdered girls was overheard saying: "We must not think evil of this man." An Amish father reminded people: "He had a mother and a wife and a soul and now he's standing before a just God." A member of another denomination, while bereaving with the Amish, noted: "I don't think there's anybody here that wants to do anything but forgive and reach out to … the family of the man who committed these acts." About thirty members of the Amish community attended Charlie Roberts' funeral. They also set up a charitable fund for the Roberts' family.

Marie Roberts, now the sole provider for her family, wrote in her open letter to her Amish neighbors: "Your love for our family has helped to provide the healing we so desperately need. Gifts you've given have touched our hearts in a way no words can describe. Your compassion has reached beyond our family, beyond our community, and is changing our world."

With hearts filled with love, the Amish recognized the pain in the shooter, the confusion and anger that drove him to such an abominable act. With a love surpassing their own loss and grief, they were able to extend love to others in the midst of their own mourning.

Bible Class Forgives Invading Killer

"A hateful person came to this community with some crazy idea he'd be able to divide, but all he did was unite us and make us love each other even more." So declared the mayor of Charleston, South Carolina, after Dylann Roof, a self-claimed white supremacist, invaded a Bible group in June 2015 at the African Methodist Episcopal Church killing nine members and hoping to start a racial war.

At the initial court appearance for Roof, a number of friends and relatives of the murdered spoke directly to the killer. The daughter of a seventy-year-old victim said: "I forgive you and have mercy on your soul. You hurt me. You hurt a lot of people. But God forgives you. I forgive you." The mother of a twenty-six-year-old victim, who survived by pretending to be dead, declared: "Every fiber in my body hurts, and I will never be the same. We welcomed you … with open arms. May God have mercy on you." The grandson of another victim affirmed that those killed by ignorance and hate were themselves so filled with love that others in the church could only respond with love, asserting that "hate won't win." (*WKPD* 6-12-17; *YHN* 6-19-15)

Warring Imam, Christian Pastor Discover Forgiveness

Animosity, hatred, and war prevailed for many years between the Christian and Muslim communities in Northern Nigeria. During this time, James Wuye and Muhammad Ashafa were fundamentalist street fighters recruiting others to join their battle to intimidate and kill those of the other faith. James Wuye became a Christian pastor, without change of heart, and headed a militia against the imam of the local mosque, a position now filled by Muhammad Ashafa, then also without a change of heart. Ashafa responded to the threat by instigating a retaliatory strike. In the battle, a fighter using a machete slashed off the pastor's right hand. The exoteric difference between the two religions had escalated into a merciless war no one could win. The two men were out to kill each other and almost succeeded.

The two religious leaders eventually realized they were not practicing the forgiveness their traditions taught. A journalist convinced them to meet and they gradually got to know each other as honest and loving persons. The warring between them ended, and they brought their respective communities together in mutual appreciation and support. Neither felt any desire to convert members from the faith of the other, but each openly affirmed the common faith they shared and were able to openly demonstrate that Christianity and Islam, in spite of many differences, share the most important dimensions of true faith, namely, love, reconciliation, and peace.

Imam and pastor now work together in the Interfaith Meditation Centre they founded. Now they instruct and counsel boys and young men in an effort to "deprogram" them from the misunderstandings and hatreds they themselves had promoted. They sponsor a television talk show and frequently appear internationally to describe their mutual forgiveness and reconciliation. (*PRI*)

Forgiveness Follows Unjust Imprisonment on Death Row

As a black boy in Alabama, Walter McMillian had worked the fields "plow'n', plant'n', and pick'n'," too useful working to be sent to school. His work skills enabled him as an adult to start his own business producing pulpwood, and thereby to support his family. On occasions, he was seen in public with a white woman. In 1988, 'out of the blue,' he was charged with murdering a young white woman and sent to death row ... even before his trial. He remained there for six years in spite of evidence that his accuser had lied in court, that he was not even near the crime scene at the time of the murder, and repeated earlier attempts to win his release. The denial of justice was based on the obvious prejudice against blacks and especially any hint of black-white alliances. Against great odds, and after years of detailed and dedicated work, his volunteer legal team finally won his freedom. When asked if his faith had been restored in the American judicial system, he replied with an emphatic, "No. Not at all." And yet Walter said he "wasn't angry or bitter, just grateful to be free." His attorney affirmed: "'Walter genuinely forgave the people who unfairly accused him, the people who convicted him, and the people who had judged him unworthy of mercy [i.e., those burdened by racial hatred]'" (*NYT*). With clear perception and a loving heart, Walter made a proper distinction between the injustice of the judicial system, which needed reform, and the people carrying out its laws and procedures, who deserved only forgiveness. (JM)

Forgiveness Between Enemy Combatants

One of the most remarkable occasions of group forgiveness is found in the first (1970) and following reunions of soldiers who fought in World War II on the island of Iwo Jima. The island is only eight square miles of volcanic sand and dirt, but would be a crucial landing site for US bombers when the invasion began in February 1945. Nearly seven thousand Americans died, with twenty thousand wounded. Of the twenty-one thousand Japanese soldiers who tried to hold the island, only two hundred and sixteen were taken prisoner, the rest died underground in bunkers or committed suicide.

The 2015 reunion included a visit to the island itself, now returned to Japan after the US victory. The declared purpose of the reunions is "to honor the fallen on both sides, ... to remember, to reconcile, and to heal." The effect is that "former enemies become friends." As the combatants meet, they learn from each other that neither side *wanted* to kill the other; they discover how they had been "brain washed" into believing the others were enemies.

An American pilot, Jerry Yellin, suffered intensely from the stress of battle and contemplated suicide. He joined the reunion reluctantly out of fear of returning to the battleground and facing his former enemies. His is a particularly remarkable change since he now has a Japanese daughter-in-law and three Japanese-American grandchildren. Yellin openly confesses that his one-time hatred has transformed into friendship and now to love.

Because the Japanese soldiers were older than their American counterparts, and so many died on the island, only one survivor, Tsuruji Akikusa, was able to attended the reunion. As a Japanese citizen after the war, because of an overwhelming sense of guilt, he kept his story to himself for years. He had not killed at least ten enemy soldiers but nevertheless allowed himself to be taken prisoner, thereby violating Japanese military custom. His eventual willingness to admit this culturally serious lapse and participate in the reunion added to the desire of the Americans to shake his hand in respect and forgiveness.

When addressing a joint session of the US Congress, the visiting Prime Minister of Japan singled out the American lieutenant general of the Iwo Jima battle, who stood in the balcony next to a younger Japanese man whose grandfather was the Japanese equivalent of the general. The Prime Minister than asked, "What can we call this but a miracle of history?" In a similar vein, the media reports on these reunions refer repeatedly to their value in the friendship and mutual honoring that occurs. Note that "miracle," "friendship," and "mutual honoring" all occur on the foundation of forgiveness. Without forgiveness, the reunions and their life-change effects would never have occurred. Apparently in government and military circles, the change of heart we call forgiveness in religiospiritual circles must be translated into secular terminology. (*PBS*)

Forgiving My Father and Myself

My father was an alcoholic, not a daily drinker but a binge drinker. The drinking only took place on weekends and not every weekend. When life became too difficult, given his self-doubt and confusion, no other alternative was as appealing as alcohol. It eased the pain for a while. There was a different suffering for him when the binge ended, which was always Sunday night: he always went back to work on Monday morning. Why? He didn't want to be compared to his father, an inept, impossible non-functioning drunk.

My siblings and I each took a different attitude and approach toward life, and how we would handle growing up in a house sometimes filled with stress and sadness. I chose to protect my mother as much as I could. She had opportunities to leave, but she chose to stay. Maybe what I presumed was weakness on her part, made me stronger. Now I realize it wasn't strength at all but fear.

A time came when my father realized how I really felt about him. By then, I didn't care how alone or hurt he was. When he was on the receiving end of rejection and loss, I had no sympathy. That he was alone and aging meant nothing. This came from the years of emotional abuse and abandonment that he imposed on my mother, my siblings, and me.

I now realize that I gave my father too much power, an almost God-like power that caused him to become a very negative influence on me, one that colored my entire world. The God he represented was one of power and anger, on the one hand, and disappointment, frustration and weakness, on the other hand.

By the time I entered my sixties, I'd had a number of years in Al-Anon and had gained some self-awareness and forgiveness. But I never married.

I didn't want to take a chance on anyone ever having power over me. There were relationships and some loves. Eventually, I took a chance on a live-in, long-term relationship that lasted more than a decade. Pete too, however, had a problem with alcohol. I told him I could not live with anyone who had a drinking problem. He entered A.A. and this time succeeded. Life with him in retrospect, given our individual histories, was remarkably successful. We were kind to each other. Perhaps we were both healed in some way since we lived together in an atmosphere of peace, love, and kindness. When he suddenly passed away, I was alone again.

That would be devastating for any woman in her early seventies, particularly the alone part. Because I had lived so much of my life feeling alone, I didn't think being alone again would be so bad. I had had a peaceful, quiet, and serene life with my partner. I figured it would continue. Well, alone doesn't feel comfortable at all. I manage, I date, and I make friends, and live a busy life. And thanks to Pete, my emotional door is open to the possibility of loving again. I know that love can replace fear, loneliness, and insecurity. Trust and good judgment are also needed.

The spiritual meetings I've been attending have enabled me to focus on forgiveness. I've come to realize how important it is for a truly spiritual life. I see the truth in some of the quotations I've found. I use them to further the process of healing from my father's abuse and the loathing and hate I had for him. Yes, I did feel hate and loathing towards my father at times. Forgiveness has enabled me to "recognize my innocence." I no longer see myself as guilty. I was a child at the time. All I could see were people around me being emotionally hurt. "Forgiveness will remove all sense of weakness, strain and fatigue from your mind." It will take away all fear guilt and pain. I remember these quotes because I want to be happy. "My function is to be happy."

I now think of my father positively and fondly. I recognize his intelligence, his love of poetry, his sense of humor, and his great love for his children. I feel him around me, as if he is protecting me. I make a conscious effort to always think about him with love. And I get that back. He is continually giving me his love and protection. I am letting his love in – at last. (Kay Kelly)

Forgiving My Parents

I grew up the oldest of three children and felt stifled. My parents were always trying to control and dominated me. I couldn't do anything right. I should be doing this; I shouldn't be doing that. I was threatened. I was often told I was so naughty that I should be taken to the woodshed and spanked. I never was, but now looking back, I wish I had been. Get it over with instead of wondering when it would happen. I couldn't wait to get away from home. I couldn't stand to be around my mother and dad. I really felt like they didn't know anything.

I finally did get away from them. I married at a young age, had two sons, and then was divorced. To survive, my children and I went to live with my parents. Still, my feelings for them had not changed much. I did realize, however, how fortunate I was to have their help.

Two years later I remarried, and several years later I had a daughter. It was a happy marriage. My husband now was a good listener and very helpful. I received lots of love and support from him. There was a span of thirteen years between the boys and our daughter. I was now able to enter motherhood in a more mature way. I've often said that the boys and I grew up together. I made so many mistakes raising them, said things I should not have said, did things that I wish I had not done. I had very little patience with them. As I raised my daughter, I was haunted and tormented by memories of how I had raised my boys. I wished I could have been the mother to them that I was for my daughter. I felt terrible guilty and was filled with remorse.

Over the years, I read books about parenting, forgiveness, and other topics. I talked to and listened to others. It was a gradual process, but eventually I realized my parents did the best they could. They both were raised under difficult circumstances. They really did love me. They too have changed over the years. Their outlook on parenting has changed a great deal as well. Having grandchildren may have contributed to their softened attitudes.

Eventually, even some happy memories of my childhood surfaced. I forgave my parents and realized how much I appreciated and loved them. The hardest part was forgiving myself. Sometimes when looking back, I think of myself as 'her.' I look at that woman and realize how young she was. She had never worked other than babysitting. She did graduate from high school but had no life experience. She was very insecure and naive. Her brother died in an accident when he was fifteen. Her sister committed suicide when she was twenty-six. I am the only one of the original three still alive. I mostly have forgiven myself, but it is a lifelong process I think. I have come to realize that I too, like my parents, did the best I could at the time. (Judy Lapham)

Is Abuse of a Son Forgivable?

If there is any act unforgiveable, this would seem to be it, or at least to be very close to the top of the list. When Jesus was asked how many times one would be expected to forgive, he reportedly replied: "Seventy times seven." I suspect he was really saying that the number is more or less irrelevant. What really matters is the quality, the depth, and the sincerity, of the forgiveness.

The father in question was in a doctoral program and challenged to the limits of his abilities and endurance. The mother was teaching in a ghetto school with children of different racial backgrounds, and many students had problems of one sort or another. The family was recently returned from five years aboard, with their children having spent half or more of their lives in foreign countries. Each was challenged by big cultural differences and the need to make big adjustments. It was a trying time for all.

None of this excuses the 'unforgiveable' act of the father. The boys were arguing one afternoon over a toy, itself of almost no monetary value. The older son threw his brother's toy out of the second floor window. Dad made his firstborn son go downstairs, outside, and retrieve the toy. When he watched from the window, he saw the older son purposely step on the toy and break it. When the son returned to the apartment, the father became a raging bull and spanked his son mercilessly, all while other members of the family pleaded for him to stop. (Tears are flowing as this is being written; the pain is still there.)

When sanity returned, the father apologized. The son was bewildered and deeply, deeply hurt. His trust and admiration had been shattered, but happily, not forever. As the son got older, he became interested in self-understanding, read widely in the area, and attended many conferences, workshops, and transformational sessions. When his father recalled the horrible injustice, the son replied that he had long ago forgiven him. He explained that he had learned to appreciate and value the incident because it gave him a crucial issue to work with. It became something from which he learned vital lessons, something that contributed to him becoming the person he is. The father, of course, heard this, but found it unusual and difficult to grasp.

The issue rarely returned in their adult interactions. On one occasion, however, when both sons and the father were sharing openly from their respective lives, the father confessed his continuing sorrow about his action more than fifty years earlier. Again, and from the depths of his heart, the son expressed his total forgiveness. Even though they were at the time in a public place, the father's heart opened, and he heard the forgiveness as never before. Uncontrollable weeping broke forth. Forgiveness was felt and acknowledged. Healing occurred. (Jim Royster)

Forgiving and 'Over-mothering' Mother

On the maternal side of the family, I was the first girl after six boys – happy, happy news for my mother and grandmother. As the first girl, I became "a princess" and got everything I could possibly want "on a silver platter." My mother doted over me and seemed to know what I wanted even before I did. I was dressed to her liking and took the dancing lessons that she hadn't.

I was an extension of my mother's dreams. Until, that is, the rebellion began in my freshman year of high school. I quite dancing – and now I had to do chores, like a normal kid. Life at home was always one of black and white: you do this and not that; you can't have that, only this. My mother would not tolerate me becoming my own person. My teenage rebellion was in full force until I was twenty-eight. At that time, my husband pointed out that I liked someone or something only until I found one tiny thing about them that I didn't like. I was unconsciously living in the black and white world of my mother. This is when I finally started to grow up and see through my own eyes, rather than how I was (so masterfully) taught.

Jump ahead twelve years. Life was wonderful – or should have been. I had everything that marked success: a faithful, hardworking husband, two lovely daughters, a beautiful home, enough money, friends, a full and interesting life – what more could I want? Yet, I wasn't happy. That was the start of a slow, evolving spiritual journey.

Circumstances had brought my mother to live with us during her final days. When she died, I heard myself – without thinking – say, "the wicked old witch is dead." I had no idea that I harbored such hatred, that I was even capable of such loathing! After all, I was the "dutiful daughter."

So I was far from free or happy. I unwittingly took on the depression that plagued my mother. My inner life was dominated by despondency and darkness. I began to come out of this self-hatred by tuning into comedy programs and watching the news. I entered personal therapy and discovered insights about myself, including the relief that comes with crying. I began reading books on shamanism. I found Mary Ann Williams and read her book, *A Return to Love.* This led to *A Course in Miracles* and later to *A Course of Love*, two books from which I've gleaned a great deal of spiritual wisdom.

I've had a series of meaningful dreams: my mother and me, with each smiling; my grandmother, mother, and me all smiling; my mother, grandmother, me, and Jesus – all smiling. These were so meaningful because no one in my family ever smiled, or even knew how to smile! I now summarize my life-long relationship with my mother like this:

> She did a terrible job.
> She did a terrible job, but it was the best she could do.
> She did the best she could do.
> She did the best she could do and it was OK.
> She did the best she could do and I love her.

These five statements represent a twenty-year journey.

Today, as I look back over my life, I am grateful for all of it. Every phase, negative and positive, has enabled me to become the happy, contented, and loving person I believe I now am. (Johanna McKeever)

Forgiving a Premature Death

My birth family gathered at my mother's home on Thanksgiving Day in 1965. It was an annual affair with a wonderful meal. My older brother Duane came a bit late, and his family not at all, undoubtedly due to the separation from his wife and impending divorce. He was a pharmacist and owned his own pharmacy. We were all happy to see one another and even Duane's spirits lifted as we all interacted happily. At the time, I was a junior in college and had to leave the family early for a college event I needed to help plan. When I left, the home it was filled with love, happy memories and a feeling of a positive future.

Duane stopped and saw his wife and family on his way home. The next day the police called my mother with the shocking news; they had found his body at his home. He was the first of my siblings to pass away. His death was a great shock and loss for me. He seemed so full of life; he had always been the big brother mentor to me. We fished together and shared many life experiences. He had even offered to pay for my college education if I became a pharmacist. However, I felt I had a different path. Because of the circumstances, the funeral was tense and I cried throughout the service. How could this happen? He was well educated and brilliant, with an effervescent personality, and seemingly so grounded.

There were official investigations, probate hearings, theories, and considerable pain, anger, etc. My mother cried often but handled it all with dignity. Duane's body was buried next to the plots of our mother and father. There remained estrangement with his family.

It took many years for me to let go of the anger and the inability to make sense of his death. After reading the autopsy report, trying to understand his state of mind and the turmoil in his life, it began to be easier. My own healing process involved getting together with my former sister-in-law, my nieces and nephew, where we shared our disbelief, confusion, and pain. I was able to offer consolation from my profession training as a therapist. I also arranged for my nephew to have a Big Brother. All of this helped me in my healing process, helped me continue my growth and development, and helped me come to forgiveness. (Jerry Lapham)

Forgiveness for a Deserting Father

My father was a successful businessman and leader in community affairs. He married my mother, his high school sweetheart, and they had seven children. My parents hired a maid whose husband was away fighting in the Second World War. Not long after this, my father deserted the family and ran off with the maid. My parents remained officially married, but it was as if my siblings and I were raised in a single-parent household. My father raised a second and then a third family.

When I was in college, my father was hospitalized with terminal cancer. I visited him in the hospital; most of my siblings didn't. During my visits, I was able to express my anger and frustration at being raised in a single-parent home. These were authentic, truthful, but brutal confrontational times together. After our confrontations, I realized how much my dad really cared for us children: two of my siblings graduated from college and entered healing professions; three owned their own businesses; and two were in college completing their degrees. We all became successful in our careers.

Until I visited my father, it had never occurred to me to wonder where the finances came from for our care, education and general livelihood. My mother was my dad's accountant, and somehow, money always appeared when we needed it, even after the divorce. Nor did I realize the love that continued between my parents. They planned their wills together and dealt with life's crises together.

My siblings held onto the pain of our father's departure, an absence of forgiveness was central in their lives. After my hospital meeting, I began to see and feel differently about my situation. I realized how lucky we were to have such a caring and forgiving mother, one who enabled us to grow and become successful, who conducted her business affairs and her relationship with her husband. My father explained to me that more of his attention was required by the other children because of their needs. He acknowledged how great my mother was in managing our growing up. He expressed his love for us, and the personal trials and burdens he had in his life. I found forgiveness for my father who went on to live another twelve years, twice as long as the doctors had predicted. (Jerry Lapham)

Forgiving My Former Wife and Myself

About the seventh year of my relationship with and marriage to my wife, we began to have constant discord. Through this stage of our marriage, there was a great deal of judgment, who's right and who's wrong. Even though we entered counseling, the differences continued to create more and more breakdown between us.

My wife began to have a relationship with a co-worker. It took me a few months to realize what was happening. Thankfully, she was honest about her affair. We continued with the counseling, but the marriage deteriorated further, and we finally separated. About six months later, we ended the marriage with a formal divorce. There was a great deal of hurt, anger, and sadness on my side. At times, I even felt hatred toward her and her 'boy friend.' This strong feeling shocked me since it was quite unfamiliar. But I couldn't deny it; it was there in darker moments. I had never felt this negative emotion in the past. I became depressed, and this was having a very negative effect on my life and other relationships. I began to realize that holding onto these negative emotions and thoughts about my ex-wife and our past life together was causing me a great deal of confusion and suffering.

I started talking as openly as I could with close family members and a few trusted friends. Slowly, over the next months, all of those feelings of anger, hurt, sadness, and fear blended into a barely controllable, deep grief. As I allowed the grief to come out through feelings of heartbreak and tears, a softening toward my former wife began to develop. This continued for about a year or so. I then began to consider how I had contributed to the breakdown of our relationship and marriage. Over the next several years, through counseling, reading, and meditating, I consciously worked on acceptance and forgiveness for her, and for myself. It took about five years after the divorce before I could begin to relate to her without feeling 'hooked' in some way.

Then, over time, I noticed a subtle openness and appreciation in me toward her as a unique person. To my surprise, a friendship began to develop. We now talk on the phone from time to time and have been to visit each other.

It's been twenty years since those days of intense trouble. We now consider each other as friends. I feel so grateful to have had the support of others and to have been able to go through the challenging feelings and difficult experiences required to forgive and let go. It has been well worth the arduous self-investigation and vulnerability to finally be free of the former animosity and suffering – and to re-discover a friend. (Anonymous)

Forgiveness in Baseball

Richard Kelly joined a mediocre baseball team that found itself in a tight game with the previous year's champions. He hit a line drive that forced him to dive into second base as the runners raced home to score. The throw from the outfield was close so he slid headfirst into the bag, was tagged out with not one but two blows of the ball to his head. He jumped up ready to fight but restrained himself as his teammates roared at the opposing team.

Richard's team won the league championship and was permitted to add players from the league in preparation for the state playoffs. Ed, the second baseman who had hit Richard on the head, was a good player. When Richard indicated to his teammates that he held no negative feelings at all toward Ed, they agreed to pick him. With the additional strength, the team ended the season in second place, not bad at all.

A few years went by with Ed and Richard working for the same company. They worked together on a few projects and eventually found themselves both in upper management. The director of Richard's division of the business left and Ed took over. Ten years later, Ed left and Richard became the director. Richard concludes his story with Ed: "Fifty years later and retired, we are still close friends. I am certainly happy I chose forgiveness rather that attack. If forgiveness was not my lifestyle already, this affirmed that it would be." (*MM* Jan/Feb 2016)

The Dalai Lama's Forgiveness of the Chinese

Many years ago, the Dalai Lama agreed to meet Victor Chan, a young American wandering the East in search of himself. Chan was racially Chinese and wondered if the Dalai Lama might harbor feelings against him and the Chinese. On meeting the Dalai Lama, he immediately discovered that this leader of Tibetans did not. Over the years, the two became good friends and frequently travelled together.

In 1989, the Dalai Lama was awarded the Nobel Peace Prize for his non-violent stance toward the Chinese in spite of their over-throw and occupation of Tibet. On this occasion, Chan interviewed the Dalai Lama and asked him: "Your Holiness, I thought it natural that you'd harbor resentment toward the Chinese. Yet you told me that this is not so. But do you, sometimes at least, experience deep feelings of animosity?"

"That almost never," the Dalai Lama replied. "I analyze like this: if I develop bad feeling toward those who make me suffer, this will only destroy my own peace of mind. But if I forgive, my mind becomes calm. Now, concerning our struggle for freedom, if we do it without anger, without hatred, but with true forgiveness, we can carry that struggle even more effectively. Struggle with calm mind, with compassion. Through analytical meditation, I now have full conviction that destructive emotions like hatred is [*sic*] no use. Nowadays, anger, hatred, they don't come. But little irritation sometimes come."

When talking about forgiveness, the Dalai Lama often shares the story of Lopon-la, a monk he knew before the Chinese occupation. After the Dalai Lama escaped from Tibet in 1959, the Chinese put Lopon-la in prison and kept him there for eighteen years. When he was finally freed, he came to India. It was twenty more years before the Dalai Lama met him again. Lopon-la was clearly older but seemed to be physically okay. His mind was still good and he was still a gentle monk.

When the Dalai Lama asked Lopon-la about his experience, he told him that the Chinese forced him to denounce his religion and subjected him often to torture. The Dalai Lama asked him directly if he ever became afraid while in prison. He replied: "Yes, there was one thing I was afraid of. I was afraid I may lose compassion for the Chinese."

Lopon-la suffered physically, but through forgiveness he kept his emotions, his mind, and his spirit untouched and without resentment. He knew he couldn't escape, so he adjusted to his lot and avoided being traumatized by it. (*WF* 47f, *passim*)

Authenticity and Freedom Through Forgiveness

Even though I knew better at the time, I entered a dubious relationship. I was in love and willing to compromise on the things that didn't quite match. That is a common thing to do when entering a long-term relationship, so I certainly wasn't unaware. Then, it hit me over the head: you are in a committed relationship, and its very foundation is wrong. I knew I was unconventional, even radical. I had grown up overseas, experienced other cultures and religions, but I was agreeing to a very conventional situation. It began with a lie – I agreed willingly to enter a closeted relationship. For me, being out-of-the-closet was no big deal, but I was sensitive enough to the fact that it wasn't as easy for others in terms of career, work situations, and family.

How much could I compromise for the stability and security I yearned for? How much of my integrity, my spiritual and intellectual curiosity was I willing to give up, when it soon became clear they were not a shared value, and even came across as a threat? How much can one adjust to another – to the point when it becomes truly destructive, and even then, maybe a bit more? I really thought we would grow together, overcome differences and enhance each other. In theory, I certainly knew what a healthy relationship should be, one of mutual respect and full support. However, any period of growth together was short-lived and founded on our enjoyment of recreational outdoor activities, which was supposed to be enough in and of itself. I found myself facing a rigidity I had never encountered before, something I could not overcome or sidestep with any grace.

I realized I was allowing myself to be controlled to the point of constriction in order to fit the relationship. I had never let anyone control me before. It happened gradually, a little compromise of myself here, then there, to make the relationship work – thinking I was doing it out of love, that I was strong enough, spiritually rich enough. Not so. I started to censure myself, impede myself creatively, socially and spiritually. The controlling situation created isolationism. I was the one "in the wrong"; I had the problem. I walked on eggshells. I realized that I could not be myself in my own home, the place that is supposed to be safe and nurturing. I had allowed myself, bit by bit, to be deeply compromised. A friend, leveling with me in my distress, told me no truly loving partner would censor your creativity, or your spirit, or decide for you how to express yourself. If you are censored to the point of losing yourself, it's simply not a healthy relationship. That was a wake-up call. There was a point at which self-sacrifice became masochistic.

I remember the day when I realized – with resignation – that I had to give up the relationship, leave the home I had helped to build. I could not continue to be seen as a threat, just by being who I was. How could I give it up when it had meant everything to me? Already the tension, pain and sorrow I lived with daily was overwhelming. There was the palpable feeling of death, very close – I had to come to an end in that relationship, never mind the love I still felt. Wasn't love supposed to encompass all, conquer all? But was that love an illusion? I didn't know where I'd go, what I'd do, what I'd become. It was the resiliency of spirit beyond my self-definition (divine intervention, instinct) that drove my act of survival – to step beyond, to cast off the bindings. My relationship was a shell I could not fit in. From the very first, I had tried to cram myself into it out of the belief of love, and in all seriousness.

I was definitely heart-broken, torn, agitated and distressed, barely functioning, but most of all, in grief. I wanted to make things right but couldn't. I had to let go of the idea of closure, of transcending one definition toward another. And that too, was painful, to realize that there had never been room for true dialog.

How many years did it take to grieve and to heal even as I began a new life full of intellectual vigor, creative freedom, delightful opportunities and terrific support? It took a long time of feeling torn apart, about five years, about as long as I had been in the relationship. It seems so long ago now, hardly remembered, but at the time it was devastating. How could I have allowed myself into such a situation? I had wanted the security of a home and a steadfast friend. It became a broken dream that involved a beloved, and we were not going to be able to heal each other. A friend said to me: "You've got to cut your losses." Another said: "Don't look back, just move on." That didn't seem like enough. So, I had to go it alone: understand my part in it and let go without bitterness, without blame, without reproach, no matter how hard. And sometimes it was really hard – wrestling that angel. I only knew I had to work through these elements whole-heartedly if I was going to find release, to realize again who I was, and to be well.

Did I heal? Absolutely yes! I didn't just move on, I healed, truly healed or I wouldn't even be able to write about it. Ever since, I have had a wonderful and fulfilling life. I'm at total peace about the relationship. I am now recognized by those I love for who I am. I am living in peace with my full creative powers – and growing all the time with new discoveries. (Rebecca Béguin)

Forgiving Siblings for Mishandling My Money

Years ago when I set out on a lengthy trip, I left a sizable amount of money with my sister for safekeeping. Upon my return, only half of the money remained in my account. She had loaned the other half to my brother – without my knowledge or permission. When I learned what she had done, I was so horrified and angry at her for violating my trust that I threw the bank book across the room with such force that it split in half. I still remember the sudden burst of anger on that occasion. I eventually came to realize that my memory of that betrayal was keeping my sister, brother, and me from having the trustful and loving relationship that I wanted. I knew I had to become free of those feelings and attitude.

It has been wonderful to release the negativity toward them that had put me in a kind of prison made of walls I built. I can now enjoy each moment without the distraction of my former grievance toward them. Through this process of forgiveness, I have also given them an opportunity to feel differently about themselves, about me, and about our ongoing relationship. (Alma Hamblin)

From Pain to Love, Forgiveoness, and Honoring

I cried throughout most of kindergarten, cried and begged for my mom like many other children. My reasons were different than most, however, because my mom had cancer, and I was afraid she'd die while I was at school. The teachers were unaware of my situation. At recess, I would sit on the curb and stare at my feet and ask myself what I was going to do without my mom, my world, my everything. Depression set in, and I often contemplated life, death, and survival at the age of five. If only an adult had explained the difference between living with cancer and dying of cancer. My mom lived until I was twenty-two years old.

My mother was afraid of ending up alone. She often said to my brothers and me: "When you get older, you're going to leave me and I'll be all alone." Because of this fear, she left her three children and our home for another man.

Abandonment by my mother was the ultimate betrayal; the pain stayed with me most of my life. My brothers and I went to live with our alcoholic father. I refused to eat, hoping my mom would be forced to take me back, but that didn't happen. I was about twelve at the time and felt that without my mother my life was over. My anger and forlorn state made me want to die – made me angry with God for allowing my mother to disappear from my life. She had no right to even bring me into the world if she wasn't going to fulfill her commitment as my mother. I longed for her presence, but her new husband wouldn't permit it.

My mother's departure left me feeling unloved and unimportant. If I had come first in her life, she would never have left me. I spent a good portion of my life needing someone to put me first in their life, for me to be the most important person for them. With every break up, I felt devastated and alone. The feelings of rejection and loss were like those of my childhood, and were repeated with the ending of every relationship. I blamed my mother for this continuing pain.

Despite these feelings, in my forties my heart began to soften toward my mom and the anger disappeared. I began to think about her life experience and her struggles. She used to dye her hair, and we believed it was Red Dye No. 9 that caused the cancer. She underwent a number of surgeries as the cancer spread down her face. More and more of her face was removed and eventually one eye. She battled cancer for twenty years. When she died a third of her face was gone.

I put my pain aside and reflected on the life of Sandra Ann Rose, my mother. I began to admire her strength, trust, and perseverance. She had a strong faith in God. Her courage inspires me in difficult times to be as she was. I now know that my mother always loved me and lived the best life she could. I was able to heal because I realized that she really did do the best she could. It was that simple realization that led to my forgiveness and healing and love. In her own way, her life was exemplary. She's a model for perseverance and strength. I regard her as a warrior and a saint. (JW)

Self-understanding and Self-forgiveness

As I develop a deeper understanding of what it means to forgive, I also have developed a different perspective of the things that seem to require my forgiveness. Families of origin and their varying degrees of dysfunction are ripe with opportunity to exercise forgiveness – my family has no shortage, and what follows is a recent example.

Four years ago my brother received a diagnosis of fourth stage terminal cancer. It was an emotional time for those who loved him; we believed in less than a year he'd be gone. There are supposedly five stages of grief, but I think Kubler-Ross may have missed a level – that one being self-centered, greedy, ego-driven, and full-scale crazy. At least that's what happened in my family.

My brother's children, ex-wife, and current girlfriend began a feud of epic proportion, replete with the most ridiculous junior high childishness that can be imagined. I'm surprised my brother didn't just die to get away from it all, but he opted instead to live his life fully and let them fight it out. I, on the other hand, jumped in the middle determined to 'fix' it. I employed reason: "What matters here is my brother, and he is sick; we need to rally around, get rid of the stress, and come together to support him." That fell on deaf ears. I followed up with shaming, blaming, threatening, and finally gave a hollow threat to gather him up and move to Canada where none of them could find us. Nothing I did mattered in the slightest or changed a thing. Then one day the light dawned, and I realized four things: first, if there was a fight to be fought at all, it was not mine; second, nothing I was ever going to do was going to change their entrenched positions; third, all I was doing was joining them exactly where I hoped they would not go; and fourth, my brother was busy enjoying his life – he had his eye on what mattered. I decided to follow his example.

It does not take an advanced level of awareness to see how all this craziness was being created at an illusory level. What interested me was how readily I jumped right into an illusion of which I had no need or desire. Even after I resigned from my self-appointed post as mediator, it was easy to get pulled back in. With time, however, I developed a technique of picturing myself driving my car and reminding myself to stay in my lane. At other times, I literally raised my hands as if about to touch something toxic as a reminder to keep my hands off – it is not my circus.

As far as forgiving the disruptive contingent of the family is concerned, I decided they were simply 'blindly' being themselves and probably didn't even consider any other ways of relating; they were driven. With this view, there's no grudge and no need for forgiveness. Since they didn't disturb my brother but did disturb me, it's my voluntary, inappropriate, ineffective, and unnecessary intervention that needs forgiveness. Thus, the situation has given me a chance to learn something about myself and to forgive myself. (Chaaron Barnes)

A Mother Forgives her Son's Killer

As a sixteen-year old in Minneapolis, Israel Oshea ran with a gang and was involved in drugs. At a party one evening in 1993, he got into a fight with the twenty-year-old son of Mary Johnson, shot and killed him. Mary attended the trial and felt such hatred toward the killer that she wanted to kill him. He was convicted and imprisoned. Years later, out of curiosity she began to visit Israel in prison. She wanted to discover for herself if he was the same person who had murdered her son. She found that he had changed and began to feel warmly toward him ... and he for her. Eventually, through subsequent visits, they began to feel deep sympathy and love for the each other, even hugging before parting.

After Oshea's release from prison, Mary arranged for him to live next door to her. They see each other and help each other often. Oshea has become for Mary the son she lost. Not able to have seen the graduation and marriage of her birth son, she now hopes that will be the case with Israel. He acknowledges receiving confidence and hope from the 'mother' love now extended to him. (*NPR*)

Forgiving Mass Killers

Black South Africans suffered under the rule of Apartheid (literally "separateness") from 1948 to 1994. During this nearly half century of ruthless subjection and wanton killing, Nelson Mandela worked tirelessly from prisons to end Apartheid. When finally released, he became the first president of the free South Africa. One of his closest allies was Desmond Tutu, an Episcopal bishop who chaired the Truth and Reconciliation Commission. This body pursued restorative justice by bringing together the victims and victimizers of the indiscriminate slaughter of the innocent during Apartheid. Even though the results of the Commission were not entirely positive, many striking instances of forgiveness did occur.

Accounts of forgiveness were remarkable. A widow described the body of her murdered husband, forty-three wounds from different weapons, acid burns on his face, a hand severed. A teenager, eight years old when her father was killed, spoke for herself and her younger brother about how much they would like to meet the killers: "We want to forgive them. We want to forgive, but we don't know who to forgive." There were instances during the TRC deliberations when perpetrator and victim publically embraced. A young woman had been forced to disrobe, her breasts slammed repeatedly in a drawer, spilling out a liquid – she too wanted to offer forgiveness.

While not all who suffered matched these accounts (some of the methods of torture and killing atrocities were even more appalling), they are representative. A final event demonstrates the effectiveness of the TRC in fostering restorative justice rather than the more common retributive judgment. In the Bisho massacre, thirty to forty people were killed and two hundred injured. The Commission's public meetings took place in a huge hall sometimes packed with angry people, many having been injured or having lost a loved one. When four of the officers who had shot and killed entered the hall, the tension and anger in the room surged. The white officer stood, and representing the black officers, acknowledged: "Yes, we gave the order for the soldiers to shoot." The commotion and anger in the room escalated. In the midst of it, he asked those present to forgive him and his comrades and receive them back into the community. Almost unimaginably, the room exploded into applause. When the applause subsided, Bishop Tutu called for a moment of silence, observing: "We are in the presence of something holy." (*BF passim, WF* 66-8)

Forgiving a Mentor's Sexual Abuse

Twelve-year-old Jeffery (a pseudonym) lived with the horror of what happened that year until he was thirty and married. Trusting his loving wife, he confessed for the first time that a teacher/coach had sexually assaulted him after a school-sporting event. After the tragedy, his personality changed. He became sullen, angry, and didn't trust adults in particular. His wife encouraged him to forgive the man, pointing out that failure to do so had caused him to continue abusing himself for nearly two decades. He confessed that he did often feel trapped, plus guilt and shame, by the painful experience. Now he could begin talking about the event with selected people. A weight seemed removed from his chest, and he no longer felt locked in a dungeon, now realizing that he held within himself the key to his own freedom: self-forgiveness. As he shared his experience with others, especially in a group of similar survivors, he became even more compassionate and was able to see even the positive side of the experience – he now had the expertise and empathy to help others. (*BF* 78-80)

Multiple Gains through Forgiveness

Amy Biehl, a twenty-six-year-old Stanford University student and Fulbright Scholar, volunteered to help in the South African effort to end Apartheid. On her way one day to help in the struggle, her car was stopped by an angry mob. Mistaken as another one of the oppressive whites, Amy was dragged from her car, beaten, stoned, and stabbed to death. Four men were convicted and granted amnesty by the Truth and Reconciliation Commission. Amy's parents, Linda and Peter Biehl, had already forgiven the murderers. Their commitment to replace evil with good led then to establish a foundation and trust in Cape Town to help the very community where their daughter was murdered. Two of her murderers came to work for the foundation, doing what they could to make restitution for the evil deeds of their former lives. This account demonstrates the undeniable benefits that can follow a horrendous event when full forgiveness occurs. The transformative power in forgiveness and restitution is unquestionable. Individuals and the world are the better for it. (*BF passim*)

Forgiveness Translated into Political Goals

Twelve-year-old Bassam Aramin, a Palestinian, saw a boy of his age shot and killed by an Israeli soldier. The rage he felt led him to join a group of freedom fighters in hope of revenge. Five years later, he was imprisoned for plotting an attack on Israeli soldiers and subjected to beatings while stripped of his clothing. Notwithstanding the odds, he and one of his Israeli guards became friends and frequently exchanged views. In spite of previously regarding each other as the terrorist who immigrated to a land not theirs, through their conversations they realized their mutual humanity and how much they had in common.

After his release, Bassam eschewed violence and cofounded Combatants for Peace. Two years later, his ten-year-old daughter was shot and killed by an Israeli soldier as she stood outside her school. His forgiveness of the shooter came with its usual benefits, but additionally in the garden voluntarily built at her school by the a hundred former Israeli soldiers. Changes of heart like these will bring reconciliation and peace eventually to this 'intractable' problem plaguing these two nations for decades – and only such changes. Political changes alone will be deemed forced and endlessly violated by both sides. (*BF* 34f)

Forgiveness for Murder of Husband and Daughter

In November 2008, an American father and his thirteen-year-old daughter were eating in the Oberoi Hotel in Mumbai (formerly Bombay), India. Foreign terrorists opened fire in a shooting, murdering rampage. The father and daughter were killed. In America, the mother, Kia Scherr, relentlessly watching TV on the unfolding crisis, finally received a call from the US Consulate in Mumbai: her husband and daughter were dead. Even though she did not regard herself as a religious person, her immediate response was to exclaim: "Father, forgive them, they know not what they do." Facing her family, she affirmed: "We must forgive them."

Kia founded One Life Alliance (with its website, onelifealliance.org), which is designed to building on the values of religion to unite people around the world in opposition to terrorism. Summarizing her response to the loss of her husband and daughter, she declares: "Forgiveness has allowed me to keep my heart open and soft. I chose to forgive because I knew that if I did not, the unforgiving would have kept me closed and hardened inside. I made an instantaneous choice when Alan and Naomi were murdered to let go of anger, hatred, and any desire for retaliation" (*BF* 122-25, 220, passim).

Forgiveness Extended to Attacking Animals

A grizzly bear near Yellowstone National Park mauled Wyoming rancher Nic Patrick. With his dog and carrying a shovel one day in 2013, he headed out across his property to open some irrigation ditches, something he been doing for fifty years. Suddenly, he heard his dog in a furious fight, ran back to him, and was himself attacked. After slashing his face and knocking him to the ground, the bear left. When returning home, Patrick heard the bear returning; she had gone in the wrong directing and left her cubs on the far side of the rancher. Again, the bear knocked him down and began biting his head and clawing his back. Suddenly, she left with her cubs. He held no grudge toward the attacking bear. Patrick appealed to wildlife officials to not kill the bruin; she was only protecting her young, as any good mother would do.

Jim Cole, a wildlife photographer in Montana, wore a pirate's patch over his left eye and deep scars on his face; he too had been mauled twice by grizzlies. Just weeks before his death at sixty, Cole exclaimed: "How lucky I am to still be ambulatory and in a place to bring more respect for the Great Bear." Cole never felt any animosity toward bears.

Not all victims of bear attack are so forgiving, and some die. But those who live and work around them are familiar with their natural behavior and hold high respect for them. These survival accounts followed by forgiveness clearly demonstrate the importance of understanding. When one understands the situation of those who attacked or offended, only someone without much compassion would forge an attitude of unforgiveness. The Buddha is credited with saying that when one understands, one holds no grievances. (*NG* 9-18-15)

Forgiveness as a Process with Ups and Downs

The process is ongoing – sometimes painful, at other times freeing and peaceful. After years of struggling to make the marriage whole, I left. The three children I bore were in mid-life with their own struggles. It came as a shock when my two sons 'divorced' me. They took sides, perhaps from male bounding and loyalty to their father. They were both aware that the 'match' of their father and mother was not the best. But they had had nearly a half-century of dependable, loving, solid family life, with support from both parents when they had their struggles with life.

It is now nearly six years since the divorce. And still they do not speak to me or respond to correspondence. They have never inquired of me about the family split. They have heard nothing negative about their father from me – and won't. He was a good father and provider. No one knew or will know what went on behind closed doors. The separation did not result from the children. It was between only their father and me.

It is difficult for me to understand their position. I left to take care of myself after serving as caretaker of others my whole adult life. My dad had taught: "Everyone must do their own thinking, and decide for themselves." I believed this and taught it to the children. They had always been encouraged to explore new things, to exclude nothing from their thinking, to decide for themselves. When events in their adult lives arose, both parents supported them, regardless of how we thought.

At first, I appealed to them by phone. Letters and cards followed, without details of my own struggles, but explaining that the split had nothing to do with them, and that it was between just their father and me. There was never any response. I don't know if the letters were even read. I couldn't believe they would take a position like this. Their father lived close to them and even with them for a time. I was far away. Disbelief dominated my thinking. I didn't feel anger (perhaps it was), but disbelief and an aching heart – all because of loss of contact. I cried a lot and wallowed in sorrow over a missing part of myself. At the same time, I was freed from years of confinement in a stressful relationship, one based on my commitment to marriage vows long honored. My life had become one of 'walking on eggshells.' Spells of depression and despair were secrets held within. It became more and more difficult to recover from the explosive rage directed at me and from the escape into silence when rational discussion ceased.

I have grown to understand that accepting 'what is' leads to peace. Being present in the Now and not laboring in the past or worrying about the future is the center-point between happiness and sadness. I know that place is peace, though sometimes I forget.

My sons now do their own thinking and decision-making. I must allow and accept that; in doing so, I free myself from attachment. They will never be separated from me in my heart, and in the sense of eternal love. The separation is temporary, of this world. I must remember this. By detaching from the desire to be with them physically, I can continue to love them, and let the hurt go. If forgiveness plays its role here, so be it. I know I must forgive myself for any offense I caused them by my decisions. My decisions and journey have led me to a peaceful life. Perhaps their decisions and journeys will do the same for them someday. (SM)

Learning to Forgive, and its Benefits

Forgiving is an unending process that yields the most precious gifts of the human heart. As a younger person, I felt my heart would break (to be forever broken!) as I faced, my deepest personal wounds. Over the years, more and more, forgiving has become a daily, ongoing, self-generating process, motivated by an expansiveness of heart that is its reward. Forgiving becomes an irresistible, beautiful, generous, and fulfilling experience.

At this time in my life, the impulse to forgive comes from noticing my heart is withholding, that a part of me has shut down, is closed off. I find this feeling to be painful. Along the way, I came to realize that forgiving does not have much to do with the other person, what they did or didn't do, or how they acted. Their gift to me is the opportunity to forgive. Forgiveness has to do with the state and quality of my own heart and mind. I am only harming myself by not forgiving.

Another important insight came as I realized that forgiving doesn't mean ignoring or not using good judgment in relating with people. Forgiving means my heart opens to others regardless of their behavior, good or bad. With forgiveness, I see even more clearly how to interact in a way that is skillful and wise – no matter what the circumstances. I'm able to see the other person's pain, their disturbance and confusion. With forgiveness, my heart softens into compassion and blessing, wishing that the other person become free of suffering as well.

Now, after many years of practicing forgiveness, I can begin to forgive even the seemingly unforgiveable – both personal and universal – as the unconsciousness of the human mind plays itself out in the world. I am beginning to see that we are all simply seeking love. We become the generators, the very source of love as we realize that our true nature is this limitless exuding of acceptance and joy. The uplift and expansive love that begins to shine in our hearts becomes so wonderful that nothing could limit or contain it.

Everyday, there is this letting go, this forgiving, this handing over to the All the process of living, so far beyond my personal mind's preference or ability to decipher or define. What I have realized so far in my lifetime is a knowing beyond learning that comes from trusting the deepest knowing of my heart. This knowing 'remembers' that love is foundational, indestructible, and unlimited.

It may be hard to forgive at first because we feel like we are giving up something precious of ourselves. The result of forgiving, however, is actually the opposite. When we are able to give up our self-image and our 'treasured wounds,' we actually become alive to what can't be wounded and is ever available, never threatened. It is who we are beyond anything we could ever hold ourselves to be. It is Love – bigger and more potent than any one person. (Joti Royster)

Forgiveness Overcomes 'Unjust' Courtroom Verdict

In 1990, thirteen-year-old Ian was given a handgun by older boys and joined them in a holdup. When the victim resisted, Ian shot her in the face, a shot that wounded but did not kill her. He was arrested, convicted, and sentenced to life in prison without parole – and put in solitary confinement. He was permitted one call a month; in 1992. he called the woman he had shot and "spilled out an emotional apology, expressing his deep regret and remorse."

The heart-felt sincerity of the apology moved the victim to become an ardent supporter of her shooter. Her forgiveness and confidence in the teenager led her to work tirelessly to convince the court to reduce his sentence. After eighteen years of uninterrupted solitary confinement, Ian was finally released from the cruel severity of his punishment for a non-lethal assault. The assiduous help from the victim-benefactor, along with the Equal Justice Initiative (an organization founded and led by Bryan Stevenson), enabled Ian to regain his freedom. (*JM*)

* * * *

In these events, we see how social and legal resistance to a remedial rather than punitive attitude in our courts may be softening slowly through individuals and organizations that recognize the liberating value of forgiveness.

A Heart of Unimaginable Forgiveness

Immaculée (im-<u>mac</u>-u-lay) Ilibagiza (i-lee-bah-<u>gee</u>-za) was a young university student in Rwanda during the 1994 genocide who spent ninety-one days in a three by four foot room with seven other women while the massacre was underway. The pastor of a local church secreted the women, ages seven to fifty-five, in the space behind the bathroom door, itself hidden by a self-standing wardrobe cabinet. Because of the sporadic invasion of the home by the rampaging killers, the women had to remain silent, communicating with hand gestures and lip reading. Only during the deep of the night, and then with risk, could they use the toilet. There was no sink and showering was out of the question. They took turns sitting, standing, and sleeping; they became grubby and odorous; they all lost weight (only meager quantities of food was available, also restricted to night delivery). Immaculée lost forty pounds from her former weight of one hundred fifteen pounds. When the women finally left their three-month confinement, they passed a mirror in the pastor's house: their cheeks had shrunk; their eyes had receded; their ribs stuck out; and their worn, soiled clothes hung loosely.

For centuries, the somewhat shorter in stature and larger in numbers Hutu mixed harmoniously with their Tutsi cattle-herding neighbors, sharing the same language, religion, and culture. With the arrival of European colonialism, however, differences and tensions appeared, stimulated by the economic and political aims of the occupiers. One authority declared that the hatred between the communities arose from the political propaganda of the German and Belgian rulers, who asserted their divisive objectives in many ways, one by requiring the Hutu and Tutsi to carry identity cards.

The mass killings began when the more populous, less well-educated peasant Hutu, then governing the country, turned against their former, more aristocratic Tutsi rulers. As better-educated and wealthier Tutsis, Immaculée's family came under attack by their neighbors, in spite of the fact that her parents had been their benefactors. The family home was ransacked and then completely burned out leaving only mud block walls.

The enraged Hutu mobs invaded packed churches where Tutsi refugees had sought safety, thereby unwittingly permitting the killers to mutilate and murder in mass. None were spared, male or female, elderly or infant, healthy or handicapped. Guns were rare; spears, knives, and machetes were most often used. I won't describe any actual murders; only indicate that they often entailed ridicule, mockery, torture, and mutilation, ending in gruesome death. A million are believed to have died.

Immaculée requested a Bible, which she carefully studied and assimilated. Long periods of time were spent in prayer, using a rosary and addressed to Mother Mary, Jesus, and God. Learning to forgive did not come easily. At times, intense hatred toward the killers rose in her; she wanted to take up weapons and kill those doing the killing. Her intense study and prayer, however, in spite of her confinement and suffering, led eventually to an unshakable conviction that only forgiveness powered by love can heal and restore harmony, within oneself and among people.

Having previously learned French in school, Immaculée requested a French to English dictionary along with a couple of English books. By the time the fighting ended, she had learned enough rudimentary English to get a low-paying job with the United Nation peacekeepers in Rwanda. Her continued self-improvement enabled her to gain on-going employment with the U.N., move to New York City, become an American citizen, marry an American, and raise two children. After describing her experiences in *Left to Tell: Discovering God Amidst the Rwandan Holocaust*, Immaculée received so many requests for public talks that (at this writing) she travels the world describing the forgiveness she discovered under the unspeakable horrors of her life in the country of her birth.

Forgiveness has come to occupy a central, essential, and powerful position in Immaculée's life. We'll conclude this brief account of her life by describing one event during the nation-wide effort in Rwanda to bring about reconciliation between the Hutus and Tutsis. After the extensive fact-finding that identified the murders, Immaculée was invited to meet face-to-face with the man who had led the gang that killed her family, the same man who had come to her 'sanctuary' twice, calling for her by name in order to kill her as well. Hearing him madly screaming, knowing he was only inches away, nearly caused her to succumb to fear. This man, Felicien by name, formerly a successful businessman with whose children Immaculée had played, was required to come before her and admit his crimes of killing members of her family, burning her home, and stealing her father's farm machinery. When he entered the room, he fell to the floor, his head down, shaking with fear and shame. On insistence from the officer, he looked up, his and Immaculée's eyes briefly met. Immaculée wrote: "Felicien was sobbing ... I could feel his shame. I reached out, touched his hands lightly, and quietly said what I'd come to say. I forgive you." (*LTT* 204, *passim*)

* * * *

This and the previous chapters have confirmed for me – beyond any doubt what-so-ever – that the two most powerful assertions one person can offer another, each leading to accord and harmony, are: "I love you," and "I forgive you." "I love you" is limitedly in its sincerity, however, if it is conditional. "I forgive you" is impossible without unconditional love.

Finally, in its fullness – in its absolute fullness – "I love you" requires no forgiveness; there is never need for it.

Chapter Six: Death, The Final Detachment?

> Birth and death are arbitrary lines drawn in the sands of time, ever disappearing into the eternal. (Jim Royster, with a nod to Lao Tzu)

Part I: Setting the Framework for Our Investigation
A. Intrinsic Challenges in the Study of Death

Everything in this chapter written by the author as well as a fair amount from other contributors is little more than hearsay – along with a bit of speculation, guessing, and hoping. Even if someone were medically certified as dead and returned to report his or her experience, it would be one person's memory and interpretation of their dying experience. The only way we can know what dying is like is to die.

This observation by no means minimizes the importance of the topic. We're all going to die. Many of us want to know as much as we can about the experience of dying. And that is exactly what we're going to be covering: the experience of dying. The phrase *the experience of dying*, however, represents a related issue that seems to weaken further the prospect of gaining any degree of certainty about what we will encounter in our own dying. What we learn from others lacks the precision we'd like when learning about death. This is so because we can never know the experience of another since all experience is entirely personal and private. We can't even know our own experience except when and as it is actually happening. When we recall it (to review it for ourselves or to share it with another) we are already interpreting it, which is not the same as the experience itself. We have no choice but to interpret all experience in light of the range of our previous experiences, broadly speaking, through our culture, our religion, our education, our activities, and our involvements. Even as this is true for each of us, it is true of every experience – actually, interpreted experience – that we ever come to know.

Since the existence of an afterlife is a controversial topic and one without the possibility of logical, rational, or scientific proof, this chapter offers evidence for an afterlife without expecting to settle the questions once and for all. If our commitment is to truth no matter where truth leads, then we must stay open to the possibility of life after death even while respecting the viewpoints of those who deny it, and also acknowledge our own doubts and reservations. The underlying assumption/presumption in the chapter is that we human beings – created as we are by whatever it is that created all that is – will experience and be aware of an afterlife. After briefly considering some common views about death, we'll delve into the evidence for an afterlife, that is, for the continuity of consciousness beyond death.

B. Common Views and Attitudes toward Death

Talk about death is unwelcome for many, maybe most. It's a virtual elephant-in-the-room topic – obvious to everyone but not to be mentioned. When faced with the inevitability of death, some will share Woody Allen's sentiment: "I'm really not afraid of death; I just don't want to be there when it happens." Not being there may be impossible even for those who die instantly, while in a coma, or during sleep, because some investigators believe that awareness continues for a period of time even after the death of the body has been medically established. This may be the case for those who experience the dying process and then return to life, what is known as the Near-Death Experience (NDE). We'll soon look at some of these experiences.

When the death of someone we know occurs, the degree of shock and sorrow is typically deepest for children and the young, then steadily lessens as the age of the deceased has advanced and health conditions have deteriorated. The emotional disturbance may be heightened when death is the result of an accident, violence, or in the line of duty, such as war. Our reaction moderates somewhat in cases of terminal illnesses, when pain can be reduced no further, and when the dying person feels their life is over and they want to die. My mother used to visit an elderly friend to provide a little companionship. On entering the lady's home one afternoon, she found her rigid, motionless, and stretched out on her couch. When asked what she was doing, she replied: "I'm trying to die."

Denial and utter resistance to death is front and center for a few. Some contend that human life can be sustained more or less indefinitely and are trying to work out ways by which this can be done, perhaps even extending individual life for centuries. Others focus on techniques like cryo-preservation – freezing the body just before death in hope that at some time in the future science will develop the ability to cure the disease in question and restore life. Futurist Ray Kurzweil believes that digital immortality (uploading our minds into computers) will be possible before mid-century; these digital uploads will then be able to hop from electronic host to host. Kurzweil also maintains that nanobots can be put into our bodies that will strengthen our immune systems and eliminate disease.

Rather than extend life, some cut it short voluntarily by committing suicide. This kind of death seems welcomed by some, and endured by others who succumb to it. Sometimes, no reason is given but may be discovered after the fact (e.g., drug induced mental disturbance). Some people cite hopelessness, a lost sense of life's meaning and worth, or terminal medical prognosis insuring progressive suffering. When Arthur Koestler, a political journalist, award-winning novelist, and philosopher, was diagnosed with terminal leukemia, he intentionally and methodically prepared for his death and that of his third wife. Though his wife was not ill, she voluntarily assisted and accompanied him – presumably out of love. Michael Scammell describes what happened:

> On Tuesday, March 1, 1983, Arthur Koestler and his wife, Cynthia, entered their sitting room at 8 Montpelier Square, London, sat down facing each other, he in his favorite leather armchair, she on the couch, and poured themselves their usual drink before dinner. Arthur's was his favorite brandy; Cynthia's was scotch. The only difference between this and a thousand similar evenings was the presence on a small table between them of a bottle of wine, a large bottle of ... sleeping tablets, a jar of honey, and some extra wineglasses. Arthur and Cynthia swallowed about half the tablets each, washed them down with wine and honey, then sipped their brandy and scotch. Within half an hour or so they were unconscious, within an hour completely dead, and they remained there, fully clothed, for a day and a half, until their Brazilian maid came to clean the house on Thursday morning. (*K* xv)

Culturally, suicide is almost universally opposed, even scorned and deemed to be illegal. It may be time, however, for liberal, progressive communities to re-evaluate the issue. Koestler's reasoned and deliberate death offers the opportunity for seriously considering the legitimacy of euthanasia under special circumstances (although his wife's reasoning might still be questioned). The rationale for this position is implicit in the overall viewpoint and contention of *Undoing*, but will become apparent only as the book is thoughtfully read and finished.

Additional striking examples of voluntary death exist. Hindus recognize the legitimacy of autonomous death by fasting. Elderly Jain monks of India may also embrace death by giving up food and water. Dozens of contemporary Tibetan Buddhists have undergone self-conflagration to demonstrate their opposition to Chinese occupation and repression. These forms of voluntary death are usually honored in the cultures where they occur. Quite different are terrorist attacks by means of suicide that cause the death of innocent people and massive destruction. While relatively small religio-political groups support and applaud these horrendous attacks, the vast majority of humans worldwide are appalled. Many other unusual and anomalous ways of dying could be discussed. Our main objective, however, is to investigate what we may call natural, usual or customary ways of dying.

C. Stages in the Dying Process

Our understanding of the dying process today is largely due to the research of Elisabeth Kübler-Ross, Swiss physician and author of twenty books, who mapped specific stages of dying based on tens of thousands of encounters with dying patients. The stages in the death process are remarkably similar to those faced by the family and closest friends during their grieving process. The stages begin with (1) denial, then move through (2) anger, (3) bargaining, (4) depression, and finally (5) acceptance just prior to (6) death itself. Background hope for the return of health and continuing life is absent in the denial stage but runs through the rest. There may be some change in progression through the stages as well as shifting back and forth. In other words, the stages are not fixed and absolute. They are, nonetheless, reported by multitudes of dying persons as well as those who offer love, support, and guidance. These are the stages we are all likely to experience.

How does detachment figure into the dying process? The main point in detaching during the dying stages is not different from what we've already discovered. Whatever is currently occupying my attention is not me; I am the witness of that, prior to it. I can rest in and as the prior awareness that is intrinsically without attachment. This occurs naturally when I drop/withdraw/ release the personalized meanings of me-ness that I have projected (which are now seen to be non-essential and arbitrary). Emotions of resistance have been released (undone), and therefore the changes sensed are not happening to the *never-changing I*.

We release attachment to the idea that I am dying; we let go of the presumed sense of the one dying being who/what I am. We don't struggle against the thought of me dying. On the contrary, we take the stance exemplified by the world's sages and saints, the contention affirmed throughout *Undoing*, namely that I am prior to what I witness, to what appears in my mind. I am the Subject that is observing mental and emotional objects. This stance is taken at each stage in the dying process. We endeavor to be fully present with the current state of mind by acknowledging the thoughts, resistance, and fears that may constitute the immediate content of the mind, all the while knowing that the content is not my true identity. Not getting caught in it, detaching from it, smoothly ushers in the next stage. Acceptance of each emerging stage – freely allowing however much time it may require – serves as the psychospiritual base from which the subsequent stage will arise.

When coming to the sixth and last stage, those returning from a Near-Death Experience (NDE) say that sometimes a choice is given, for the imagery during the final stage may include departed relatives inviting the one that is dying to join them in the Hereafter, or alternatively suggesting they return to earthly life as the second option. Indications of the nature of each choice may also be given. Often one returns to his or her previous life on earth, perhaps to learn or to do more. However, some people that have experienced NDE have reported that there was no option offered for choosing whether to live or die. Nevertheless, a prevailing Western worldview seems to be that at death, the person will continue to exist in some way that reflects the quality of life he or she lived on earth.

Part II: Evidence for Life After Death

A. Near Death Experiences (NDE)

I personally or with a family member or friend frequently conclude that a NDE is, or can be, a vital, moving, and rewarding experience. Whether it is or isn't depends on: (1) the depth and breadth of maturity and understanding gained in one's lifetime; (2) the quality of the moral and spiritual life lived; and (3) the ability to release blockages that may still exist by means of detachment. Evidence in support of this three-fold claim is set forth in the pages that follow.

* * * *

1. Anita Moorjani's Illness, Coma, And Cure

After two close acquaintances died of cancer, Anita became fearful of the disease and took up a lifestyle designed to avoid it. "It seemed to me," she wrote, "that everything caused cancer. I read about how pathogens in the environment and foods that were carcinogenic. Microwaves, using plastic containers for food, eating anything with preservatives, using mobile phones – they all seemed to cause cancer." Her inordinate fear of the disease expanded to a fear of the treatment. Chemotherapy had not saved her best friend. "My experience of life was getting smaller and smaller, ... the world was a menacing place. And then I was diagnosed with cancer."

Even though most people advised against it, Anita opted for alternative forms of healing and reported:

> I tried faith healing, praying, meditation, and energy-healing sessions. I read every book I could get my hands on about cancer. I worked on forgiveness therapy, and forgave everyone I knew – then forgave them again. I traveled through India and China, meeting Buddhist monks, Indian yogis, and enlightened masters, hoping that they'd help me find answer that would lead to healing. I tried being vegan, meditating on mountain tops, yoga,

Ayurveda, chakra balancing, Chinese herbal medicine, pranic healing, and Chi Gong.

All her efforts were to no avail. Her body stopped taking in nutrients. Her breathing required a continual supply of oxygen from a tank. Her strength diminished, and she could no longer walk. Her weight fell below ninety pounds. On February 2, 2006, she became unconscious and was rushed to a hospital. En route and in a coma, Anita exclaimed to herself: "Oh my God, I feel incredible! I'm so free and light. I'm not feeling any more pain in my body. Where has my fear gone?" When arriving at the hospital along with her emotionally distraught family, the oncologist said to her husband: "Your wife's heart may still be beating but, she not really in there. It's too late to save her."

Anita was fully conscious while in the coma. From her expanded consciousness, she was aware of the events happening around her and even in other rooms of the hospital and at great distance. With her inner voice (words could not be sounded), she tried to comfort her family and to assure her brother, who was rushing in an airplane to reach her, that she would be waiting for him, and he need not be anxious. Free at last from the confusion and perplexity of her life, especially the pain caused by the lemon-size tumors from the base of her skull to below her abdomen, and the large, open, seeping lesions that covered her body, she never felt more confident, relaxed, and free. She asserted:

> I felt no emotional attachment to my seemingly lifeless body as it lay there on the hospital bed. It didn't feel as though it were mine. It looked far too small and insignificant to have housed what I was experiencing. I felt free, liberated, and magnificent. Every pain, ache, sadness, and sorrow was gone! I felt completely unencumbered. I couldn't recall feeling this way before – not ever.

From the vantage point of her expanded consciousness, Anita could see how she had curtailed and convoluted her previous life to meet the expectations of others; how she had repressed her own feelings, understanding, and viewpoints; and how she had unwittingly denied her own authenticity. The words and expressions she used to identify her inauthenticity include: "my fears," "my worries," "I wasn't expressing my true self," "I realized how harshly I'd treated myself and judged myself," and "I'd never loved myself, valued myself." Her outlook not only prohibited her from forgiving herself but forgiving others as well. This inauthentic pattern of living, she came to believe, gave rise to a reversal of the natural energy and power of her body so that instead of being directed inwardly and outwardly in a manner appropriate to the uniqueness of Anita herself, it reversed and turned against the healthful trajectory of her life in the form of cancer. In her own words, the cancer "was just my own life force expressing itself as cancer because I didn't allow it to manifest as the magnificent, powerful force of Anita."

Anita came to this understanding of her personal role in the cancer as part of a much larger view regarding the universe and the divine. She exclaimed: "The universe makes sense! Why do I suddenly understand all this? Who's giving me this information? Is it God? Krishna? Buddha? Jesus? And then I was overwhelmed by the realization that God isn't a being, but a state of being ... and I was now that state of being." Reflection on these insights led Anita to conclude: "The greatest truths of the universe don't lie outside. They lie deep within us, in the magnificence of our heart, mind, and soul."

Drawing from insights gained during her coma and NDE, Anita credited the actual beginning of her dying process to her earliest 'indoctrination,' an indoctrination that – with her unwitting cooperation – impeded the free expression of her inherent nature as a divine, magnificent human being. This inevitable cultural, familial, educational, religious conditioning overpowered her birthright authenticity and caused the distortion and repression of her uniqueness and magnificence.

What Anita Moorjani Learned About Life And How To Live

The following words, reversing much of what she had previously assumed and consciously believed, depict some of the main insights Anita gained during the thirty hours of her coma and NDE experience:

I saw divinity in everything.

I found myself with nothing but compassion for all the criminals and terrorists in the world, as well as their victims.

I was no longer able to view the world in terms of 'us' and 'them'. There's no 'them'; it's all 'us.'

We're all spiritual, regardless of what we do or believe. We can't be anything else, because that's who we are – spiritual beings.

There's no separation except in our own minds.

It was *me* I hadn't forgiven, not other people. *I* was the one who was judging me, whom I'd forsaken, and whom I didn't love enough.

In my NDE state, I realized that the entire universe is composed of unconditional love, and I'm an expression of this. Every atom, molecule, quark, and tetra quark, is made of love. (*DTBM passim*)

2. Dr. Jill Bolte Taylor's Stroke of Insight

Strokes caused by too little or too much blood to the brain usually leave their victims paralyzed and severely handicapped for life, even after extensive therapy. This stroke victim not only survived and recovered but was aware of her stroke as it was occurring – and also aware of heretofore unknown and incomparably appealing sensations.

Jill Bolte Taylor is a Harvard-educated brain anatomist who, at thirty-seven years of age, experienced a massive stroke that wiped out the normal functioning of the left hemisphere of her brain. Excessive bleeding permeated this half of her brain to such an extent that it took her nearly five hours to marshal enough of her customary skill and resources to summon help. Given the nature of the injury, it's amazing that she could do this at all. In her own words: "I could not walk, talk, read, write, or recall any aspects of my life." Such obvious efforts as dialing 911, calling her landlady, or hailing a stranger didn't even occur to her. Somehow, she struggled against all odds and managed a phone call to her office. A colleague recognized the sound of her voice amidst the "grunts and groans" and sent an ambulance. Jill describes the extraordinary split occurring within her self-awareness:

> Deep within a sacred cocoon with a silent mind and tranquil heart, I felt the enormousness of my energy lift. My body fell limp, and my consciousness rose to a slower vibration. I clearly understood that I was no longer the choreographer of this life. In the absence of sight, sound, touch, smell, taste, and fear, I felt my spirit surrender its attachment to this body and I was released from pain.

Thus far we have seen the struggle of Dr. Taylor with the nearly total absence of her familiar and highly developed left brain, the brain most valued and cultivated in nearly all contemporary cultures. Even as the two hemispheres interact in processing information, the left tends to be dominant in about eight-five percent of the US population. This half of the brain excels in rationality, language (including verbal 'chatter'), mathematics, linear thought, the sense of individuality (the ego), and making judgments. Jill's stroke wiped out these and comparable functions, abilities on which she had built her identity and skills. In her own words: "Dr. Jill Bolte Taylor died that morning and no longer existed."

What did she experience in her intact right brain during this excruciating ordeal? We have seen above her newly discovered capacity for surrender and the loss of pain. In addition, her self-sense expanded beyond the boundary of her body, she "felt like a genie liberated from its bottle." She felt euphoric, as spirit flowing smoothly; she felt what it's like to simply be, not constantly doing; she felt joyful, tranquil, and blissful.

Absent were such previously burdensome emotions as anger and hostility. Gone was the constant drive to hurry, to achieve.

A summary statement focuses on the extraordinary expansion of her usual self-sense:

> I was no longer isolated and alone. My soul was as big as the universe and frolicked with glee in a boundless sea. My eyes could no longer perceive things as things that were separated from one another. Instead, the energy of everything blended together. We all flowed *en masse*, together as *one*. I was not capable of experiencing separation or individuality.

Two weeks after the onset of the stroke, Jill underwent surgery that left her with a nine-inch scar above her left ear. Inestimably more important was the possibility first of regaining her former health, life skills, and medical expertise, and second of modeling her new life based on the remarkable discoveries during her near-death experience. Requiring multiple forms of extensive therapy and steady patience, her healing and restoration slowly progressed over a period of eight or ten years (*MSOI passim*).

Dr. Taylor's stroke – given her expertise in brain anatomy and astute perception of her experiences during the stroke – has enabled her to offer valuable insight into our human identity. Although as a scientist she continues to function within the assumptions of the dualistic world, her new understanding has given her the ability to *decide* and *choose* how she will respond to what she experiences. She can *decide* now on the spot whether to respond from her left brain or her right brain. If an emotion arises from the left brain, she allows herself ninety-seconds to *decide* if or how she'll manifest that emotion. For example, if anger arises, a minute and a half is what she has determined sufficient time to *choose* her response. If her *decision* is to allow expression, she then will *choose* just how to do so, rather than responding automatically. Without a doubt, this exemplifies a significant understanding and skill in overcoming uncontrolled outbursts. Who would not have high regard for Dr. Taylor's discoveries and her astute conclusions?

* * * *

The dual-hemispheric view of the brain (coupled with Dr. Taylor's stroke experience) provides several helpful metaphors – not assertions of proven fact, but "as if" parallels. The Self-self and Divine-human distinctions originate with the right and left brain (Self and Divine from the right brain, and self and human from the left brain). Sometimes this idea is expressed thus: We are spiritual beings (right brain) having a human experience (left brain). The right brain symbolizes our essential birthright and the left brain our human potential. Our origin at birth may be seen as if we enter the world with a right brain informed by the qualities of the divine and in the course of growing up receive into the left brain the 'humanized' features of our cultural world. The process of detaching from left-brain conditioning presented throughout *Undoing* will allow free manifestation of the right brain qualities.

In conclusion, I'd like to offer a view for which there is growing evidence, namely that it is possible to so thoroughly integrate the conditioning and impulses of the left brain into the 'consciousness' of the right brain that the latter will naturally predominate and prevail so that an individual will neither react impulsively nor need to deliberate and decide how to respond, for the response will occur spontaneously as a result of that total integration. Many of the founders, saints, sages, and others of the world's spiritual traditions have proven their ability to respond instantly out of unconditional love. Their ability to do this may stem from their spiritual discipline, practices that have synchronized the left brain so thoroughly into the right that, in actual fact, the right brain has become dominant and the left brain simply supportive. The brain's anatomical link between the two halves (the *corpus callosum)* would seem to make this possible. How hopeful is this prospect for humanity's future!

B. *After Death Communication (ADC)*

1. A Personal Indication

Until about ten or fifteen years ago, I oscillated between denying, doubting, and holding an open mind about what I – and most others – then called reincarnation. However, one morning when leisurely reading the autobiography of Huston Smith, arguably the most prominent historian of religions in America at the time, I discovered that he believed in reincarnation and provided evidence for it. For the first time in my life, I suddenly found myself believing in the likelihood of past-life communication. At just that moment, a crash occurred in our TV room. My wife and I rushed in to find a photograph of my deceased mother lying facedown on the hardwood floor. The photo, the glass, and the frame were all undamaged. A light wind was coming in from an open window, but the photograph had been setting back into the bookcase where a breeze was unlikely of reaching it. Was this an event confirming my revised view, an event from beyond the supposed assumption that death represents a 'solid' boundary in consciousness? Events like these offer evidence of possible communication from beyond the grave.

2. Scholarly Documentation

Dr. Gary E. Schwartz, Harvard graduate, professor at the University of Arizona and a specialist in studies of the evolution of consciousness and the foremost authority on trans-temporal communication, is one of the scholars currently employing the full scope of reason and scientific method in the study of life after death. His many publications, based to the extent possible on careful scientific controls, present convincing evidence of the reality of trans-death communication. Drawing from his criteria for evaluating the afterlife, Schwartz concludes: "The probability that our consciousness survives physical death ... is the same probability that the light from distant stars continues long after the star has died. And just as the information of individual stars is not lost in the vastness of space, neither is our individual information lost as well" (*AAIH* 449). This is an extraordinary declaration.

Applying his rigorous approach to the study of afterlife evidence, Schwartz contributed the scholarly component of a recent book with the improbable title, *An Atheist in Heaven*. The book focuses primarily (though not exclusively) on communication from a deceased elderly atheist who had agreed with his younger friend that he would try to make contact in whatever way he could after he died. Over a hundred and fifty of these phenomena are described in the book. Examples of these After-Death Communications include: the sudden appearance of an object previously absent; apparitions; a portrait painted before a person's death showing a clock with the exact time of the subject's death; a blank piece of paper that was found later with printing on it; a dormant, unwound clock suddenly ticking; and many more (*AAIH* 475ff).

While somewhat different in import, events in the natural world that accompany death are frequently reported. When my granddaughter learned one morning that her mother had died during the night, she discovered that her wristwatch had not only stopped running (perhaps due to not winding) but had actually broken at the precise time of her mother's death. Ken Wilber has noted that at the moment of his wife's death, a gale-force wind that had been blowing suddenly stopped. During my mother's last night on earth, the bouquet of daffodils that had leaned during the day toward the light of the nearby window shifted nearly a hundred and eighty degrees in her direction. While events such as these prove nothing, their timing warrants consideration.

C. Past Life Memories (PLM)

1. The Case Of Shanti Devi

In 1902 in Mathura, India, a girl was born and named Lugdi. As was the custom then, when she was ten years old her parents 'married' her to a shopkeeper. After puberty, she became pregnant but lost the child at birth. Following another pregnancy at the age of twenty-four, she gave birth to a son through Cesarean section, but died a few days later.

Slightly less than two years later in 1926, a girl was born in Delhi, some one-hundred and twenty-five miles from Mathura (a three-and-a-half hour journey by car today). Named Shanti Devi, she was a quiet child who hardly spoke until she was four years old. Then she surprised her family by telling them that her real home was in Mathura where she had a husband and a son. She said her real name was Chaubine (which means the wife of Chaubey), her husband owned a cloth shop, that he was fair-skinned (a positive quality in India), wore reading glasses, and had big wart on his left cheek. She described the dresses she had worn during that previous life and the kind of sweets found in her former home. She gave specific evidence about the medical procedure that preceded her death, details that amazed the family physician.

By the time Shanti Devi was six, her parents realized that these memories were more than just a child's fantasy. Over the years, she revealed many additional details about her former life and began to insist on going to Mathura. A relative and high school teacher in Delhi told Shanti Devi he would take her there if she would tell him the name of her husband, something she had not done previously. She whispered in his ear that his name was Pandit Kedarnath Chaubey. On other occasions when asked his name, she blushed and said only that she'd recognize him when she saw him. (Reluctance to name one's husband is customary in India.) When asked if she could find her way to her former home from the railway station in Mathura, she said she could. She also spoke of a well in the courtyard, and a place where she had buried some money.

The relative contacted the former husband in Mathura, who confirmed most of the details. He then arranged for one of his relatives who lived in Delhi to meet Shanti Devi. When this took place, Shanti Devi recognized him as her husband's cousin. The cousin then persuaded Kedarnath Chaubey to come to Delhi himself and meet Shanti Devi. When this occurred, a test/trick had been previously arranged; her former husband was introduced to Shanti Devi as her uncle. She immediately blushed and turned aside while saying, "No, he is not my husband's brother. He is my husband himself." As Kedarnath Chaubey became further acquainted with Shanti Devi and the details she revealed, he readily acknowledged that she was indeed his former wife, Lugdi.

The number of specific details recounted by Shanti Devi created a lot of interest in India and began to be reported in the newspapers. Mahatma Gandhi heard about the case and contacted her. He personally arranged for a committee of fifteen well-known authorities to investigate and, if possible, accompany Shanti Devi to Mathura. The delegation traveled by rail in November 1935; Shanti Devi was nine at the time. Not only did she guide the party successfully to places previously identified, she also added details about conditions existing when she had lived in Mathura, conditions confirmed by residents.

What makes the Shanti Devi event unusual is the extent to which it has been studied since the 1930s, namely, by hundreds of scholars, researchers, critics, religious authorities, and the media. It remains the most thoroughly documented and substantiated PLM case during that period. Several contemporary authorities who study these events with rigorous scholarly standards acknowledge the authenticity of Shanti Devi's account. One of these is Dr. Ian Stevenson, an internationally respected professor at the University of Virginia where he worked for fifty years, wrote around three hundred papers, and published fourteen books. He travelled for forty years around the world investigating about three thousand cases of children who claimed to remember past lives. On one of his trips, he interviewed Shanti Devi, her father, other witnesses, and the husband she claimed from a former life. Stevenson concluded: "She made at least twenty-four statements of her memories that matched the verified facts" (*SSD*).

Sture Lonnerstrand of Sweden was a staunch skeptic and critic of PLM. He set out to disprove what seemed preposterous in light of his rational, scientific stance. When he heard about Shanti Devi and the mounting evidence supporting her memory and claim, he decided to go to India to prove the evidence wrong, intending to settle the matter once for all in his own mind. In the end, he reversed his view and wrote a book about his own investigation, concluding that the evidence was conclusive (*IHLB*).

2. The Case of James Leininger

This case undermines a common rationalist objection to examples of reincarnation that dismisses them because they so frequently occur in Asia where such things are routinely believed, perhaps even encouraged and promoted. Rather than carry any validity, however, this seeming objection is only calling attention to the fact that children will not reveal their inner selves if doing so is met with rebuff and ridicule. On the other hand, if allowed, or even encouraged, their sharing will occur more frequently and often lead to verifiable facts.

My wife, a retired primary school teacher, tells about one of her pupils who said she saw colored lights around people (i.e., auras). When my wife acknowledged this in a positive tone, the child replied: "My mother tells me to stop talking like that." Children clearly learn to reveal or hide themselves depending on the attitudes they meet in adults.

About the time of his second birthday, James Leininger, who lived in Lafayette, Louisiana with his parents, began to have the same nightmare: it would wake him screaming, kicking his feet in the air, and flailing his arms. A year or so later, when his mother was able to hear his words more clearly, she heard: "Airplane crash. On fire! Little man can't get out." James's favorite toys had been airplanes, but he had never fanaticized about them crashing or burning, and he had never watched war movies or TV programs. His parents, Andrea and Bruce, were puzzled but recalled that his nightmares began after his father took him to a flight museum. When he played with his toy sit-in airplane, he would do a walk-around inspection before getting into it. When his mother referred to a bomb under one of his models, he corrected her by calling it a "drop tank," which she later learned was flight parlance for a fuel tank suspended under planes.

When James' nightmares continued, his parents took him to a therapist who treated disturbed children. He encouraged the parents to talk with James about his memories when he was relaxed, sleepy, and preparing for bed. James began to reveal many details: he was a pilot who flew a Corsair airplane, a plane that often got flat tires; he flew from a ship called "Natoma"; he was shot down by the Japanese in the battle of Iwo Jima; he had a buddy named Jack Larson, also a pilot. Each of these and other memories were eventually confirmed.

James's mother found it much easier to acknowledge and consider her son's stories than did his father. Bruce was a well-educated businessman who approached puzzling issues with reason and logic. He also regarded himself as a faithful Christian and one who did not believe in reincarnation. This disbelief – and the resulting effort to find other explanations for James' nightly disturbance and strange talk – required that he demonstrate the absence of any connection between his son's assertions and historic fact. Given his personal integrity and regard for reason, Bruce undertook an honest, systematic, and thorough investigation of his son's statements. His personal authenticity and love for his son required it.

Over the next several years, Bruce followed every lead he could find in order to confirm or deny the many things James had said and was continuing to say. He secured relevant documents, photocopied them as necessary, organized them into binders, and studied them carefully. He made countless telephone calls, wrote myriad of letters, travelled by car and air to near and distant places, became a specialist on the Natoma aircraft carrier, attended reunions of seamen and pilots who served on it, and interviewed anyone who might confirm or discredit something James had said about his former life. Several shelves were filled with well-organized material in his home office.

Bruce verified each of James' statements listed above and many more revealed in the next few years. He learned that an aircraft carrier named Natoma Bay fought in the Pacific in the Second World War, and that it supported the US Marines in their invasion of Iwo Jima. In a book on Iwo Jima, he found an aerial photo of Chichi-Jima, a Japanese supply center for battles in the area, where a devastating aerial fight had occurred in March 1945. After James announced that his previous name was also James, his father documented a James M. Huston, Jr. who had flown in the attack at Chichi-Jima, had been shot down, crashed into the harbor, and died on March 3, 1945. Bruce was able to interview a pilot who had flown in the same battle, who had made actual eye contact in the air with James Huston just before his plane was hit and then crashed into the harbor.

Bruce learned that James Huston had a sister living in California. She was able to confirm much of what young James had disclosed. Bruce sent her some of the documentation he had gathered about her younger brother. He also informed her that his son James mentioned paintings stored in the attic that their mother had done of his sisters ... information so specific that it amazed her. She sent back some of her brother's war possessions that had been returned to her, including his model of a Corsair, one of two planes her brother was known to have flown.

The number of specific memories that young James Leininger recalled about the life of the twenty-one-year-old World War II pilot, James M. Huston, Jr., who died in an air battle over Japan, remains uncounted. Most of them by far have been validated, making this one of the most accurately document cases of its kind, particularly among those originating in the West. In the end, Bruce became convinced that his son's memories were factual. He learned to live with the tension this caused with his disbelief in reincarnation.

Few if any additional memories are likely to come to James Leininger, now approaching adulthood, since specialists maintain that memories of this sort typically appear between the ages of two and four, and wane thereafter (*SS*).

D. Evidentiary Medium Messages (EMM)

1. Academic Research and Authentication

Mediums fall into groups: fake mediums (charlatans who prey on the public's gullibility); self-deluded mediums (those who think they're mediums but aren't); weak mediums (those who inject their own thinking); mediocre mediums; good mediums; and finally authentic, competent mediums. The latter group has developed their talent by studying at reputable schools of instruction, and have practiced and continued to learn from their experience over the years. Among these are some who have proven themselves reliable and trustworthy in previous careers, thereby giving evidence of personal competence and integrity.

2. Suzanne Giesemann

Suzanne Giesemann, is one of those competent mediums, and is currently involved with Dr. Schwartz and his research. He has declared: "Suzanne is among the most gifted and among the most credible of any genuine medium I have had the privilege to meet and work with over the past 15 years."

Schwartz created and has used for over ten years a rating scale of seven standards for evaluating the evidential reliability of medium transmissions. These include: 0, insufficient information to rate; 1, a clear miss; 2, a stretch (too vague); 3, possible; 4, probable; 5. a clear hit (obviously accurate); and 6, a super hit (accurate and meaningful). The message recipients are asked to rate each item received from the deceased, and provide a single sentence supporting their score. To serve as a control for authenticating the appropriateness of the messages from the departed, the recipients are also asked to do the same rating of the messages with someone they know well who is also close to the departed in age and experience. This is to determine the extent to which the specific messages given to them would ring true if they were from the alternate subject. (*WM* 173)

* * * *

Before the fall of the Twin Towers in New York City on September 11, 2001, Suzanne Giesemann was a Commander in the Navy, and aide-de-camp to the Chairman of the Joint Chiefs of Staff. She flew on Air Force One with the President, attended top-secret hearings on Capitol Hill and at the Pentagon, and participated in official business meetings in the Oval Office. A second calamity, this one even more personal, interrupted Suzanne's life when lightening killed both her twenty-seven-year-old stepdaughter Susan and her unborn son. Shortly before learning of the deaths, Suzanne had awakened from a dream in which Susan appeared and said: "We're fine. The baby and I are very happy." On numerous occasions since then, Susan has appeared to Suzanne and confirmed this first message.

These disastrous events – unexpected and astounding – precipitated an abrupt change in Suzanne Giesemann's life. After formal study at respected schools for medium training and extensive experience, she is now broadly recognized as a competent, evidentiary medium, one capable of bringing accurate messages from beyond death. Suzanne's former high-level of professionalism adds authenticity to her trans-temporal skills.

Before taking up specific examples, it will be helpful to discover Suzanne's state of awareness when receiving information from the other side. Fortunately, she has freely described her state of awareness when receiving 'downloads' from beyond, which generally come in the form of clairvoyance, clairaudience, and clairsentience (i.e., by seeing, hearing, and sensing). She notes that her energy field is more one of feeling or sensing with openness than one of thinking, which tends to be more confined and precise. She affirms: "When the energy fields is good, ... it's as if I become that person. I feel as if I know him or her, because for a short while, I *am* that person. With our consciousness joined, we become *one*." Suzanne was once concerned by the strong waves of vertigo that accompanied messages she received, until she realized that this simply represents "the higher vibration of those in spirit" (*WM* 24, 31).

Rather than summarize reports from several mediums, I've decided to provide examples of evidence only from Suzanne Giesemann because of her exceptional credibility. We will look at four cases, each in format quite different from the others: (a) separate sessions with three subjects who, unknown to Suzanne, were sisters; (b) Suzanne's communiqués from a young man killed by lightening; (c) public presentations with messages from a small coterie of departed souls known as Sanaya; and (d) a personal session with me.

a. Three Sisters

My two sisters, Joanne and Margaret, and I had individual readings with Suzanne over a three-month period, without Suzanne knowing we were related. Mother and Dad, both deceased, made their presence known to each of us with many common factors of their illnesses, life habits, and family patterns. In addition, each of us received evidence specific only to us, with most facts confirmed by the other sisters in light of our shared memories. Most memorable were evidence of the near drowning of Margaret, Mother's adoption, and Dad's career as a banker who 'counted every penny,' as he did in the family as well. [Author's note: I have read all three transcripts of these readings, studied the comparative spreadsheet of the evidence revealed to each of the sisters, and can confirm the accuracy of this testimonial.]

Joanne had lost her husband eleven months prior to her reading and had hoped to hear from him, but did not. A week or so after Joanne's reading, Suzanne was awakened at night with a "presence" and made notes of the message. It was my sister's deceased husband, Homer, with specific evidence and the message, "I hear her." Joanne confirmed the evidence of "fingering the necklace" (a gold cross from Homer she constantly fingers), roses and their scent (Homer's passion), his membership in a fraternal organization, his love of hunting and fishing, and a hammer and the words "cast in stone," referring to his skill as a stone mason. Joanne had "talked with him" since his death, but had never sensed his presence; thus, the message, "I hear her!"

Since these readings, I have been present for literally hundreds of messages through Suzanne from Sanaya, and have asked and received answers from this Spirit source to specific questions concerning both personal and global issues. Recently through a second reading after a loss of a dear friend, the messages I received from the deceased provided evidence known only to the deceased and me. Some were of physical items; others were of events. I was again 'blown away' by the accuracy of these messages from beyond. (Connie England)

b. 'Wolf' Pasakarnis

Given the similarity in their experiences, Suzanne readily scheduled a private reading with a couple whose son had been killed by lightening. Two days before the sitting, the son appeared to Suzanne unexpectedly and gave her a number of specific images. He also asked that the message be evaluated by Schwartz.

Suzanne typed the notes she sometimes takes when downloading from the spirit world and emailed them to Mike and Beth Pasakarnis, parents of Wolf. They readily confirmed most of the fifty-eight items. Mike was hugely impressed. Beth confirmed: "There was no doubt that it was him with a few powerful specific messages" (*WM* 29). The parents scored the specific items from their son, and a second time *as if* they were from his cousin (as the control) according to the Schwartz method, as Wolf had requested. Dr. Schwartz performed a statistical analysis and tabulated the hits as 73.9% accuracy for Wolf and 5.6% for the cousin, with the misses at 13% for Wolf and 89.5% for the cousin. Based on these results, Dr. Schwartz concluded: "This visit is one of the best of its kind I have ever seen" (*WM* 44).

There remained uneasiness in Suzanne because of the items that carried no apparent significance for Mike and Beth, the so-called misses. She sensed that even these items carried significance for Wolf, though unknown to his parents. The puzzling images in question included a Radio Flyer wagon, unfamiliar words that Suzanne recorded as "Pajamas ... Jama Mama," and "messages chiseled in stone." The continuing communications between Wolf and Suzanne in her efforts to find the links is remarkable. She and her husband were travelling in the West for speaking engagements during the months following the onset of the communication from and with Wolf. Through a process of verbal exchange between the two, and attending to strange happenings, heeding coincidences, following hunches, and dogged persistence, Suzanne was finally able to discover the significance of the items in question from Wolf ... and to expand her own repertoire of knowledge at the same time. (A full account of this process is given in *Wolf's Message*.)

c. Messages from Sanaya

Sanaya often communicates through Suzanne to the public. These sessions take place in Central Florida as well as nationally and internationally. She also offers worldwide sessions by means of webinars that occur in her home. I have been present at a number of sessions with Sanaya and have high regard for the content of the messages and the manner in which she receives them.

After general comments and perhaps some music, Suzanne quiets herself and shifts into a different state of consciousness, apparent from the change in her voice, slight facial shifts, and arm and hand gestures. The messages that come forth are entirely positive and universally inclusive. I have not heard anything I would question ... not a single idea fails to accord with the teachings of the world's wisdom and spiritual traditions. The underlying message is one of unconditional love, with all supportive comments affirming the undying value of harmony and peace. Toward the end of these sessions, the audience may be invited to ask questions. Sanaya's responses tend to be specific to the questions and to have broad import as well. (Details can be found on Suzanne Giesemann's website.)

d. A Personal Session With Suzanne

I spent forty-five minutes with Suzanne while she communicated messages and impressions from deceased members of my family, identified by their role (mother, sister, for example). Some of the dates and specific names had no meaning for me, which could be due to my limited memory or to not ever having known them. I have evaluated most that came through as probable, definite, or strikingly on the mark. While some of the specific items could fit other families, for all of them to fit another family as specifically and accurately as they did mine would be exceptionally unlikely.

According to my evaluation, using the scale produced by Dr. Schwartz, there were sixty-seven probable, clear, and super hits. I have merged the categories because of the occasional subjective subtleties between them. I have not included possible hits since I regard these as quite likely among post-Great Depression families who share a common cultural status (education, religion, profession, income). Where needed for clarification or import, I have added an explanation between brackets depicting the relevance and significance of the message. Suzanne passed along from several family members the following details:

- There was a house fire. [My large, newly built family home burned down when I was in grade school.]
- I had two brothers and one sister.
- My sister and one brother are deceased.
- My parents lost an infant child, as did my wife and me.
- My parents farmed; lived in Illinois.
- Dad was a hard worker; worked with hand tools; wore a military type uniform for four years [Civil Air Patrol during WW II]; wore a Fedora.
- Brother followed dad in same business. [Both brothers did.]
- Church permeated family life and was Protestant.
- Accurate description of my childhood dog.
- Parents did not attend high school.
- Dad liked reading Zane Grey; had scholarly books. [He owned the Five Foot Shelf of Harvard Classics.]
- Parent's deaths were due to pancreatic problems; they died fairly close to each other in time; died at home.
- I was the only family member to get a college degree.
- Mother dangled car keys. [Once when visiting, I borrowed her car; on returning at lunch time, I put the keys on the kitchen counter; Mom had a doctor's appointment after lunch; extensive searching produced no keys; I finally gave up, resigned to the fact of lost keys; unthink-ingly, I walked to a kitchen drawer, opened it, and there found the keys; Mom made her appointment; this became a memorable family event.]
- Dad apologized for pushing me. [As a pre-school kid, I had to recite the ABCs before going outside to play; was given money inducements to get A and B grades, and obey church moral standards (no smoking or drinking before 21; no sexual activity until marriage); had to become an Eagle Scout to go deer hunting. After my higher education and during my teaching career, my dad pressured me to "return to the faith of my childhood and youth." When my mother was slowly dying in her final hours, my dad accused me of being the reason she would not pass on; she wouldn't die because I wasn't a Christian. This made no sense to me, to other family members, or my parent's minister. My mother actually died in apparent peace.]
- My deceased siblings also offered apologies. [While I have never felt any need or desire for apologies, I now suspect (after thinking about this following my session with Suzanne) that apologies might well flow naturally from the hearts of loved ones in a realm

where unconditional love prevails. For traditional Christians, a belief of unconditional love and non-judgment in what they call Heaven is common, and has been expressed by departed souls according to many accounts.]

The number of specific items (called evidential evidence) expressed through the "messages" from my deceased family members is striking. To regard the extent of accurate information I received as luck, or fabrication, or chance, or coincidence would require a degree of skepticism hardly imaginable.

E. The Prospect of Life after Death

While the standard of truth and reliability expected for strict rationality and scientific conclusion is not yet equaled in the human experiences cited above, it seems to me that outright denial, especially *a priori* denial, of the countless reports of trans-death evidence is premature and unjustifiable. Such a position is, in fact, unscientific. Good science requires the careful investigation of evidence that seems exceptional, even contradictory, to prevailing views. This open-ended requirement has led to significant scientific discoveries and breakthroughs.

As a result of my investigation in the course of writing this book, my position on this subject is firmer that ever. While short of full-fledged proof, evidence for continuity in trans-death consciousness seems to me stronger than ever. It now seems entirely probable that the entire time/space continuum emerges from, resides in, and returns to Ultimacy – from which it never separated. Thus, I am now comfortable in affirming the singularity of the eternal/infinite and temporal/finite. Energy, frequency, and vibration might well provide a rationale bridging any assumed discontinuity. From this perspective, to argue against trans-death continuity signifies an arbitrary and needlessly truncated view of unbound reality.

Part III: Peaceful Transitions to the Afterlife

> When you were born, you cried and the world rejoiced.
> Live in such a manner that when you die the world cries
> and you rejoice. (American Indian Saying)

1. Final Days of a Buddhist Abbot

Peter John Morgan, born in India of English parentage, became Ajaan Paññāvaddo and served as abbot at the Thai Forest Monastery in Thailand until his death in 2004 at the age of seventy-seven. After a lifetime of practicing and teaching Buddhism, he died exemplifying the life he had lived. Internal bleeding led to the discovery of colon cancer, which was initially treated unsuccessfully with herbs. He refused surgery, and when he could no longer eat, he declined artificial feeding and allowed his death to come peacefully, as he had lived his life.

During his final days, he experienced extreme exhaustion but no pain. Finally, his breathing became shallow and then stopped. Ajaan Paññā's passing was not just the death of a respected monk; it represented the power of his realization and the teaching he embodied. By the example of his death, Ajaan Paññā exhibited the caliber of the underlying qualities of his personhood and character. According to those who knew him best, to be in Ajaan Paññā's presence was to sense his palpable inner peace and serenity. His gaze was open, calm and benevolent – free of conflict, bias or judgment. With his warmth, his wisdom and his compassion, Ajaan Paññā personified the nobility of the principles of Buddhism. By his personal example, the *Dhamma* [Buddhist teachings] was rendered practical and vibrant with life. His teachings inspired in others an unshakeable confidence in the *Dhamma*, and a conviction in the central importance of a trusted teacher. Those who encountered his virtuous qualities tended to become acutely aware of the greed, the aversion and the selfish instincts clouding their own hearts. Earnest practitioners saw in his exemplary manner and freedom from attachments the qualities they longed to emulate. He had learned to accept the circumstances at hand without resistance and to allow the present moment to be, accepting the changing nature of all things and conditions.

Ajaan Paññā never indulged in feelings of satisfaction or disappointment. When things went smoothly, he did not feel especially elated, and when encountering obstacles or failure, he was not dejected. He did not struggle against the inevitable; he simply persevered. The determination to proceed resolutely, regardless of obstacles or difficulties, was a guiding principle in his life. As he approached death, he still kept his feet planted firmly on the Buddha's noble path, never taking for granted that his work was completed.

The revered monk's funeral took place on a sunny, cloudless afternoon during the usual rainy days of a monsoon:

> For a moment, as Ajaan Paññā's casket was placed atop the funeral pyre, the whole crowd was still. Then, an extraordinary occurrence attracted everyone's attention skyward. Against the clear blue sky shone a fiery, white light from a blinding, seemingly boundless source; a diamond-bright heart radiating outwards and fading to a softly diffused, circular glow. Around this white diamond was a second circle: a ring of rainbow light with an outer border of luminous white down. It was the sun, resplendent in breathtaking purity, encircled by a

magnificent rainbow, which suffused the translucent, wispy clouds with a prismatic glow. This sudden apparition drew the gaze of the whole congregation and transfixed it on the heavens. (*UW* 123-124)

The display seemed to add significance to a life that needed nothing added. Ajaan Paññāvaḍḍho had a keen and incisive mind dedicated to reason; yet in his teaching he went beyond the rational to penetrate the realm of the heart. This made him highly respected and well loved by many. He exuded genuine warmth and vibrant kindness.

In his talks and responses to questions, Ajaan Paññā often described the habits and conditions that constrict the human heart, such as greed, separation, and anger. Following this, he inspired glimpses of the pure, original, liberated mind. He often referred to the core teachings of the Buddha, which encouraged basic ethical conduct and virtues as well as the development of concentration and the cultivation of wisdom and discernment (paññā). Ajax Paññā was gifted in his ability to make advanced Buddhist teachings accessible and relevant for monks and lay people, and for Westerners and native Thai villagers alike (*UW* 120-28).

2. The Extraordinary Death of a Hindu Sage

At the age of sixteen, not yet named Ramana Maharshi, a schoolboy more interested in sports than books, came home from classes to his uncle's house where he was living. He reports the crucial event of his life in detail:

> I was sitting alone in a room on the first floor of my uncle's house. I seldom had any sickness, and on that day there was nothing wrong with my health, but a sudden violent fear of death overtook me. There was nothing in my state of health to account for it, and I did not try to account for it or to find out whether there was any reason for the fear. I just felt 'I am going to die' and began thinking what to do about it. It did not occur to me to consult a doctor, or my elders or friends; I felt that I had to solve the problem myself, there and then.
> The shock of the fear of death drove my mind inwards and I said to myself mentally, without actually framing the words: "Now death has come; what does it mean? What is it that is dying? The body dies." And I at once dramatized the occurrence of death. I lay with my limbs stretched out stiff as though *rigor mortis* had set in and imitated a corpse so as to give greater reality to the enquiry. I held my breath and kept my lips tightly closed so that no sound

could escape, so that neither the word 'I' nor any other word could be uttered.

"Well then," I said to myself, "this body is dead. It will be carried stiff to the burning ground and there burnt and reduced to ashes. But with the death of this body am I dead? Is the body I? It is silent and inert, but I feel the full force of my personality and even the voice of the 'I' within me, apart from it. So I am Spirit transcending the body. The body dies but the Spirit that transcends it cannot be touched by death. That means I am the deathless Spirit."

All this was not dull thought; it flashed through me vividly as living truth which I perceived directly, almost without thought process. 'I' was something very real, the only real thing about my present state, and all the conscious activity connected with my body was centered on that 'I.' From that moment onwards the 'I' or Self focused attention on itself by a powerful fascination. Fear of death had vanished once and for all. Absorption in the Self continued unbroken from that time on. (*BSR* 10a)

Not long after this event, the schoolboy left his uncle's home, and found his way to the most sacred mountain in South India, Arunachala. He meditated for months in temples and caves on the mountain. The extent and depth of his meditation attracted countless devotees. Eventually, a spiritual center (ashram) was established to provide accommodation for the many visitors from India and abroad. They would simply sit silently with him, absorbing the power and love of his presence and receive his occasional instruction. During these sessions, he sometimes addressed questions of death and did so in reference to birth also. He denied the reality of both birth and death by indicating that they pertain only to the body and the mind, with mind understood as thinking. For Ramana, the Self is the true 'I,' not the ego self that produces and identifies with the body and its thoughts. Birth and death exist only for the ego self. The true Self is neither born nor dies; it neither comes nor goes. It simply *is*.

Ramana's lifelong teaching message centered in detachment, that is, detaching from everything other than the Self. He formulated the practice of detachment positively in the question, "Who am I?" Investigate the I-thought and discover that it springs from the ego self. Investigate the ego self and discover its non-existence. Only the Self, the 'I' is. And that 'I' is eternal, untouched by time – and therefore has neither birth nor death.

Ramana never left the ashram. After a lifetime of conveying the Self through his silent presence, through his speaking and writing, in his late seventies, he developed cancer. It proved incurable in spite of his doctor's efforts. His devotees pleaded for him to heal himself. He refused, saying this body is all worn out, so why hold on to it. Distraught at the thought of their sage/saint's absence, some cried out, "Ramana, don't leave us." He calmly replied, "Where could I possibly go?" On April 14, 1950, using language common in India, Ramana "dropped the body."

3. From Dehumanizing Origin to Death as a Saint

Dominique Green was born in Houston, Texas in 1974. In his earliest years, his mother, Stephanie, devoted herself lovingly to him; as a consequence, he developed a basic self-trust. However, as family responsibilities increased and tragic events occurred, Stephanie's own childhood degradation began to take over and she became "a mother from hell."

Stephanie had been forced as a child to have sexual relations with the adult males in the household. As a consequence of these encounters and hardly in her teens, she gave birth to a daughter. The baby's grandmother, who eventually banned Stephanie from the home, raised the little girl. Later, in her own family and undoubtedly against the best of her intentions, Stephanie eventually succumbed to the 'rule' that we treat others as we have been treated, a rule miraculously transcended and reversed in the case of her son Dominique.

When Dominique was six, his father's drug associates broke into their home planning to rape Stephanie and kill Dominique and his brother, all with the intent to threaten his father, Emmitt, for failing to follow through on a drug deal. Even though their objective failed, it left a deep impression on Dominique. A year later, a priest at Dominique's Catholic school raped the now seven-year-old boy. Stephanie withdrew her son from the school but informed no one of the atrocity.

From then on, family life degenerated further. Stephanie succumbed to alcoholism, and Emmitt to both alcohol and marijuana. Unsavory characters began to hang around. When Dominique failed to inform his mother of a telephone call, she held his hand over a gas flame, repeating what her mother had done to her. A few years later, Dominique was forced to endure the same abusive cruelty once again.

When in his mid-teens, Dominique's parents separated and his mother was admitted to a mental institution and diagnosed as schizophrenic. She had previous shot a pistol twice at her firstborn, fortunately without success.

Dominique went off on his own. Having attended seven different schools, he gave up on education. He bunked with friends for a short while, learned to sleep under bridges and in abandoned cars, and

187

eventually rented a storage shed. He had previously been admitted to a juvenile detention center for possessing a small amount of marijuana and an illegal weapon. There he was sexually abused by staff members, and at times found himself lying in bed in his own blood from having been sodomized. These experiences compelled him to stay out of detention centers.

Dominique's love for his two younger brothers and his desire to protect and care for them required money. He confessed that he "didn't have the nerve to be a burglar, ... the cunning to be a thief, the will to be a pimp, or the hate to be a hired killer." Given this self-knowledge and the conditioning of his environment, he chose to deal in drugs. For a time, he managed to avoid the authorities. However, at the age of eighteen, he was arrested for the fourth and last time. The previous day he had been driving a stolen car that crashed into a ditch after a fifty-mile police chase. Dominique escaped through the fields and woods but was captured the next day by police using dogs. Two other young black men were captured at the time of the crash with a handgun and a BB gun in their possession.

During the immediate past, there had been several armed robberies in the area. Ballistic tests showed that the gun had been used previously in the killing of a black man, Andrew Lastrapes. Dominique's two black companions and a white youth accused Dominique of the shooting. The white youth was neither booked nor charged, and the two black youths were convicted as participants in the robberies but not charged with capital murder, which fell solely on Dominique. He was the youngest and the poorest, and the one least capable of a competent defense.

Law enforcement aberrations, failures, inadequacies, illegalities, erroneous interpretations, injustices, gross prejudices, outright lies, and withheld evidences prompted an unjust arrest. The ensuing trial, courtroom procedures, conviction, and imprisonment fall unconscionably short of being American, moral, Christian, or just in any sense of these terms. To summarize: Dominique Green was unjustly doomed to a life on Death Row for eleven years – ever moment facing the eventual execution that came as a lethal injection when he was twenty-nine years old. The rest of this account reviews his personal transformation from a naturally gifted youth who survived a harsh and demeaning life to become a man who manifested the most laudable of human qualities.

As he became aware of what his life in prison was going to be, Dominique knew that he would have to depend primarily upon himself for survival – and that he would need the help of others as well, inside and outside the prison. This insight, profound in itself as recognition of the interdependency of human life, motivated him throughout his endeavors to help both himself and others. He received the aid of several attorneys, some caring and competent, others not. By reaching out even internationally, he secured the help of a lay Italian group, the Community of Sant'Egidio (Saint Giles) that works to implement the values portrayed by Christ, including opposition to the death penalty, into personal and social life. This community arranged for a skilled attorney to represent Dominique at his final appeal, and raised funds for this effort.

In addition to his appeals outside the prison, Dominique worked hard within the prison. He undertook an extensive study of law in order to understand better his own situation. With this knowledge, he helped other inmates as well. He repaired a broken radio and listened to newscasts to stay current with the outside world and shared news with others. He arranged activities involving his fellow inmates, all the way from football pools to individuals writing their personal experiences and bringing these together in a composite document.

Dominique's self-appraisal led him to discover his need to forgive those who had wronged him, including his mother, which he was able to do. He discovered the compassionate and insightful work on forgiveness of South African Archbishop Desmond Tutu, which greatly deepened his understanding. Almost unbelievably, but through the help of some of Dominique's supporters, the Archbishop (while on a book promotion tour in the States) was persuaded to visit Dominique. There was an immediate heart-level rapport between the two, evidenced by the joyous laughter overheard by those nearby. Long an opponent of the death penalty, Archbishop Tutu wrote a letter on Dominique's behalf for his final appeal, as did other notable, respected persons. The family of the man whose murder had been charged to Dominique also pleaded on his behalf. All this and more proved fruitless.

Dominique's work on behalf of others is symbolized by a necklace he created. It was made of one hundred and one beads and hung below his waist (until the authorities finally forbad him to wear it because it had suddenly became a security risk). When asked about this unique rosary, he explained that he added a bead for each "friend, mentor or spiritual guide ... who has died and who gave me the chance to use their knowledge and wisdom to touch other lives." Eleven years after Dominique came to prison, more than two hundred and fifty of his fellow inmates had been executed. Dominique knew almost all of them. He stopped adding beads when he felt that he had learned enough to "have an impact on the lives of others and to help make a difference."

Dominique capitalized on his life in prison by effectively using the discipline and skills of an ancient anchorite in a desert setting, working on himself and serving others. He confessed that life in prison made him "the man I always wanted to be." Having successfully come through several previous identity crises, Dominique was able to assert, "One of the first things I learned in coming to Death Row was how to be myself."

On the day his execution, Dominique had a final meeting with his mother followed by his sweetheart from before his imprisonment. He fully forgave his mother, even warmly calling her "Mom." His former girlfriend, Jessica, now his common law wife, was about to become a physician and was still in love with Dominique. She observed that: "Dominique had blossomed exponentially," and that he "was now a presence that overcame any other energy in the room."

Dominique had become a man exhibiting the qualities of sainthood. Thomas Cahill, an acclaimed author and astute observer of Western culture, entitled his book on Dominique's live and death, *A Saint on Death Row: How a Forgotten Child Became a Man and Changed a World.* Cahill describes a saint as "a person of extraordinary kindness and patience." He notes further that most Christians regard those in heaven as capable of appealing to God on behalf of both the living and the dead, therefore, themselves worthy of receiving prayers. Cahill attests to knowing many who do this, who pray *to* Dominique. On the last day of his life, the condemned man promised, "Where I am going I'm going to take care of everybody."

Implicit in the recognition of Dominique as a saint is the belief that we can discern sainthood in the extraordinary gulf that exists between the deplorable and limiting conditions of early life in contrast to the exceptional qualities that emerged in final years, qualities such as pervasive inner peace, acceptance of what is, gratitude for life, and unbound regard for others. Though greatly different in time and outer conditions (birth in extreme dysfunction and birth in a stable), a similar life development is apparent between Dominique and the historical Jesus of Nazareth. If the one is regarded as saintly, why not the other? (*ASODR passim*).

4. Orthodox Jew, Skeptic, Philosopher, Christian, Mystic, and Saint

Edith Stein was born into a devout Orthodox Jewish family in Germany in 1891. She was the youngest of eleven children and possibly the brightest, least conventional, and most outgoing. Her independent spirit and 'headiness' led her to deny a personal God during her adolescence and early adult years. At the same time, her inner sense of an "underlying coherence of human existence" prompted her to study psychology, a study abandoned, however, when she discovered that her professors where promoting a view of human nature without "spirit, meaning and life." Her brilliance then led her to graduate study with Edmund Husserl, an exceptionally creative German philosopher whose international influence continues in many and varied fields today. Husserl selected Edith as his personal assistant and charged her with introducing his basic views to new students and clarifying them for established students who misunderstood them.

Her early denial of a personal God notwithstanding, Edith held firmly to her personal sense of human nature as integral and spiritual. This fundamental perspective, coupled with her wide-ranging intellect, and perhaps linked to Husserl's advocacy of agnosticism, led her to hold views contrary to her mentor. Nonetheless, Husserl's views on how we know what we know were so clarifying that they ingrained themselves deeply into his students. He taught them "to look at everything with strict impartiality and do away with their rationalist blinders." These views have contributed to the well-established acceptance today of what is called "the transrational mind" (i.e., reasoning beyond the strictly dualistic framework of customary rationality). Though not realized by Husserl himself, these perspectives on how to know what is real, the truly real, were leading many of his students to convert to Christianity.

This background, along with a number of other factors, converged in Edith's life and produced a personal crisis. Her awareness of the tragedies of World War I and the agonizing developments during the war years in Germany contrasted with the acceptance and hope that she found in the widow of her cherished and respected colleague and personal friend, Adolf Reinach, who had died on the battlefield in the war. Prior to his death, Reinach and his wife had been baptized as Lutherans, and he had written from the field that in the future, his role as a philosopher would be to bring others to faith. Intellectualism could not forestall Edith's crisis of faith. As a result of these events, Edith began to read the *New Testament* and Christian philosophers. She came upon the autobiography of Saint Teresa of Avila and was profoundly moved by it. Conjoined with other negative factors, and with her emerging self-awareness, there arose in Edith a sense of the 'shadow of death,' suggesting the impending loss of her core spirituality and integrity if fundamental change did not occur. She was impelled to relax her intellectualism and open to faith, to transrational knowing. Her expansion beyond the intellect was a surrender comparable to St. Augustine's relinquishment of his sensuality that freed him to compose the first Christian spiritual autobiography (*The Confessions of Saint Augustine: The Autobiography of a Prodigal Who Became a Saint*) and St. Teresa's departure from her wordliness to become a model saint for countless others down through the centuries.

How did Edith understand her conversion? She regarded it as an ahistorical event, not simply the result of a sequence of personal developments, but "a transformation accomplished by some transcendent power, a power outside the individual and the entire nexus of natural circumstances." She affirmed: "God is a lover who requires the surrender of the will from those he loves [if they are] to achieve this transformation." No longer would she deny the reality of a personal God. This personal God became foundational and central in her self-understanding and her eventual service to humanity. She held firmly to her belief in the "'inextinguishable uniqueness' of the human person who lives at the same time in a state of spiritual 'interconnectedness' with the rest of reality." Each of us is always in relation to even that which we may seem not to be. Given the interconnectedness of reality, nothing exists in isolation and separation from the whole.

Rather than her intellectualism blocking her way to the divine, as it had previously, now it enabled Edith to formulate interpretations of biblical teachings and principal Christian thinkers (such as Thomas Aquinas, foremost theologian in the Roman Catholic Church) that enabled her to become a major teacher in the Church. Her original nature as an outgoing youth took on a new boldness as she came to "a sense of tremendous security" following her surrender. This extraordinary "sense of resting in God" would become tellingly apparent in her final days.

Edith entered the Carmelite Order in Cologne, Germany, as a novice in 1933. She became a full-fledged Carmelite nun the next year in a formal rite that invested her with the traditional brown garb of her discalced order. (Discalced refers to the custom of going barefoot but is more commonly expressed today by wearing sandals. The practice is a sign of discipline, an ascetic life of poverty, and loving devotion to Christ through service.) Shortly after her induction into the Order, a law was passed in Germany declaring that Jewish converts to Christianity were no longer safe. For the security of the convent and of Edith in particular, she was transferred to the Netherlands. Soon after the move, the same edict fell on her new homeland, and Edith was brutally arrested and forced onto a train to begin the weeklong, torturous journey to Auschwitz.

Years before circumstances offered the opportunity to demonstrate the depth of her commitment, Edith confessed: "I joyfully accept in advance the death God has appointed for me, in perfect submission to his most holy will." In her personal reflections, Edith discovered that "Holiness is a form of the soul that has to emerge from the inmost core, from a level inaccessible both to external influences and to the efforts of the will." It is ahistorical, beyond time and space, and available only through unreserved trust and submission. It isn't so much learned as known.

On this final journey, transportation halted periodically and the prisoners were herded into army barracks. Here Edith continued attending her fellow travelers as she set about cleaning the facility, washing clothes, and aiding the hungry. A survivor noted Edith's care for the women and children, including mothers so distraught they no longer looked after their own children. Her Carmelite sisters remembered her as "as unfailingly serene and cheerful". She was calm and self-possessed while consoling and helping others. Her personal attitude seemed unworried and even cheerful as she addressed specific issues. Another person noted that "the influence she exerted by her tranquil bearing and manner was undeniable." A biographer acknowledged "her quiet composure, ... the lighthearted happiness in the way she spoke," and "the glow of a saintly Carmelite [that] radiated from her eyes."

The last known contact with Edith Stein came from the stationmaster where the train carrying her and the other prisoners stopped briefly on its fateful journey. Edith called from the train to the stationmaster and asked if he knew the family of Dean Schwind, who had been Edith's spiritual director. His family had virtually adopted her into their family. When the stationmaster replied that he knew the family well, she asked him "to convey Edith Stein's greetings to the ... family, and let them know she was on her way to the East" (a euphemism for Auschwitz). Even in her final hours, Edith sent greetings to cherished friends, seemingly oblivious to her own impending fate, definitely unattached to it.

Earlier in her career, with poetic depth and clarity, Edith penned her innermost awareness, thereby indicating the merging of her self-sense into the Source of All:

>Who are you, kindly light, who fill me now,
>And brighten all the darkness of my heart?
>You guide me forward, like a mother's hand,
>And if you let me go,
>I could not take a single step alone.
>You are the space,
>Embracing all my being, hidden in it.
>Loosened from you, I fall in the abyss
>Of nothingness, from which you draw my life.
>Nearer to me than I myself am.
>And more within me than my inmost self.
>You are outside my grasp, beyond my reach.
>And what name can contain you?
>You, Holy Spirit, you, eternal Love.

Edith Stein's pilgrimage to sainthood culminated in 1998 when she was canonized by Pope John Paul II. She had been beatified as a martyr in 1987 and awaited canonization until credited with the healing of a little girl who had swallowed a substance that destroyed her kidneys. Subsequent to the prayers of many, including the child's father and a priest in the Greek Orthodox Church, the intensive care nurses attending the little girl saw her sit up one day completely cured ... a cure confirmed by the pediatric doctor at the Massachusetts General Hospital. (*ESAB passim*)

* * * *

My original heading for this final section in the final chapter of *Undoing* was "Easeful Deaths." When discovering the conditions and dying process of Edith Stein, I could not imagine her death as easy. Almost immediately, the word "peaceful" came to mind. It may be that few deaths are ever easy, but they can be peaceful. A sense of peace can prevail when the loving and accepting qualities of the life actually lived continue into our final days, when we have detached from our cultural identities and rest in and as our original, divinely established identity.

* * * *

The world is holy! The soul is holy! The skin is holy! ...
Everything is holy! everybody's holy! everywhere is holy!
(*sic*) (Allen Ginsberg)

Epilogue: How Far Do We Take Detachment?

Detachment will prove to be a crucial tool throughout all our coming years. We will continue to detach until we are confidently and comfortably centered in ourselves as unique persons, until we are content inwardly regardless of outer conditions, until we feel free to live our personal values openly without regard to criticism, and until our compassion and care extend to the universe. Detachment, as the active agent of nonattachment, may be needed until awareness itself comes to an end, or is presumed to end (i.e., up to the final dying moment). Nonattachment, calm, neutral, non-reactive, sheer awareness, is required even at death – especially at death. Therefore, how far do we take nonattachment?

On Detaching from God

Views about God have evolved over time to include a myriad of forms. Of the making of ideas about God, there seems to be no end: paganism, polytheism, henotheism, monotheism, pantheism, agnosticism, atheism, to name the most common. Then there's the view that God is so totally beyond human conception that any description would be inaccurate. Even this unknowable god is believed to exist and is approached either by means of negation (naming what he/she/it is not), or by means of silence. In the mid-1960's, the 'Death of God' Movement reached its peak in America, having been introduced in Europe in the previous century. This view, as one would expect, stimulated extensive debate and discussion. A number of prominent theologians supported the idea, and traditional religion fought hard to defend its God.

Accompanying these diverse perspectives on God are the many religions, which have had an equally checkered career. Religion has inspired the purest and highest human achievement in literature, music, art, architecture, theology, and philosophy. It has inspired selfless service to the distraught, elderly, sick, dying, poor, homeless, and marginalized. Religion has encouraged generosity and beneficence to aid the needy. These contributions of religion are commendable and undeniable, and all in the name of God.

But there has been a dark side to religion as well. It has distorted truth for its own ends and aggrandizement. It has opposed and curtailed education. It has purposely destroyed the religious products of other religions. It has enflamed prejudices and stimulated hatred. It has set up regulations and boundaries that have alienated and divided people. It has demeaned, persecuted, and killed its perceived opposition. It has secretly planned murders. It has demonized its enemies and provoked hatred. It has fostered mass killings and instigated devastating wars. All of this too was done in the name of God.

It is time – well past time – to reevaluate god. My contention is that the 'idea' of god has always been a product of human thought and imagination. Critics of religion believe they have undermined and dismissed religion when they note that it is just a case of anthropomorphizing, of creating a god-in-man's-image. It's all sheer projection they claim. Of course, it is. It can't be otherwise. Everything that we recognize 'outside' ourselves originates and remains 'inside' ourselves. Strictly speaking, there is no outside. To know an 'outside' would require being outside our own consciousness – utterly impossible.

Outside is merely a convenience (for language, for communication, for a sense of connection) required by the inability of the thinking mind, of rational thought, to know reality directly. As indicated in Chapter One, for reason to operate, it must divide that which is whole and undivided into discrete parts, into entities and things that exist only by right of their relationship to multiple other so-called specific things that have occurred before and arise along with. When reason gets close to the end of its rational functions, it may succumb into paradox. If the paradox is to be resolved, it will merge into the transrational mind and its unique abilities to transcend and resolve contradictions, thereby becoming the greater wholeness of consciousness where it disappears.

The outside/inside distinction disappears when the fragmentation of the interactive, unfolding whole gives way to seeing from the stance of nonduality. Entrapped within duality as we are, the fragmented world sets up a ready arena for fostering both the negatives and the positives of human existence.

The verdict is out concerning whether religion on the whole serves human interest or not. Personal bias undoubtedly shapes all 'guesses. It takes a good bit of 'step back,' 'think objectively,' along with extensive surveys and massive tabulations to consider fairly the comparative worth of the positive and negative effects of religion. There is unlikely to be a resolution of the issue as long as religion operates with the assumption that god is other than us.

Both the best and the worst of god and religion originate in the human mind, and then are acted out. The noble and ignoble are projected, embodied, and formalized in an 'idea' of what's worthy and commendable for my 'tribe' and me. This 'idea' takes on human values and is then projected on and envisioned in an all-powerful being external to mankind. That which is human is ascribed to this imagined being. This concocted entity takes on these qualities, and then requires, encourages, and inspires these same qualities in those who acknowledge and worship this God. The humanly imagined deity becomes a reality that fosters the ideas that have been imputed to it. It's all mental and emotional. There is no difference *in the operation of the mind* between the god and religion positively envisioned, and the god and religion negatively envisioned. In origin and manifestation, they arise identically – in and as projected imagination.

I am not suggesting that god, and the religions centered in god, be abandoned. Rather, I am contending that since the idea of god has always been a human creation, we jettison the notion of an external god and declare that we now openly and consciously occupy the role that god has played throughout history. As conscious beings who have evolved to become integral, all-inclusive, and caring, *we have become* much of what has been projected onto the gods throughout the ages. It is time for us to assume *the role* of god. What god has represented in the past has now devolved onto humanity.

Obviously, we did not create the cosmos, the planets, or life. But, so far as we know, we are the highest and noblest achievement of this mysterious and magnificent process. The future of the planet depends on our most brilliant, conscientious, and caring minds. Nothing any longer can be left up to a god. God has become manifest in and as us!

* * * *

Reality is the only god there is. An acquaintance of mine wrote a book several years ago entitled *Reality Is All the God There Is* in which he drew extensively from Hindu and Buddhist sources. *(RGI)* He could easily have found more. From the Western religious world comes a book entitled, *Everything is God* (*EIG*). Many if not most of the world's mystics and nondualist affirm the same (e.g., Jean Klein, Leo Hartong, Joseph Kloss, Greg Goode, *et al.*). Once the idea is seriously entertained, one finds repeated assertions by other thoughtful people and may begin to see how perfectly obvious the claim is. "Why did it take me so long to realize this perfectly obvious Truth?" might be one's exclamation.

Increasing numbers of intelligent and thoughtful people who live eminently moral lives and are committed to humankind (not just to themselves) question or deny the notion that god is an agent apart from the cosmos or even a separate agent operating in the cosmos. For them, religion as found in most societies today is *passé*, obsolete, and irrelevant – except for the evil and nonsense it promotes.

* * * *

Postscript

Now more than ever: Who am I? What is Real? What gives my life meaning and significance? What gives me the deepest satisfaction? How do I want to be remembered?

George Bernard Shaw attests: "Progress is impossible without change, and those who cannot change their minds cannot change anything."

Bibliography

For the convenience of readers, the Bibliography is arranged alphabetically by the letters used as abbreviations in the in-text citations.

AAIH — *An Atheist in Heaven: The Ultimate Evidence for Life After Death?* by Paul Davids and Gary E. Schwartz, Los Angeles, CA: Yellow Hat Productions, 1916.

ACIM (key: T, Text; W, Workbook; MT, Manual for Teachers) — *A Course in Miracles:* Combined Volume, Third Ed., Mill Valley, CA: Foundation for Inner Peace, 2007.

ADL — *The Art of Dying and Living* by Kerry Walters, Maryknoll, NY: Orbis Books.

AFLP — *The Art of Forgiveness, Lovingkindness, and Peace* by Jack Kornfield, New York: Bantam Books, 2008.

AG — *Avadhuta Gita* by Dattatreya, (Trans. Ashokananda), Madras, India: Ramakrishna Matt, 1981.

ASODR — *A Saint on Death Row: How a Forgotten Child Became a Man and Changed a World* by Thomas Cahill, New York, NY: Anchor Books, 2010.

BF — *The Book of Forgiveness* by Desmond Tutu and Mpho Tutu, New York: Harper One, 2014.

BG — *The Bhagavad Gita.* (Trans. Elliot Deutsch), New York: Holt, Rinehart and Winston, 1968.

BSR—*Bhagavan Sri Ramana: A Pictorial Biography.* Tiruvannamalai, India: Sri Ramanasramam, 1981.

CW 6 — *Sex, Ecology, Spirituality,* The Collected Works of Ken Wilber, Vol. 6, Boston, MA: Shambhala Publications, 2000.

D — *The Dhammapada*: *The Saying of the Buddha.* (Trans. Thomas Cleary), New York: Bantam Books, 1995.

DFP — *Detroit Free Press.* freep.com. Web. 15 June 2017.

DHB — *Diamond Heart Book II.* by A.H. Almaas, Berkeley, CA: Diamond Books, 1997.

DS/SHN — *The Diamond Sutra and the Sutra of Hui-Neng.* (Trans. A.F. Price and Wong Mou-lam), Boston: Shambhala, 1990.

DTBM — *Dying to be Me: My Journey from Cancer, to Near Death, to True Healing* by Anita Moorjani, Carlsbad, CA: Hay House, 2012.

EHS — *Essence of the Heart Sutra* by Tenzin Gyatso, (Trans. Geshe Thupten Jinpa), Boston: Wisdom Publications, 2002.

EIG — *Everything is God: The Radical Path of Nondual Judaism* by Jay Michaelson, Boulder, CO, Trumpeter Books, 2009.

ESAB — *Edith Stein: A Biography* by Waltraud Herbstrith, (Trans. Bernard Bonowitz), San Francisco: Harper & Row, 1985.

GII — *Go In and In: Poems from the Heart of Yoga* by Danna Faulds, Kearny, NE: Peaceable Kingdom Books, 2002.

HTM — *Have This Mind: Supreme Happiness, Ultimate Realization, and the Four Great Religions: An Integral Adventure* by James E. Royster, Bloomington, IN: Balboa Press, 2014.

I — *Islam* by John A. Williams, Ed., New York: Braziller, 1962.

IHGL — *I Heard God Laughing* by Muhammad S. Hafiz, (Trans. Daniel Ladinsky), New York: Penguin Group, 1996.

IHLB — *I Have Lived Before: The True Story of the Reincarnation of Shanti Devi* by Sture Lönnerstrand, Huntsville: Ozark Mountain Publishing, 1998.

JM — *Just Mercy: A Story of Justice and Redemption* by Bryan Stevenson, New York, NY: Random House Books, 2015.

K — *Koestler: The Literary and Political Odyssey of a Twentieth-Century Skeptic* by Michael Scammell, New York, NY: Random House, 2009.

LBLC — *Living Buddha, Living Christ* by Thich Nhat Hanh, London: Rider, 1996.

LT — *Lao-tzu's Taoteching* by Red Pine (Bill Porter), San Francisco, CA: Mercury House, 1996.

LTT — *Left to Tell: Discovering God Amidst the Rwandan Holocaust* by Immaculée Ilibagiza, with Steve Erwin. Carlsbad, CA: Hay House, Inc., 2014.

MM — *Miracles Magazine.* Jon Mundy, Ed., Washington, NY: Institute for Personal Religion.

MSOI — *My Stroke of Insight* by Jill Bolte Taylor. New York, NY: Plume (Penguin Group), 2009.

NG — *National Geographic.*

NGP — *Natural Great Perfection* by Nyoshul Khenpo, (Trans. Lama Surya Das), Ithica, NY: Snow Lion Publications, 1995.

NPR — National Public Radio. 5-20-2011.

NYT — *New York Times.* Article by Bryan Stevenson, 3-3-93.

PBS — *Iwo Jima: From Combats to Comrades* (DVD).

PE — *The Point of Existence* by A.H. Almaas. Boston, MA: Shambhala Publications, 2001.

PRI — Public Radio International.

RGI — *Reality Is All The God There Is: The Single Transcendental Truth Taught by the Great Sages and the Revelation of Reality Itself* by Avatar Adi Da Samraj. Rochester, VT: Inner Traditions, 2008.

RSS — *The Royal Song of Saraha.* (Trans. Herbert V. Guenther), Berkeley, CA: Shambala, 1973.

SSD — "The Story of Shanti Devi." www.viewzone.com. Web. Nov.15 2016); K.W. Rawat, "The Case of Shanti Devi," www.carolbowman.com. Web. 23 Nov. 16)

SIEM — *Self in Integral Evolutionary Mysticism* by Marc Gafni. Tucson, AZ: Integral Publishers, 2014.

SS — *Soul Survivor: The Reincarnation of a World War II Fighter Pilot* by Bruce & Andrea Leininger. New York: Grand Central Publishing, 2009.

T — Sifferlin, Alexandra. "Forgiving Other People Is Good for Your Health." *Time Magazine.* 16 Jun. 2016. Web. 24 June 2016.

TD — *The Deal: A Guide to Radical and Complete Forgiveness* by Richard Smoley, New York: Jeremy P. Tarcher/Penguin, 2015.

TMS — *Three Muslim Sages* by Seyyed Hossein Nasr. Cambridge, MA: Harvard University Press, 1964.

TP — *The Prophet* by Khalil Gibran. Mumbai, India: Jaico Publishing House, 1988.

TSOS — *The Study of Spirituality.* Edited by Cheslyn Jones, Geoffrey Wainwright, Edward Yarnold. New York: Oxford University Press, 1986.

UW — *Uncommon Wisdom: Life and Teachings of Ajaan Pannavaddho* by Ajaan Dick Silaratano, Lexington, VA: Forest Dhamma Publications, 2004.

WC — *A Workbook Companion.* I, 2nd. Edited by Allen Watson and Robert Perry, West Sedona, AZ: Circle Publishing, 2005.

WF — *The Wisdom of Forgiveness* by the Dalai Lama and Victor Chan, New York: Riverhead Books, 2004.

WJ — *Wandering Joy: Meister Eckhart's Mystical Philosophy* by Reiner Schürmann (translations and commentary), Great Barrington, MA: Lindisfarne Books, 2001.

WM — *Wolf's Message* by Suzanne Giesemann, Self-published, 2014.

WOTW — *Wandering on the Way* by Victor H. Mair, Trans. New York: Bantam Books, 1994.

ZL — *Zero Limits: The Secret Hawaiian System for Wealth, Health,*

Peace, and More by Joe Vitale and H. Hew Len, Hoboken, NJ: Wiley, 2007.

ZTB — The Zen Teachings of Bodhidharma by Red Fox, Intro. & Trans. New York: North Point Press.

Undoing draws from and makes readily accessible Dr. Royster's former book: "*Have This Mind: Supreme Happiness, Ultimate Realization, and the Four Great Religions – An Integral Adventure*" *(Balboa Press, 2014)* which represents his professorial efforts.

Praise for *Have This Mind: Supreme Happiness, Ultimate Realization, and the Four Great Religions – An Integral Adventure*:

Have This Mind is an ultimately optimistic argument for the essential, ecumenical, unifying functions of religion – "to facilitate fundamental transformation in … our very nature as human beings" (John Miller PhD).

As Dr. Royster discusses the deeper meanings of our major faith traditions, he focuses upon ways in which our spiritual faith impacts the quality of our lives as human beings on planet earth – our minds, our consciousness; our supreme worth as persons; our goals for a life that fosters supreme happiness; our interrelatedness with one another; our oneness with all that is; and the wholeness of all that is (Vern Norris PhD).

Made in the USA
Columbia, SC
11 January 2018